Strategic Shopper Marketing

Strategic Shopper Marketing provides a uniquely strategic perspective on the "anything, anywhere, anytime" retail revolution.

Following the principles set out by leading global consultant Georg August Krentzel, a practitioner can connect shopper marketing principles with strategic concerns, aligning it with other disciplines like marketing, sales and distribution to connect their route to purchase with their route to market. Providing professionals with a theoretically well-founded understanding of shopper marketing, the book charts the history and development of shopper marketing and describes the newest developments and changes in the marketplace that impact how shoppers need to be activated to generate profitable sales and loyalty. The book presents a guideline with examples and numerous illustrations to develop successful shopper marketing strategies across different sales channels.

Focused on practice, but with solid theoretical foundations, practical insights and methodologies, and enriched with examples, this book is ideal for marketing practitioners at strategic levels looking to integrate shopper marketing principles into their organization, as well as for those less experienced practitioners learning the principles, and those in marketing education.

Georg August Krentzel is an expert in sales and distribution, marketing and shopper strategies with a PhD from the University of Economics and Business of Vienna. He is a former editor of the *Bonnier Management Handbook* in Sweden and author of books on international management and shopper marketing, as well as various articles.

Strategic Shopper Marketing

Driving Shopper Conversion by Connecting the Route to Purchase with the Route to Market

Georg August Krentzel

LONDON AND NEW YORK

First published 2021
by Routledge
2 Park Square, Milton Park, Abingdon, Oxon OX14 4RN

and by Routledge
52 Vanderbilt Avenue, New York, NY 10017

Routledge is an imprint of the Taylor & Francis Group, an informa business

British Library Cataloguing-in-Publication Data
A catalogue record for this book is available from the British Library

Library of Congress Cataloging-in-Publication Data
Names: Krentzel, Georg August, author.
Title: Strategic shopper marketing : driving shopper conversion by
connecting the route to purchase with the route to market / Georg August Krentzel.
Description: Milton Park, Abingdon, Oxon; New York, NY: Routledge, 2020. |
Includes bibliographical references and index.
Identifiers: LCCN 2019059782 (print) | LCCN 2019059783 (ebook) |
ISBN 9780367192587 (hardback) | ISBN 9780429201417 (ebook)
Subjects: LCSH: Marketing. | Consumer behavior. | Consumers' preferences.
Classification: LCC HF5415 .K6728 2020 (print) |
LCC HF5415 (ebook) | DDC 658.8/342–dc23
LC record available at https://lccn.loc.gov/2019059782
LC ebook record available at https://lccn.loc.gov/2019059783

ISBN: 9780367192587 (hbk)
ISBN: 9780429201417 (ebk)

Typeset in Times New Roman
by Newgen Publishing UK

Contents

Figures

Tables

1 Shopper marketing and society

Economic development has lifted millions of people out of poverty in emerging and developing economies, and has turned developed economies from markets of scarcity into markets of oversupply. Industrialization has made more and cheaper products available. Combined with more free time and access to cheaper money, shopping has turned from a necessity into a mass and leisure activity. Shopping is today a key engine of the economy. Infrastructural and technological development have profoundly changed the way we shop through improved availability and reach of products and services, and have made the management of shoppers, retailers, distributors and other partners more complex.

Successful shopper marketing strategies are dependent on a good understanding of the economic, sociopolitical, and technological environment. The development of this environment has a direct influence on shoppers and their behavior in terms of omnichannel shopping, segmentation and personalization, and values.

The relevance of shopper marketing

Private consumption is an important engine of the economy. With the ending of the gold standard and the Bretton Woods system in the seventies, the amount of money, as well as credits, that were available in the marketplace multiplied exponentially. In the 1980s, during the era of the new conservatism led in the United States by Ronald Reagan and in the United Kingdom by Margaret Thatcher, political decisions with important implications on the economy were taken. The ideas had academic support from the liberal theories of free market economics from the University of Chicago that were critical to demand-side economics and Keynesianism. Among the academics who gave theoretical support for that political development were Milton Friedman with his theory of monetarism (Nobel Prize winner in 1976)[1]; George Stigler with his description of how lobbying formed economic policy in its favor (Nobel Prize winner in 1982)[2]; Gary Becker, describing that rules of economics could also be applied to social situations outside the economy (Nobel Prize winner in 1992)[3]; or Robert Lucas who won the Nobel Prize in 1995 and was a strong critic of Keynesianism[4]; and other important academics such as Frank Knight, who is seen as one of the founders of the Chicago School and who showed the important role of the entrepreneur.[5] The Chicago School of Economics was the driving force behind the famous Chicago Boys, the economists in the 1980s who had a major impact, first in Chile and then in other South American countries, on economic policy.[6]

The 1980s were the point at which the idea of the free market won against opposing political ideas, such as communism as well as many of the more socialist ideas in Western

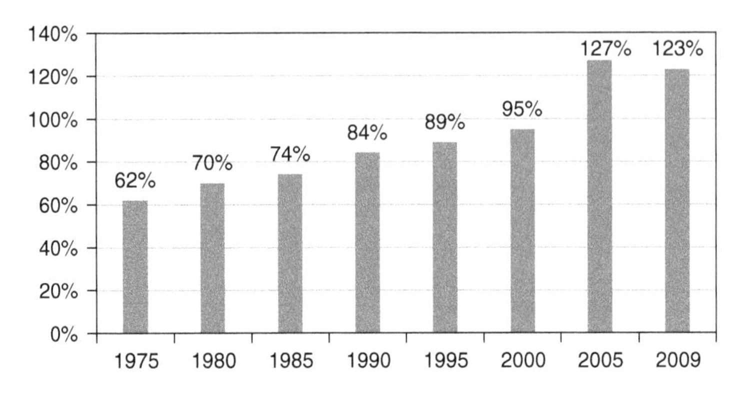

Figure 1.1 Debts in relation to disposable income
Household debt in the United States relative to disposable income.
Source: Stewart, 2010

societies. Francis Fukuyama, in his famous article, even proclaimed the end of history, as with the collapse of the Soviet Union, the last ideological alternative to liberalism had been eliminated.[7] From the communist bloc only North Korea really remains today. Other communist countries, such as China, have strong ingredients of market economics. Countries with strong socio-democratic traditions, like Sweden or Austria, started to introduce important privatization reforms in the 1980s, and more heavily in the 1990s, based on the conviction that the state can never distribute products or services as effectively as a functioning free market.

The idea of the benefits of free market forces, especially when it comes to efficient distribution of scarce resources, is increasingly coming under criticism when it comes to public services. In addition, with the growing income divide, globalization is under criticism,[8] a criticism that is strongly associated with the economic crisis of 2008 and the real estate bubble that started in the United States with subprime products. Those who entered late into the real estate game had less potential value to gain and those with low incomes were the ones who lost the most, in relative terms. Today, we are in a situation of high debts, low inflation and growth in most Western societies, but also countries traditionally associated with strong growth are losing speed, such as China and South American countries.

Private debts have grown very strongly in recent years as the money has been decoupled from tangible securities, like gold, and with the lowering of strict bank security rules, i.e. the ratio between credit and security. The increase of available money, and more credit has given a boost to shopping. The situation of high debt and low growth is forcing companies to become more professional and competitive to convert shoppers into buyers.

With increased productivity and economic development, countries are increasingly becoming service economies.

Not only has productivity increased, important cost savings have been made through outsourcing to low-cost countries. Companies like Nike, IKEA or H&M are no longer production companies, they are marketing and sales companies. They produce through subcontracted companies in low-cost countries, while they focus on innovation, design, marketing and sales.

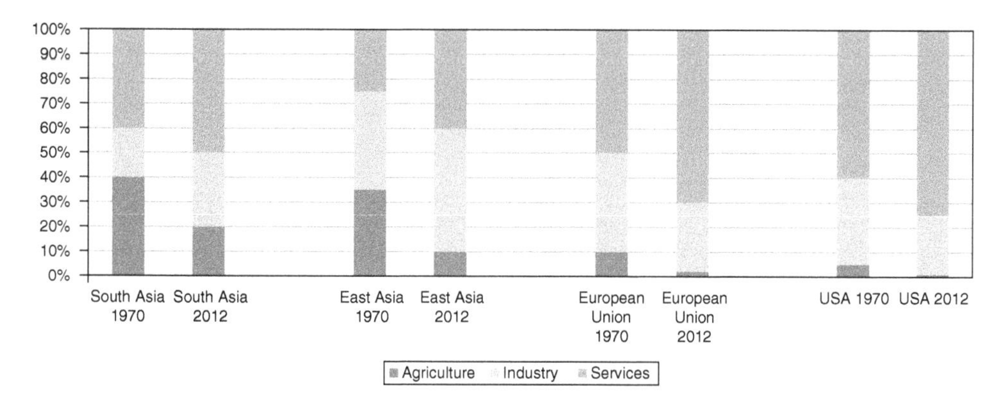

Figure 1.2 Development of the composition of GDP in different parts of the world
Composition of GDP in South Asia, East Asia, the European Union and the United States in 2012 compared to 1970.
Source: The World Bank, 2017

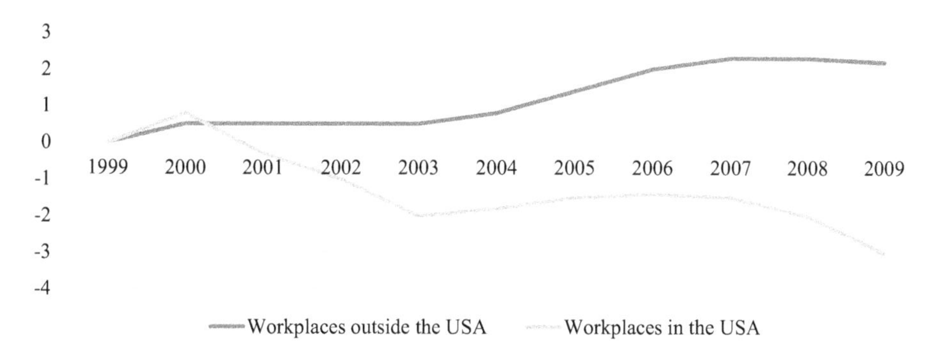

Figure 1.3 National and international job changes in the United States
Cumulative change in millions of jobs between 1999 and 2009 in multinationals in the United States.
Source: Jilani, 2017

The price of many consumer products or services, like clothing, food and electronics, has fallen in relative terms in the last 30 to 40 years.

What has increased in relative price are the cost of housing and personal insurance and pensions, while relative prices on items like groceries, clothes and services have decreased.

With the access to more money and credits and the decrease of relative prices of products and services, shopping has developed from a necessity to a leisure activity. Additionally, people today have more time because of stricter regulations on working hours and holidays. Shopping has become a social activity, about experiences beyond the mere products and services, it has become about brands, experiencing new things, being part of social groups, discussing products and brands and identifying with these. Shopping as a mass activity is something recent, something that emerged in the seventies, gained speed in the eighties, and now has a central place in modern societies.

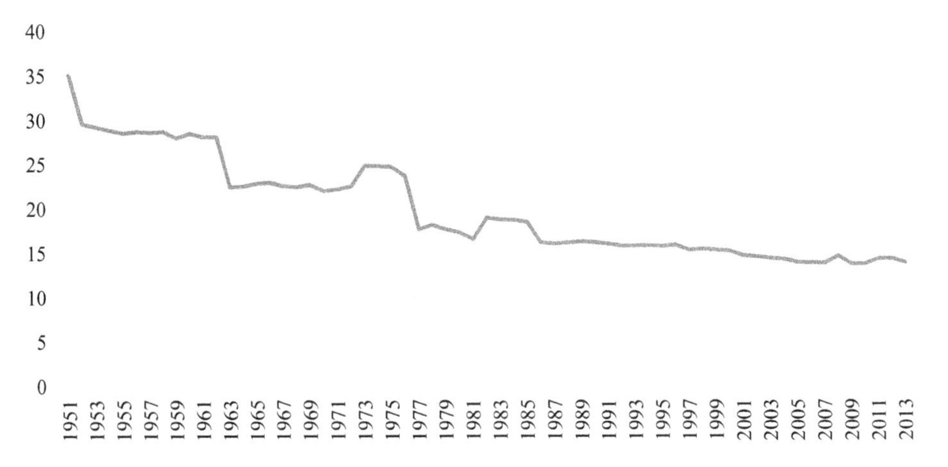

Figure 1.4 Change in food spending in the USA, 1951–2013
Relative importance of food spending as a percentage of the consumer price index (CPI) between 1951 and 2013 for urban consumers in the United States.
Source: Bureau of Labor Statistics, 2017

Table 1.1 Change in the composition of household costs
Change in average household cost composition between 1950 and 2007 in the United States.

	2011	*2002–2003*	*1996–1997*	*1984–1985*	*1972–1973*	*1960–1961*	*1950*
Groceries	13,0%	13,1%	13,8%	15,0%	19,3%	24,3%	29,7%
Alcoholic beverages	0,9%	0,9%	0,9%	1,3%	1,3%	1,7%	1,7%
Living costs	33,8%	32,8%	32,1%	30,4%	30,8%	29,5%	27,2%
Clothes and services	3,5%	4,2%	5,1%	6,0%	7,8%	10,4%	11,5%
Transport	16,7%	19,1%	18,7%	19,6%	19,3%	14,7%	13,4%
Medical attention	6,7%	5,9%	5,3%	4,8%	6,4%	6,6%	5,2%
Leisure	5,2%	5,1%	5,3%	4,8%	8,6%	4,0%	4,4%
Hygiene	1,3%	1,3%	1,5%	1,3%	2,0%	2,9%	2,2%
Books and education	2,3%	2,1%	2,1%	2,0%	1,9%	2,0%	1,5%
Tobacco	0,7%	0,7%	0,8%	1,0%	1,6%	1,8%	1,8%
Miscellaneous	1,6%	1,7%	2,5%	2,1%	1,0%	2,2%	1,4%
Support (donations, child support, …)	3,5%	3,2%	2,8%	3,2%	--	--	--
Personal insurance and pensions	10,9%	9,8%	9,2%	8,6%	--	--	--

Source: Chao & Utgoff, 2006; Bureau of Labor Statistics, 2017

Shopping and consumption have developed into key economic drivers, especially in developed economies.

Industrialization with its productivity gains has led to important decreases in prices and increases in income in relative terms. Together with infrastructure investments, products are now cheaper and can more easily reach people with more money everywhere, a situation that has led to overproduction and oversupply.

Figure 1.5 US consumption in relation to GDP
The development of consumption in the USA in relation to GDP.
Source: Federal Reserve Bank of St. Louis: Economic Research, 2017

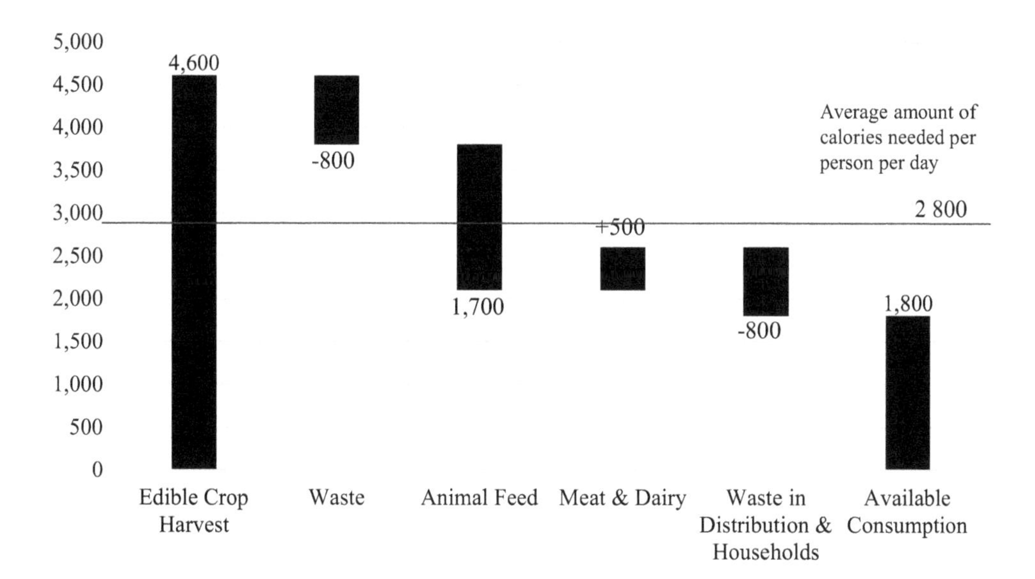

Figure 1.6 Worldwide overproduction of calories
Production and waste in daily calories per person.
Source: Stockholm International Water Institute, 2008

In many parts of the world, societies have gone from being societies of scarcity to societies of overproduction. Economic development has lifted millions of people out of poverty. In parallel, the economic division is increasing. Not only are there important differences between markets, but also within countries. On one side are educated professionals with relatively secure jobs, and on the other side a growing precariousness driven by new low-paid service jobs.

We come from a world that seemed more orderly, in which communication and knowledge generation were firmly organized. Mail, library, telephones, all had their clear place.

This has changed; everything can be found on the internet, accessed from a computer or a mobile device. Today the internet industry has developed into the world's leading industry with the world's most valuable companies.

Digital solutions will reach more and more industries, given that the productivity advantages are immense and the market reach, and its impact on the so-called consumer democracy, has no parallel. The digital revolution is not only changing the way products and services are offered and how they are purchased, but the products and services themselves. In addition, these are changes that have an impact beyond products and services; they are affecting the market and society. The emergence of the shared economy with companies like Uber and Airbnb has not only changed how we buy transportation services or accommodation during the holidays, it has also impacted the market for those services as a whole and has sparked discussions about the new job market of the gig economy.

Digitalization has made shoppers and consumers a part of the purchase process. Shoppers now follow a more deliberate cycle of search, evaluation, point of purchase choice, purchase and purchase evaluation.[9] In particular, social platforms of different types on which shoppers and consumers give advice and exchange opinions on products and services are playing a critical role in the forming of these new shopping journeys. There are information forums on how products or services are used. Consumers and shoppers can be friends with brands, products or companies through Facebook. Manufacturers and companies are trying to influence these flows of information generated directly from shoppers and consumers or other agents, such as influencers. The touchpoints between shopper, consumer

Table 1.2 Change in ranking of brands

MOST VALUABLE BRANDS	
2015	*2000*
1. Apple	1. Coca-Cola
2. Google	2. Microsoft
3. Coca-Cola	3. IBM
4. Microsoft	4. Intel
5. IBM	5. Nokia
6. Toyota	6. GE
7. Samsung	7. Ford
8. GE	8. Disney
9. McDonald's	9. McDonald's
10. Amazon	10. AT&T

The change in the most valuable brands between 2000 and 2015.

Source: Best global brands, 2016

and brands, products and services have multiplied and are no longer under the full control of manufacturers.

At the same time, shoppers and consumers have not become the active shoppers and consumers who seek out, evaluate and exchange information about every potential purchase. Rather, most people are busy with their daily lives and do not wish to devote time to this. From a marketing perspective, the involvement in the category in these cases is too low to generate engagement outside the actual moment of purchase. The involvement is clearly different whether you are buying a car or a loaf of bread.[10] In addition, most shoppers still go to existing stores (brick and mortar) to buy and/or find out about products and services. Here there are important differences between categories of goods.

Traditional sales channels continue to be key in emerging countries, and in developed countries the classic brick-and-mortar retailer, in different formats, still represents the lion's share of sales. At the same time, digital services such as MPESA, the mobile to mobile money transfer system, can radically change the game, including in emerging markets in Africa. The touchpoints along the shopping journey are in most cases the classic and more passive ones, such as television, radio, street or shops. One touchpoint that has certainly decreased in importance are paper newspapers. As an example, the *Independent* of England abandoned its paper edition in 2016 and is now available only on the internet. The *Huffington Post* of the United States was founded only for digital editions. Here a significant number of touchpoints has migrated from paper to digital click touchpoints. The shopper marketing environment and purchasing processes are under constant change, especially due to the digital revolution, the economic development in emerging markets, and the increasing economic divide. In parallel, traditional shopping processes remain, which results in a more complex shopping environment and more complex purchasing processes impacting the discipline of shopper marketing.[11] Together with a hardening competitive environment, winning at the moment of truth has become a key concern for manufacturers. It is not enough to win the preference of consumers; the critical point is to turn that preference into a purchase to generate sales.

The increasing importance of marketing became evident in Kotler's book on marketing in the eighties.[12] Kotler's classic 4Ps approach (product, price, place, promotion) already included the idea of channel management and place, but it did not treat shopper marketing as a discipline and approach of its own.[13]

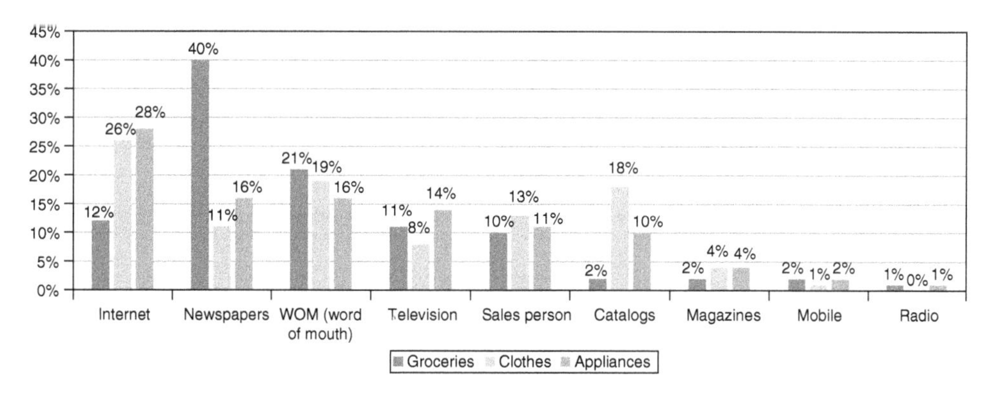

Figure 1.7 Sources of product information
Sources of product information on groceries, clothing and appliances in the UK, 2010.
Source: Cognizant, June 2011

A company can only survive and succeed if it has income, i.e. it must sell its products or services. The act of selling and buying is the fundamental act in a free market economy. Historically, this happened at markets, for example, when farmers transported their produce to villages or towns to sell their surplus production to receive money to buy products that they could not produce themselves. Today, the division of labor is much finer and more complex. The challenge of distributing products and services has decreased while the challenge of selling them has increased. To sell, companies have developed systems and academia has developed disciplines to understand and educate professionals who are dedicated to managing these more and more complex systems. Given that finances are key, subjects such as accounting developed first, which has evolved into controlling, not only to monitor but also to actively direct the company in aligning different areas with their financial objectives. Logistics is key to ensuring that products and services reach buyers and more complex and efficient systems have been developed. In many cases, it is already cheaper to produce in another part of the world and transport the goods to their destination. A company can have the best products and services in the world, but if they are not sold, the product and service will not continue. Philip Kotler emphasized the importance of marketing to the success of companies. To him, marketing was about strategy, and included topics such as product and service development and innovation.[14] Shopper marketing focuses on how to ensure the encounter between product and service and buyer and how specifically to manage that process. It touches many other marketing and company processes that have to be aligned. Shopper marketing is a discipline that ensures effective and efficient sales in coordination and coherence with the company's overall marketing strategy.

Key factors influencing shopper marketing

Introduction

Shopper marketing is a relatively new discipline. It has developed in parallel with the development of the internet and the introduction of new media. That is why one of the most important topics is the influence of digital media on shopper behavior and in particular on the shopper journey. This development has a big impact on the role of brick-and-mortar retail and the interrelationship with e-commerce and digital touchpoints.

Shopping plays an important role in our society and is heavily dependent on economic and societal factors. In order to have an idea about what the future challenges will be, both short and medium term, it is important to understand trends and the possible implications on the purchase process and shopper marketing. Understanding trends and their potential influence on shoppers' purchasing habits is important from a strategic viewpoint, as they will play a key role in the current and future success of a company. This is a challenging task, as no one can see into the future and know which trends will have an impact, what the impact will be and how important they will be.

It is always interesting to read what people have said about the future. One of the great protagonists of the internet is Bill Gates, the founder of Windows. In 1995, he said that the internet was only hype; in 2004, he commented that the problem of spam would be solved in two years and in 2010 that the iPad would not have a future, because it belonged to netbooks. To keep the internet theme, in 1998 Paul Krugmann, the famous 2008 Nobel Prize

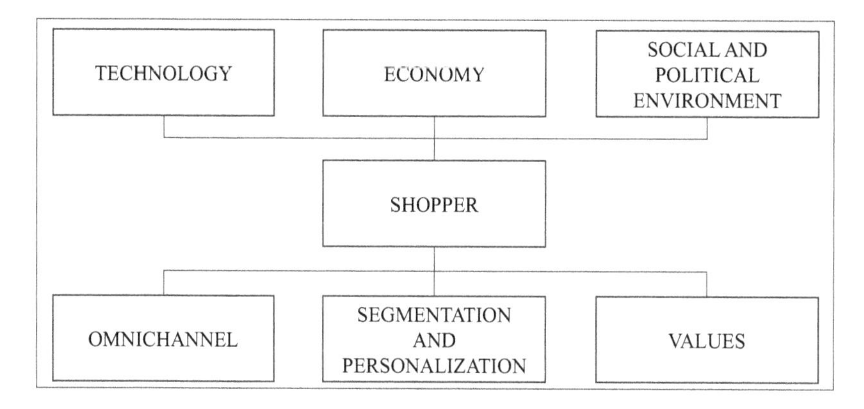

Figure 1.8 Trends influencing shopper behavior
Trends that influence shopper behavior and shopper marketing.
Source: Author

laureate, predicted that the internet would have no more influence on the economy than a fax machine. On a different theme, in 1982, the head of Philips believed that the CD had no future. Moreover, the interesting thing is that not only did it have a future; today it has had to give way to other technologies, like streaming. The CD has undergone almost all phases of the product life cycle, based on Vernon's theories from the sixties on investment products.[15] One of the most famous phrases is that of Thomas Watson in the 1940s that there is no room for more than perhaps five computers in the world. Likewise, many did not believe in the car at the end of the nineteenth century, like the German Emperor who was convinced that the car was just a fashion that would disappear. Trends are not only about products and services, but also about society. For example, in 1905 US President Theodore Roosevelt said that intelligent women did not want to vote, and in 1973, Margaret Thatcher believed that in her life she would not see a woman as prime minister in the United Kingdom. The political map has also changed in an important way. In South America from the 1970s until the 1990s, many countries were still led by military juntas, and there were two opposing ideological blocs worldwide. In the 1990s and into the new century much has been about free trade with the European Union, the North American Free Trade Agreement (NAFTA) and MERCOSUR in South America. There are now some indications of counter-developments, such as the relationship between the USA and China, Brexit and the renegotiation of the NAFTA agreement.

There are three themes that have a major impact on shopper marketing. One is clearly technology, another is economics, in terms of economic policy, but also economic differences between groups and economic development between countries. The third is society and politics, such as environmental regulations, which are becoming more and more of a focus due to global warming.

These trends affect the behavior of shoppers, and thereby the discipline of shopper marketing in three main areas: where shoppers buy, e.g. omnichanneling; their different economic realities and needs, e.g. personalization and segmentation; and what they believe in, e.g. their values. These three areas influence shoppers' behavior and purchase habits.

Technology

We are in the midst of the digital revolution and the changes have had a fundamental impact on the buying behavior of shoppers. Technology has a key impact on what and how we buy. Production technology has made it possible to offer a wide range of products and modern logistics infrastructure has ensured their availability. These developments have been the basis for the development of modern retail.

The development of modern retail was seen as a threat to traditional retail and to the structure of cities with their historically smaller stores. The car in combination with the development of infrastructure and the offer of more products at lower prices facilitated the development of large stores and the decline of small stores with their competitive advantage centered on proximity, service and expertise. The small store cannot usually compete on price or offer. With the increasing awareness of environmental issues and the growth of single households there has been a revival of city shopping, often through chains with small-format stores. In emerging and developing markets, the role of modern retail has sometimes been different. In Latin America, modern retail has been targeted more towards the emerging middle class while traditional stores are the preferred destination for the lower socio-demographic classes, often because they offer cheaper alternatives to leading brands, and also because they fractionate products or offer credits.

The internet is now putting the classic channels under pressure, as modern retail did with the traditional channels. Retailers like Amazon and Alibaba have changed forever the retail landscape, but also classical chains like Walmart are forming the new retail channel landscape. In industries where the manufacturer has a direct relationship with the customer, such as banks or telecommunications service operators, the changes have been fundamental. Digitalization is an opportunity to work more efficiently and lower costs. In this sense, technology is a key player in increasing productivity in retail. In the entertainment industry, digitalization has changed the product itself, such as books, music and movies, and not only the product, but the entire value chain, and even the production of content.

E-commerce has partly reversed the value chain. In the past, sales volumes had to be planned, and products had to be transported to shops and placed on shelves. In e-commerce, distribution comes after the purchase. Traditionally, manufacturers and retailers have been gatekeepers, and due to the limited space in retail, only big brands, or innovations that can drive traffic, have been allowed to arrive on the shelves. With category management and efficient consumer response (ECR) initiatives logistics efficiencies have been optimized, and a leading manufacturer is responsible for developing the entire category strategy in line with retailer guidelines.

Digitalization is turning this division of labor upside down, in some industries more than others. The example "par excellence" is the entertainment industry. Digital technology makes it possible to lower the production costs of books, which can then be distributed through alternative channels. Music and films are now streamed. Streaming sites, like Spotify and Netflix, have become leading distribution channels. With YouTube, people can produce and upload their own content.

Still, not all products enjoy the same e-commerce penetration, for specific categories, the brick-and-mortar experience is still important.

Technology products, such as computers, as shown by Dell, for example, work well through e-commerce and most manufacturers of consumer technology products have their support through the internet. In clothing, initiatives like Zalando are successful, as long as the system of exchanging and returning products works well. For immediate consumption products such as food and beverages, the internet has influenced the reservation system on one side, and the delivery service, through companies like Uber Eats, on the other side. As with clothing,

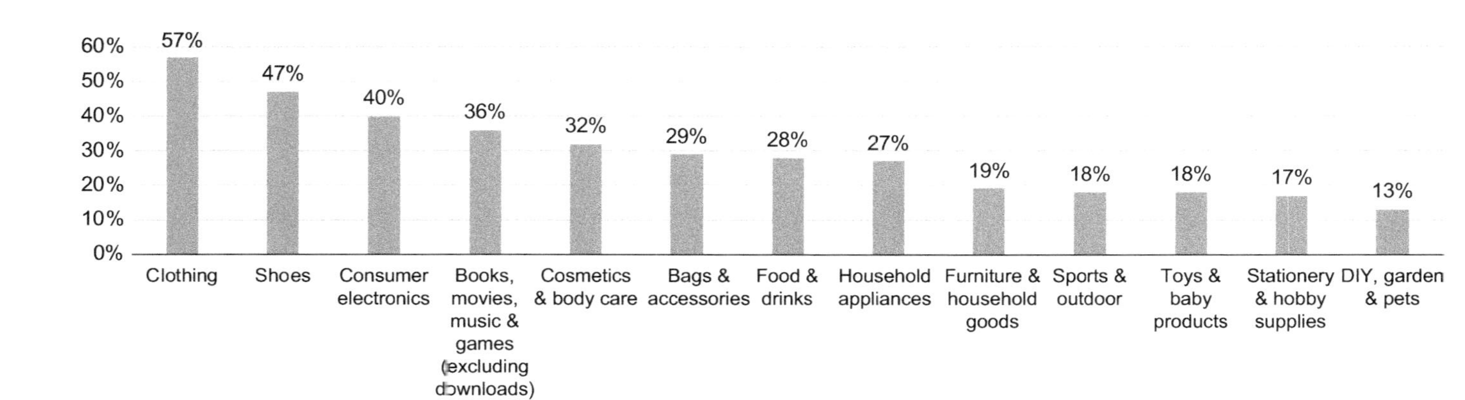

Figure 1.9 Categories purchased online
Worldwide percentage of people who have purchased these categories online, 2018.
Source: Datareportal.com

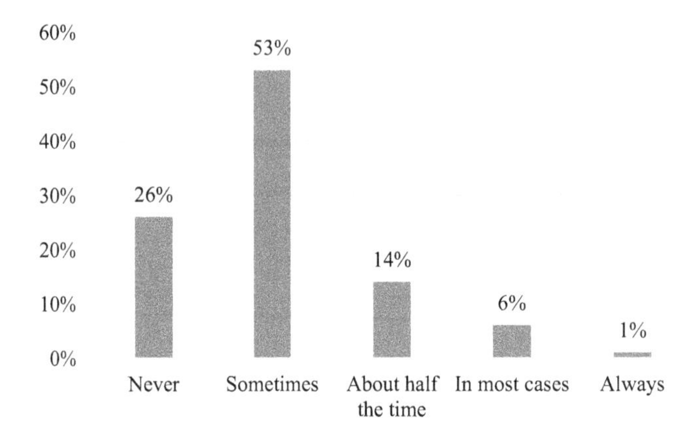

Figure 1.10 Omnichannel usage
Shoppers who ordered on the internet to pick up products in store in the United Kingdom in 2013.
Source: Cognizant, 2014

the change in technology, from telephone to the internet, has increased usage, rather than radically changing behavior. Nevertheless, in many categories, the customer experience of face-to-face interaction and the shopping and consumption ambiance is crucial.

It is not only the internet, but other technological developments like artificial intelligence (AI) and robots that are becoming more important. In countries like Japan that are facing demographic challenges due to low birth rates and very strict immigration laws there is a lack of people for service jobs, e.g. in the health sector or in hotels. Robots have been tested to replace some of the work normally conducted by humans.

Over the Christmas and New Year period 2015/2016, the most important retailers in the United Kingdom increasingly introduced e-commerce. Although there was a fear of cannibalization between sales channels, results showed that the different sales channels actually complemented each other. The retailers that had pushed e-commerce channels grew not only in that channel, but in the brick-and-mortar sales channels as well. Technology is not a zero-sum game, but opens up new opportunities to influence shoppers and their attitudes.[16]

The internet and the interaction of channels, such as ordering on the internet and collecting the products at a predetermined site, e.g. on the way home (click and collect) increases the convenience for shoppers.[17]

In addition, the interest for omnichannel solutions is clearly growing and will increasingly be an integral part of shoppers' behavior in the future. Higher levels of shopper satisfaction are positively correlated with higher levels of spend by multichannel users.[18] Multichannel means parallel channels that do not interact, while cross-channel or omnichannel is when channels interact. Shoppers show higher levels of satisfaction in omnichannel environments.[19] Depending on shoppers' attitudes, omnichannel usage has to be evaluated differently. More involvement, loyalty and experience equals more satisfaction.[20] This needs to be actively managed by manufacturers.[21]

Technology, especially the internet, not only changes how we buy and the production process, but also how we inform ourselves and how we are influenced.[22] There is a video from Scholz & Friends called 'Shift in Marketing Reality' that shows how media and advertising rules have changed in recent years.[23] Until the 1990s, the most important medium was television and many countries only had one or two networks, mostly state owned. Today, the media available to us are vastly different. From the point of view of timing, one could say

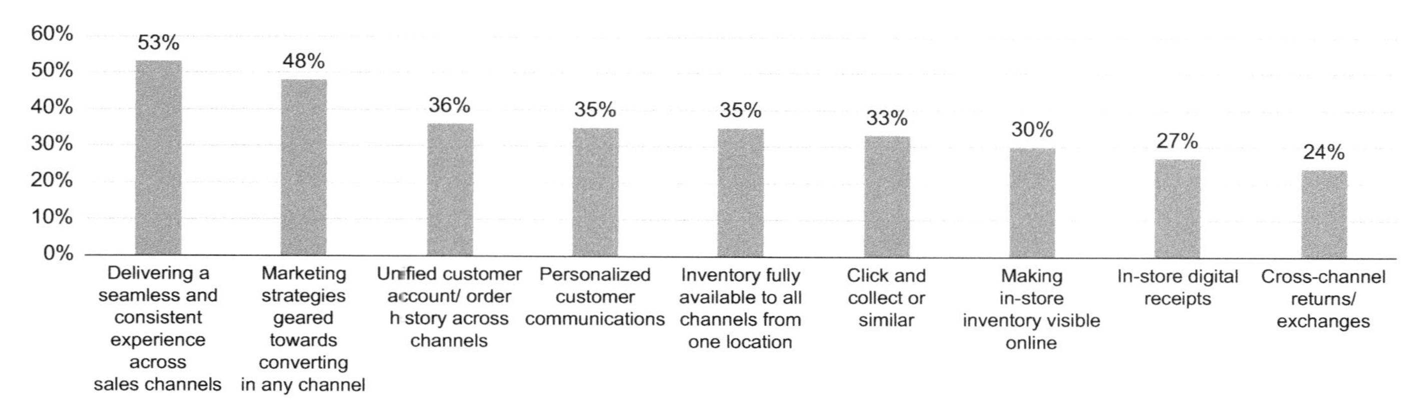

Figure 1.11 Interest in omnichannel solutions
Omnichannel capabilities that retailers worldwide planned to implement in 2018 (% of respondents).
Source: Brightpearl & Multichannel Merchant, 2017

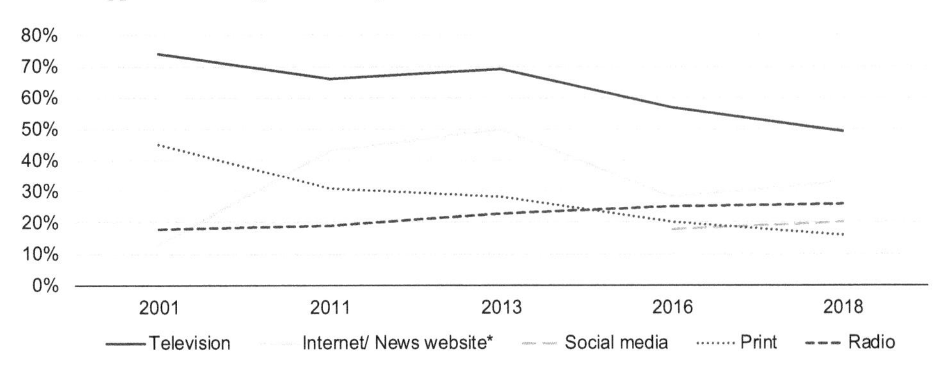

Figure 1.12 News sources
Change in major news sources in the United States between 2001 and 2018.
*Until 2013 reported as internet, after divided into news websites and social media
Source: Pew Research Center, 2013; 2018

that it has gone from prime time to right time. Moreover, the right time is in the hands of consumers and shoppers. The other big change is the equipment. If in the past the equipment of influence was the television or the radio, today there are a wide variety of media equipment and screens, such as televisions, computers, tablets or cell phones. Both traditional and social communication have a positive impact on brand equity.[24] With the increase of the number of touchpoints at the point of purchase, be it brick and mortar or digital, the point of purchase becomes even more important in the decision process.[25]

The direction of communication has changed dramatically. Previously it was a simple model of communication, from manufacturer through major media channels to consumers/shoppers. Today, there is a great variety of media channels, from classical ones, like television, radio, newspapers, peer to peer, and word of mouth (WOM) between consumers/shoppers and among other influencers, to bloggers, YouTube personalities or people who have or want to have an opinion or make fun of companies and products.[26] This has been made possible thanks to new social platforms such as Facebook, Twitter, YouTube, Instagram, etc. Social media makes it possible to better target different segments of shoppers.[27] Influencers can have an important impact, especially if the public, potential consumers and shoppers, identify with them.[28] If in the past creativity was something that only belonged to the content of advertisements, creativity today has not only to do with content but also with the mix of channels and influencers. While not too much has changed when it comes to radio the importance of print newspapers and magazines has given way to internet sources. There are already newspapers and magazines that have only digital editions, such as the *Huffington Post*, which was founded as an internet newspaper.

For billboards, electronic screens offer the possibility of changing the advertisements faster and cheaper, and adapting to different timetables and targets. With codes, such as QRs, it is possible to tailor communications via consumers' and shoppers' cell phones. Electronic coupons have been found to be more efficient than paper coupons, increasing usage rates from 1 to 5 percent and even 15 percent in some cases. Cell phones also facilitate the management of customer programs, such as loyalty programs, customer clubs, newsletters and so on. Moreover, communication around products and services can be expanded by providing additional information through cell phones, referred to as "beyond the package".[29] Location information on where to find stores, evaluation of stores and stock availability can all be accessed through the internet and cell phones. The use of cell phones can lengthen the shopping trip and spending through applications.[30]

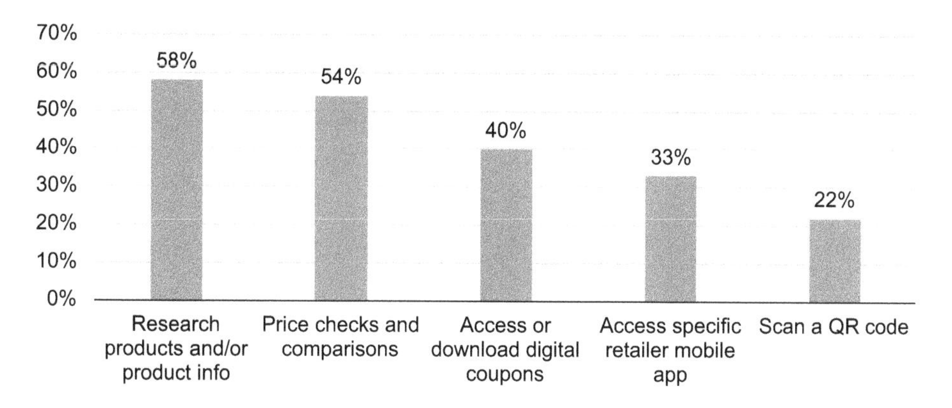

Figure 1.13 Use of cell phones during a shopping trip
How consumers use cell phones in store in the USA in 2017
Source: Skrovan, 2017

The development of technology has changed and is changing the behavior of shoppers and thus shopper marketing, especially the management of touchpoints and omnichannel solutions.[31]

Economy

It seems that the world has been in constant economic crisis since 2008. The effects of the Corona pandemic of 2020 are still to be seen. China, seen for many years as one of the most important engines of the world economy, is lagging behind expectations and many analysts believe that the growth numbers achieved in previous years have been partially pushed by the Chinese government. In addition, the other BRIC countries (Brazil, Russia and India) have continuously been below growth expectations.

The economy of the United States is still going strong. They have chosen a more aggressive monetary policy, as well as government spending path. The European Union, on the other hand, which has tried to opt for a stricter monetary policy, has experienced lower growth rates, as well as political tensions, as seen in the Brexit development.

Still, the general trend of recent decades has been to open up economies to more free trade. The Trump presidency is following a stronger America First policy, and together with the 2020 Corona pandemic, the effects on free trade are still to be seen. The trend toward free trade has been due in part to the spread of political democracy and the end of communist and military dictatorships in Europe and South America. During the decades when military dictatorships dominated Latin America between the 1960s and 1980s, only Mexico, which was under a very authoritarian government, Venezuela, Colombia and Costa Rica were not governed by military juntas. In Europe, the fall of the Berlin Wall in 1989 was the beginning of the fall of communist dictatorships in Eastern Europe. In addition, before that, countries like Greece, Spain and Portugal had left their military dictatorships behind them.

This political development has led to increased globalization of trade, a globalization that is not only about the economy and the possibility of international companies reaching new markets more easily or establishing production in low-cost countries. There is an important social aspect to it as well. This social aspect is clearly supported by the technical developments in communication. Through globalization, influences and trends become global as well. People are confronted with similar brands and products, the same fashion, the

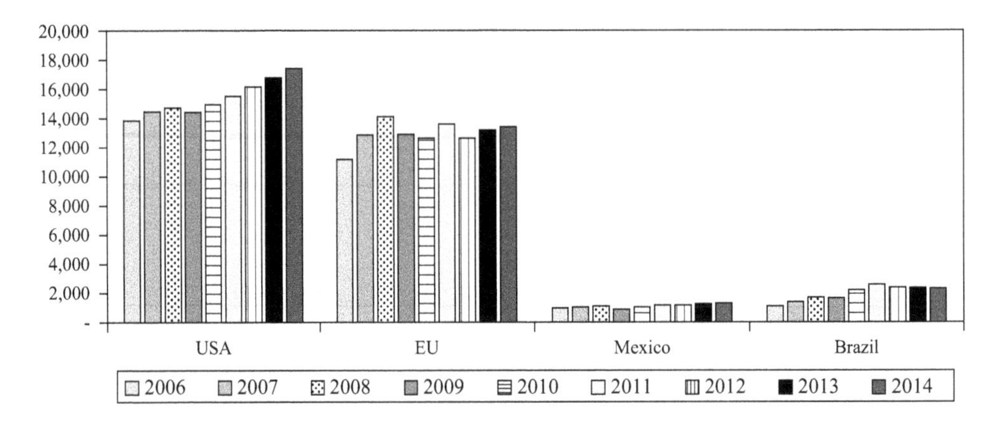

Figure 1.14 GDP in the United States, European Union, Mexico and Brazil
GDP of the United States, European Union, Mexico and Brazil in billion US dollars between 2006 and 2014.
Source: The World Bank, 2017; Trading Economics, 2016

same movies etc., although with some regional and local adaptations. Such a development is criticized by some and seen as something very positive by others.

Another important trend is the growth of emerging economies. It is clear that many economies have grown very rapidly in recent years and many South American countries have been very successful, as well as countries in Eastern Europe or parts of Asia. Through a growing middle class and purchasing power in these countries, shopping has become more important. Still, purchasing power is low in many cases, often referred to as the bottom of the pyramid economies. Although on an individual basis purchasing power can be very low, through the cumulative power of the people at the bottom of the pyramid the market becomes very attractive as a target to companies.[32]

An interesting example of companies that have been successful in reaching these groups of shoppers and consumers are cell phone companies, who have developed profitable businesses in almost all markets on all continents, reaching high cell phone penetration rates.

Globalization from an economic point of view is seen by many as a possibility to grow the economy and develop and enlarge a middle class where it did not exist before. The bottom of the pyramid economies are also developing and many working conditions in emerging countries are seen as phases of development, which over time will be surpassed, as they were in North America and Western Europe.

In recent years, there have been critical views, led by economists such as Paul Krugmann or Thomas Piketty, who point out that economic development is something enjoyed by only the richest part of the population.[33] While important population groups are rising out of poverty in emerging and developing economies, there is an increasing inequality in developed economies. The social mobility between social classes that existed after the Second World War until the 1980s has slowed down.

Neoliberalism developed as a reaction to the New Deal in the United States as academics feared a development towards "big" government, as they had seen in Europe, leading to central planning. Von Mises described in his book *Bureaucracy* the danger of central planning and von Hayek saw the danger of an oppression of individuality and a route to totalitarianism in socialist initiatives. The two founded the Mont Pelerin Society in 1947.[34] Milton Friedman built on the ideas of neoliberalism and these ideas

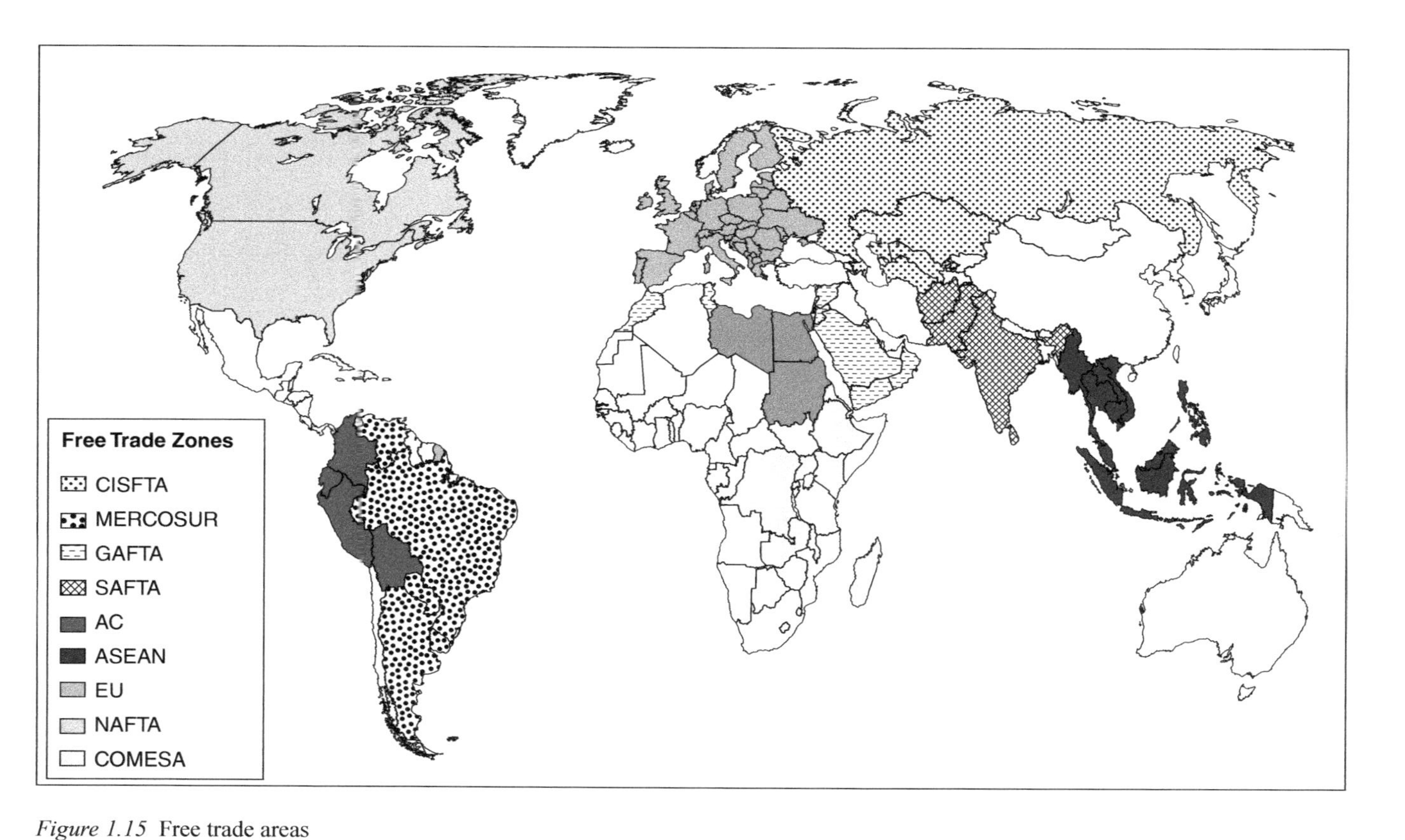

Figure 1.15 Free trade areas

The map shows the most important free trade areas: the Commonwealth of Independent States Free Trade Area (CISFTA), MERCOSUR, the Greater Arab Free Trade Area (GAFTA), South Asian Free Trade Area (SAFTA), the Andean Community (AC), the Association of Southeast Asian Nations (ASEAN), the European Union (EU), the North American Free Trade Agreement (NAFTA) and the Common Market of East and South Africa (COMESA).

Source: Danielson, 2017

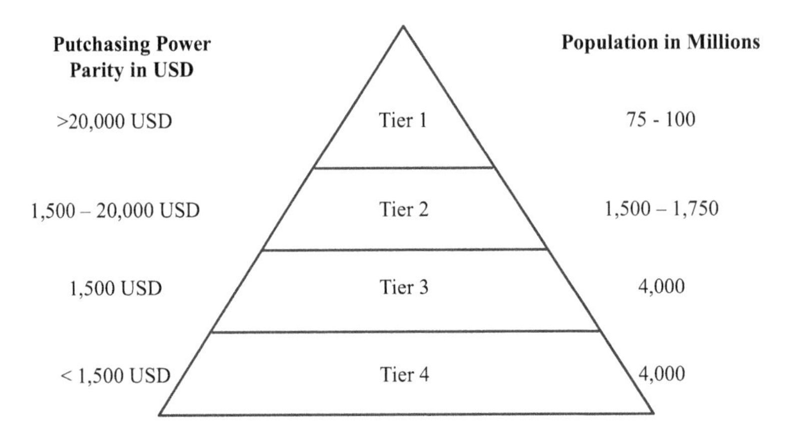

Figure 1.16 Economic pyramid
The economic pyramid depicting the world population by purchasing power parity and number of people, in millions.
Source: Prahalad & Hart, 2002

were used in the 1980s by Reagan and Thatcher as a critique against Keynesianism and demand-side economics.[35] Neoliberalism led to tax cuts, deregulation and privatization with the result of a concentration of wealth in the high income brackets.[36] There has also been strong criticism that there are vital services in which competition does not really work, like health care, or banks, as they are often not allowed to go bankrupt.[37] Some authors present the thesis that the crisis is used to introduce political change and privatizations, such as the privatization of the education system in New Orleans after Hurricane Katrina.[38] Through the privatization of common goods, some people, such as the oligarchs in Russia, have become very rich and powerful without actually developing anything themselves.[39] Given the concentration of wealth and power, normal households increasingly have had to finance their consumption through debt. With an increasing economic divide new retail formats, like discounters, and new offerings, like retail brands and low-cost services, have emerged.[40]

As society and the economic reality is changing, so are social classes. A society grows economically, but the growth is felt mostly by the richest percentage of the population, the wealth of the middle class ends-up being mainly based on their property ownership, and lower social classes become dependent on subsidies or state support. With the transformation from an industrial to a service economy, social classes are changing. What once were classes of capitalists, managers/technicians and workers have transformed into a society of capitalists and managers, professionals and a type of precariat of people in low-paid service jobs, working in the gig economy or looking for a job.

Countries are at different stages of economic development, and the economic divide impacts the lifestyle and needs of different categories of consumers and shoppers. Segmented approaches are needed within shopper marketing to address the different needs of shoppers. In addition, there are important lifestyle differences that need to be addressed with increased personalization of offers.

There is no single shopper marketing approach, but many different ones, aimed at, for example, Peru or Sweden, or various social classes and lifestyles.

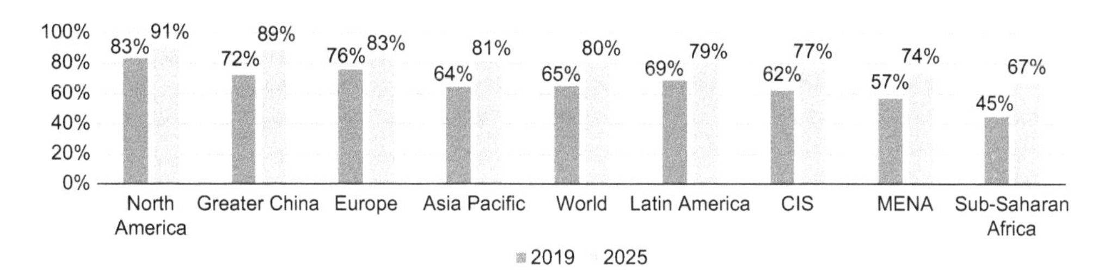

Figure 1.17 Smartphone penetration
Smartphone penetration in 2019 and expected in 2025 for different parts in the world.
CIS: Commonwealth of Independent States
MENA: Middle East and North Africa
Source: GSMA, 2019

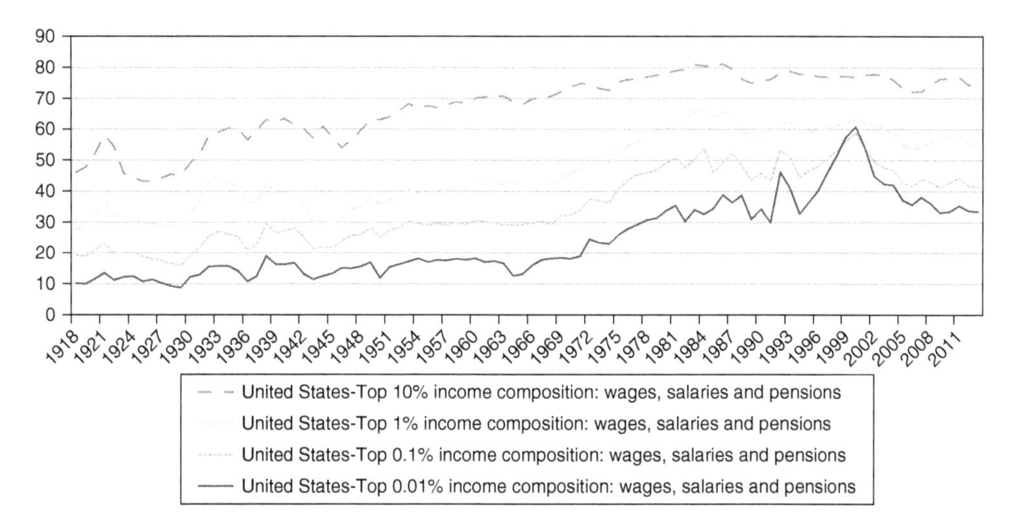

Figure 1.18 Distribution of income
Share of total income of the groups with the highest incomes (the 10%, 1%, 0.1% and 0.01% highest income brackets) from salaries, wages and pensions in the United States between 1918 and 2011. Does not include dividends or other capital income.
Source: Wid.World, 2017

Social and political sphere

Plato proclaimed that human beings are political beings, "zoon politikon". The society in which we grow up, the society in which we live and the society we desire are, at least partially, results of political aspirations. These aspirations influence our behavior and our preferences.

Utilitarianism as a fundamental piece of modern economics was introduced as a moral theory by Jeremy Bentham and John Stuart Mills, and later used in economic theories by academics such as David Ricardo. It describes the process in which activities and decisions that maximize the utility of the collective as a whole are good.[41] It is a general and practical concept in the analysis, but the problem is the operationalization of the concept of utility, given also that it is based on individual preferences, especially as those preferences can be changed. The collective utility is normally seen in economic terms, but other dimensions such as the environment,

Table 1.3 The new social classes

Class	*Importance*	*Average age*	*University education*	*Belong to ethnic minorities*	*Average savings*	*Average household income*	*Average value housing*	*Cultural activity*
The Elite	6%	57	56%	4%	> 140 000	90 000	325 000	High
Established Middle Class	25%	46	43%	13%	26 000	47 000	177 000	High
Technical Middle Class	6%	52	26%	9%	66 000	8 000	163 000	Moderate
New Affluent Workers	15%	44	11%	11%	4 900	30 000	129 000	Moderate
Traditional Working Class	14%	66	11%	9%	9 500	13 000	127 000	--
Emergent Service Workers	19%	34	19%	21%	1 200	21 000	18 000	--
The Precariat	15%	50	3%	13%	800	8 000	27 000	--

New categorization of social classes in the UK instead of the classic divisions of upper, middle and working class. In £.

Source: Savage et al., 2013

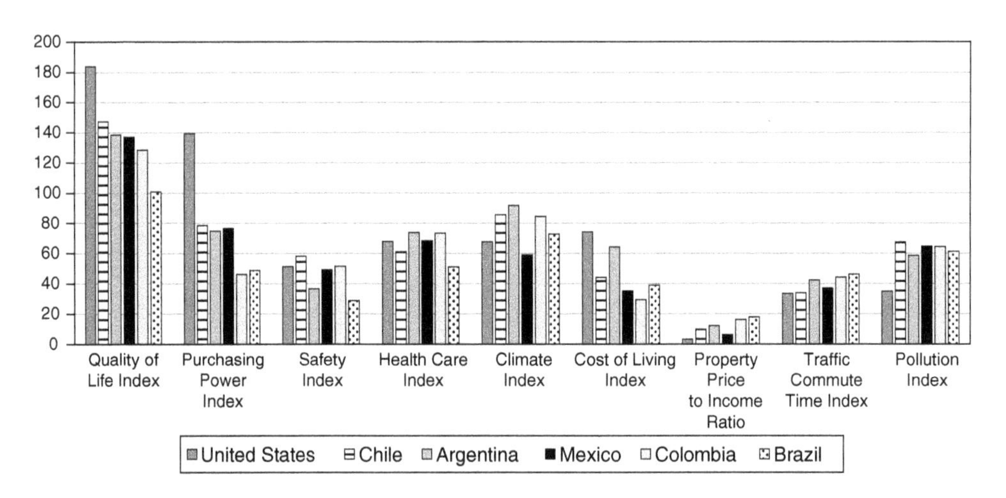

Figure 1.19 Quality of life index
Quality of life index and sub-indices for the United States, Chile, Argentina, Mexico, Colombia and Brazil in 2016.
Source: Numbeo, 2017

or even happiness, as introduced by Bhutan, are becoming more important. There are also indicators such as quality of life to measure the development of countries.

Preferences in societies change and have political impact on regulations, but also on preferred behavior. Examples are the discussions on sustainability, or the use of children as workers in sweatshops in countries such as China or Bangladesh. Something that was once normal, such as smoking, is today seen as something negative, with more and more regulations surrounding it. Another example is sugar: the UK has introduced extra taxes for products with a high sugar content, such as soft drinks. This has important impacts on the positioning of products and the image of the company and its brands.

The political sphere is influenced by values in the society, but also influences those values. The smoking ban in public spaces in many countries has affected and limited how tobacco products can be used, and the same can be said for products with high sugar levels. As an example, Mexico's sales of sugared soft drinks fell by 12 percent in the first year of the introduction of the new law in 2015.[42] In addition, such factors as fair trade for, e.g., coffee, or actions against child labor have implications on how products can be sold or consumed, and thereby influence shopper marketing. Values of consumers and shoppers, as well as trends have and will have an important impact on behavior and ultimately on the offer, and on how to communicate and activate products and services.

Implications for shopper marketing strategies

Shopper marketing solutions have to adapt to changes and trends in societal values. Certainly, there are values that are relatively stable, but others where there are important differences, such as those concerning the roles of women, the church or equality between social classes. For example, a major telephone operator in Nigeria, Zain, always has to adapt its advertisements, depending on the target region of the country. In the North, there are mainly Muslims and in the South, the majority are Christians.

A segmented approach is needed based on lifestyle, aspirations and social class. In addition, differences in economic development affect what can be sold and how to reach shoppers. As an example, banking services in Kenya were developed by mobile operators, the famous MPESA, to send and withdraw money in a society where most people had no secure income and where there were no banking structures in place. On the other hand, in many Western societies banks are closing their branches and developing digital channels. In Peru, banks have introduced

Figure 1.20 Example of ethnic advertisements
Advertisements for the service Tru from the mobile operator Zain in Nigeria in 2006 for the Southern and Northern regions of the country.
Source: Author

simple banking services in traditional grocery stores to be closer to their customers. The services are similar, but the solutions differ depending on country and population segment.

Technology will continue to have a significant impact on how we shop and how products and services are offered. Omnichannel solutions, i.e. the interaction of different sales channels, will grow in importance, and media channels will continue to change, influencing the number of touchpoints and the way to communicate with consumers and shoppers. Shopper marketing needs to understand societal changes in terms of the economy, politics and values and adapt to these changes when developing specific strategies for brands, products and services.

Notes

1 (Friedman, 1962)
2 (Stigler, 1975)
3 (Becker & Posner, 2009)
4 (Lucas, 2005)
5 (Knight & Emmet, 1999)
6 (Dezalay & Garth, 2002)
7 (Fukuyama, 1989)
8 (Piketty & Goldhammer, 2014)
9 (Shankar et al., 2011)
10 (Liebmann & Kraigher-Krainer, 2003)
11 (Underhill, 1999)
12 (Kotler & Armstrong, 2006)
13 (Kotler & Armstrong, 2006)
14 (Kotler & Armstrong, 2006)
15 (Vernon, 1966)
16 (Shankar & Balasubramanian, 2009) and (Shankar et al., 2010)
17 (Verhoef et al., 2007)
18 (Larivière et al., 2011)
19 (Chatterjee, 2010)
20 (Piercy, 2012)
21 (Egol et al., 2013) and (Cognizant, June 2011)
22 (Grewal et al., 2014)
23 (Scholz and Friends, 2008)
24 (Bruhn et al., 2012)
25 (Gilbride et al., 2013)
26 (Diehlmann, 2011)
27 (Neff, 2009)
28 (Ahrens & Dressler, 2011)
29 (GSMA, 2015)
30 (Huang et al., 2013)
31 (Neslin & Shankar, 2009) and (Neslin et al., 2006)
32 (Prahalad, 2004), (Prahalad & Hart, 2002) and (D'Andrea, Ring, Aleman & Stengel, 2006)
33 (Piketty & Goldhammer, 2014) and (Krugman, 2009)
34 (von Mises, 1944) and (von Hayek, 1944).
35 For the originals, see (Keynes, 1936) and (Friedman, 1962).
36 (Monbiot, 2016)
37 (Judt, 2010)
38 (Klein, 2007)
39 (Sayer, 2015)
40 (Wendt, 2010)
41 (Brewer, 2010)
42 (Editorial Board, 2016)

2 Strategic shopper marketing

Shopper marketing has left the store. It now also includes before and after the purchase, which can take place in brick-and-mortar or digital points of purchase. With digitalization, fragmentation of media and purchase channels, channel blurring, omnichannel shopper behavior and always connected shoppers looking for convenience and seamless shopping experiences, shopper marketing has grown increasingly complex. An outside-in approach is essential to transform shopper journey insights into a route to purchase strategy to ensure the right offering for specific consumption occasions for a defined target group at the right time and place, activated across key touchpoints.

Shopper marketing has traditionally been a discipline with much academic research focused on attitudes and in-store behavior, and more lately including online search and decision behavior. It has evolved from describing shopper behavior to driving profitable sales by connecting the route to purchase with the route to market in line with the defined marketing strategy to ensure the availability of the right product and service at the right point of purchase at the right time activated in the right way. Strategic shopper marketing is based on several disciplines, such as category management and ECR, trade marketing, channel management, consumer marketing in terms of shopper journey management, loyalty management, and sales and distribution.

Strategic shopper marketing is cross-functional in nature and integrates the management of shoppers, touchpoints, channels and distribution, and requires both business-to-consumer and -shopper, and business-to-business management skills.

The emergence of strategic shopper marketing

Shopper marketing, especially in the new digitalized era, is steadily gaining in importance.[1] The increasing investments in the field of shopper marketing show the growing importance for manufacturers of converting shoppers into profitable buyers.[2] In recent years the spending in shopper marketing activities has continuously increased. While classic shopper marketing spend is plateauing and even decreasing, the marketing spend increase is largely directed toward digital, including digital shopper activation.[3]

There is a shared view that shopper marketing brings value to manufacturers, retailers and shoppers alike.[4] With the growing importance and spread of shopper marketing, the discipline needs to develop a more scientific approach.[5] This includes moving beyond the traditional view of shopper marketing as a tool to drive conversion and sales in the short term at the point of sale, usually through presentation, promotions and discounts, which are short-term activities that could threaten brand equity in the longer term.[6]

Shopper marketing is confronted with many challenges, such as a lack of information and shared standards to measure results. Therefore, budget allocations are often not adapted to the challenges of shopper marketing, leading to sub-optimum alignments between manufacturers and retailer across multiple channels and points of purchase formats.[7]

The role of shopper marketing has moved away from being description oriented to become an action-oriented discipline, from describing buying behavior to driving purchases. Shopper marketing has traditionally been very close to research and in many companies it is clearly related to the insights function.

Shopper marketing is still a young discipline with little literature.[8] The shopper marketing service industry has traditionally been led by market research companies. Other types of consultancy have entered later or only partially. Shopper marketing is often located between several departments based on the internal organization by company activities, rather than the logic of the purchase process of the shopper.

The purchase process, the action of purchasing a product or service from a company, is one of the most crucial acts in the relationship between the company and its customers. No purchase, no revenues; and no revenues, no company. In other words, shopper marketing is of strategic importance.

Shopper marketing tries to ensure that the buyer, the shopper, meets the product or service. Then, more and more fine-tuning is needed: who is the target shopper; how to find a solution tailored to the shopper's needs, depending on the place, the time, and the situation; how to increase the conversion from shopper to buyer; and how to make the product or service available at each crucial moment. The basic idea of shopper marketing is to ensure that the shopper and product and service will meet at the right time and place to generate a purchase and thereby sales in a profitable way.

Internally, from an organizational point of view, it can be argued that shopper marketing is simply the function that ensures that consumer marketing is aligned with sales and distribution.

The roots of shopper marketing go beyond research of shopper behavior. Shopper marketing links the route to purchase and the route to market. Route to purchase, in short, is

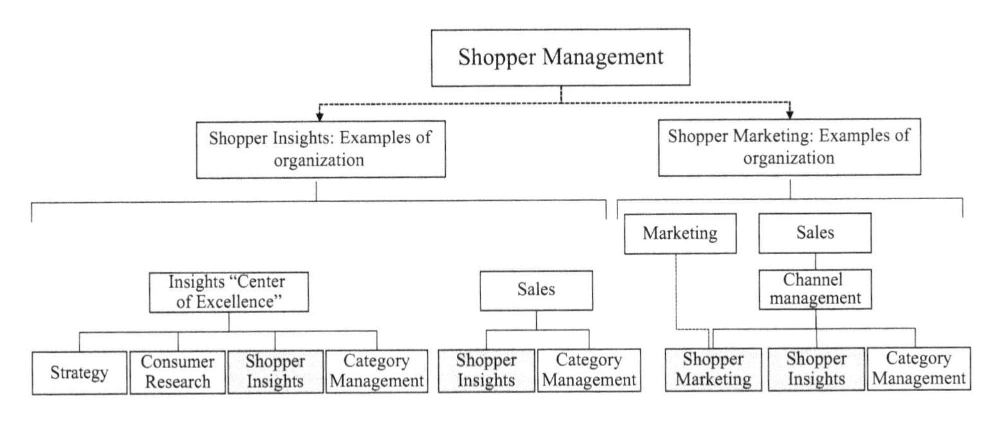

Figure 2.1 Examples of shopper marketing organization
Shopper marketing is often organized as part of research, and sometimes as coordination between sales and marketing.
Source: Weber, 2009

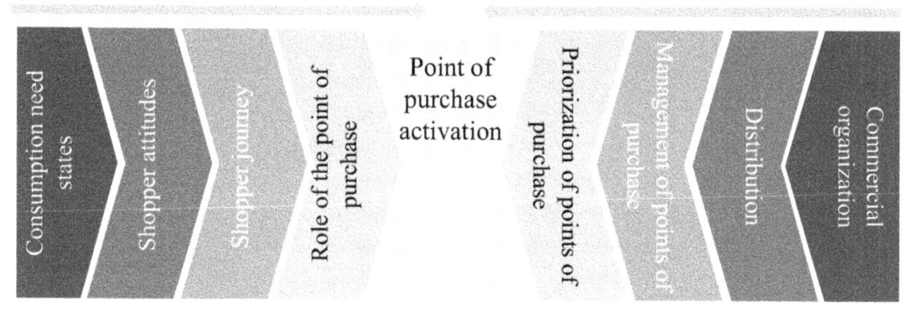

Figure 2.2 Connecting the route to purchase with the route to market
Optimal activation at the point of purchase is based on the shopper's needs (consumption need states), his or hers attitude toward the purchase (e.g. involvement and planning), the touchpoints and their interrelations with the shopper and the product/service/brand (shopper journey), the choice of the point of purchase based on its role (attributes of the point of purchase based on the shopping mission of the shopper), and the management of the points of purchase based on the prioritization and optimization of distribution to reach the points of purchase, and the necessary commercial organization.
Source: Author

the management of the shopping journey. The management of directing shoppers to products and services, the moment of truth, and how to finally convert the shopper into a buyer. The route to market is the management of the product and service to be available to the shopper at the moment and the place intended to maximize the conversion of shoppers into buyers, and the flow of money back to the company.

Shopper marketing has multiple roots. Academic research on purchasing behavior has traditionally focused on the behavior in stores, at the time of purchase, but also on the attitude of shoppers in terms of both involvement and purchase planning. Influencers have also been investigated, such as the influence of persons accompanying shoppers. Category management is another important root of shopper marketing and there are those who see the development of shopper marketing as the phase that has followed category management. Category management was born out of the need to find productive ways of cooperation between retailers and manufacturers. This includes initiatives such as ECR, in response to which many companies have installed category management functions.[9]

Category management does not end with shopper marketing, but remains key in the management of the relationship between retailers and manufacturers, especially focusing on organized trade, and the organization, presentation and activation of categories in stores. Thus, it can be said that category management is a vital part of shopper marketing, which has contributed much to the development of the discipline.

Another important influence on shopper marketing is trade marketing, to activate the point of purchase through in-store marketing. It is no longer enough to manage channels to activate consumers and sales, it is necessary to activate the shopper at the final decision point in modern and traditional channels. A long-standing discussion has been whether trade marketing should be part of marketing, to develop in-store marketing plans; or part of sales, to develop channel strategies. As shopper marketing evolved, it started to include a focus out of the store, looking at the entire shopping journey to understand how the buying process works, rather than just the act of purchase. Shopper marketing has had to understand

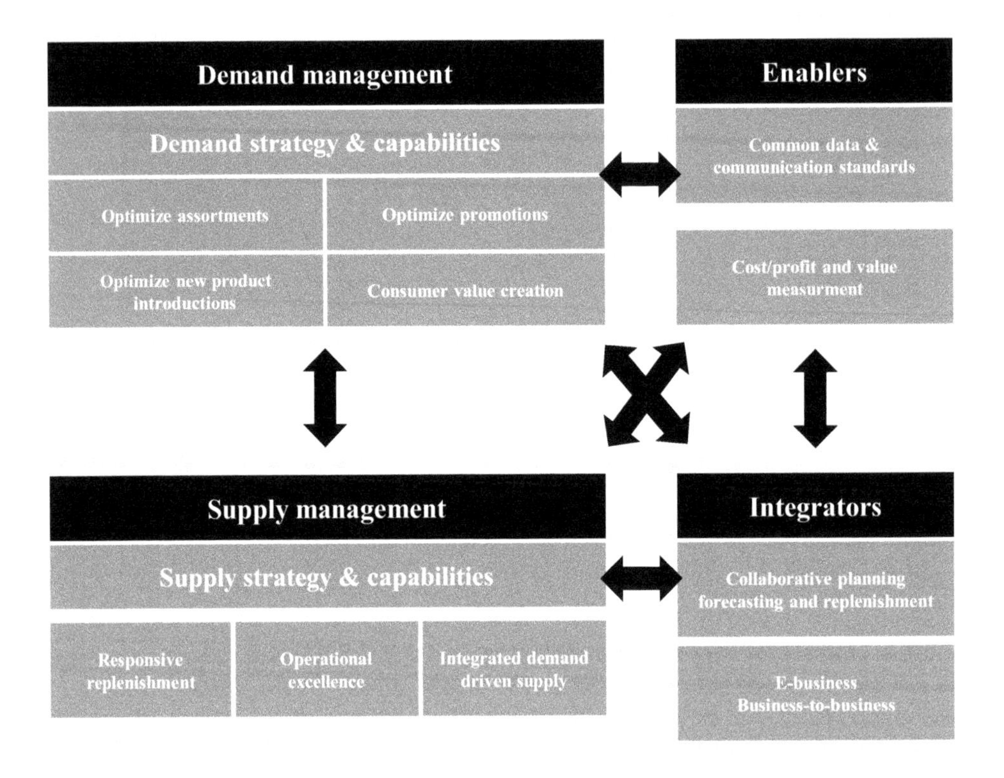

Figure 2.3 ECR Scorecard
ECR Europe Scorecard, including the main areas of the collaboration between manufacturers and retailers of demand and supply management, and enablers and integrators.
Source: ECR Europe, emnos & The Partnering Group, 2011

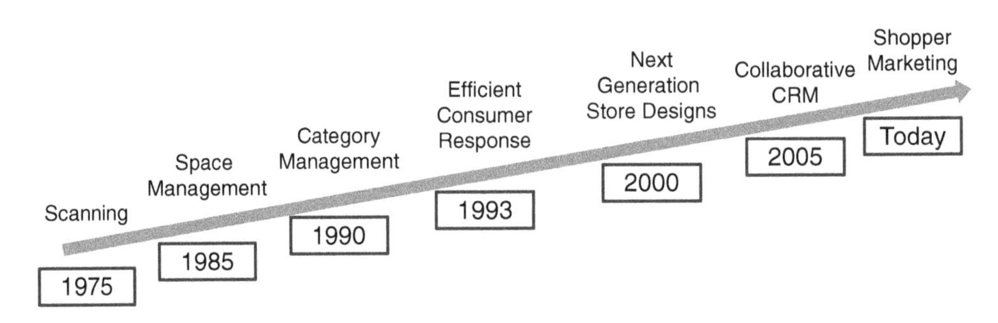

Figure 2.4 Development of shopper marketing according to the Partnering Group
The Partnering Group's view on how shopper marketing is the next step in the collaboration approaches between manufacturers and retailers.
Source: ECR Europe, emnos & The Partnering Group, 2011

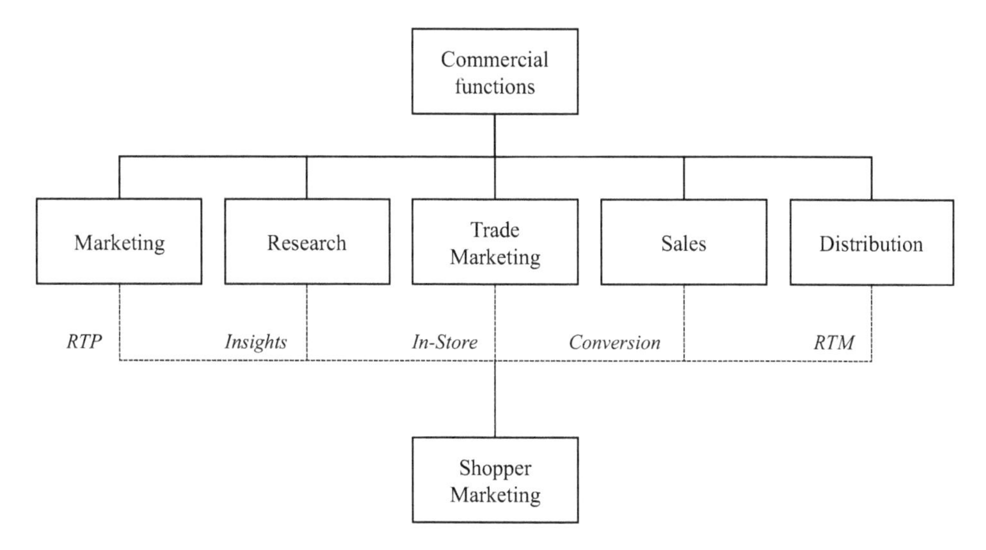

Figure 2.5 Commercial functions related to shopper marketing
Functions of the commercial organization that normally have activities related to shopper marketing.
Source: Author

how different touchpoints work between brand, product, service and shoppers and how the relationship between the shopper and the consumer works, especially in an environment in which shopper journeys become more individual.[10] In that sense, shopper marketing utilizes consumer marketing insights, knowledge and tools. Shopper marketing, as it deals with customers of retailers and manufacturers, is much about loyalty and loyalty programs. In sectors like banking and telecommunications, the relationship is continuous and direct, in contrast to individual purchases of products, in which the shopper can have a preference, but the contractual relationship ends with the purchase. Other roots of shopper marketing come from the channel management side, such as sales and customer management to align interests and ensure preferences and activation at the point of purchase. This includes the distribution and availability of products at the defined points of purchase. Finally, shopper marketing has an important organizational aspect, determining how to structure and organize for a successful implementation.

Shopper marketing has a strategic focus with many different roots and incorporates many functions, or rather, it is part of many functions that need to be coordinated. By definition, a company has shopper marketing, even if it does not have a specific department for it.

Very often the challenge is not that there is no shopper marketing, but that it is spread across the organization, following the logic of the company rather than that of the market.

The importance and relevance of a business discipline is often linked to the specialists providing solutions to companies, the people in charge of it in companies, and the resources dedicated to the discipline. Some companies have established shopper marketing departments, but often they are relatively small and are part or report to other departments, such as sales or marketing.

Shopper marketing, or rather, the activities associated with shopper marketing, are often found in research, trade marketing or key account management. Shopper marketing is often

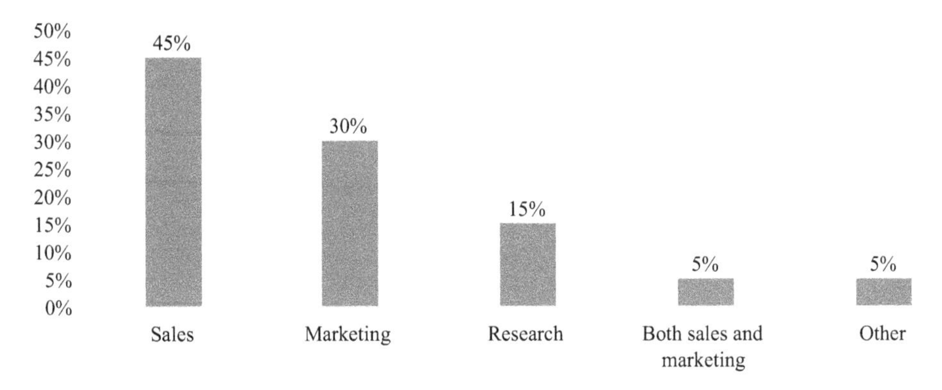

Figure 2.6 Location of the shopper marketing department within commercial organizations
Departments where shopper marketing normally is located in the organization (USA).
Source: Madlberger, 2011

a responsibility of the research department to generate shopper insights, or support in category management efforts. More rarely, it is situated within the marketing department.

Many see shopper marketing as the next step of category management. But in many companies shopper marketing is still understood as category management, and category management is equated with a decision tree. Clearly, there are many cases and companies that focus successfully in the area of shopper marketing, but broadly speaking they are more the exception than the rule. However, by definition, every company is doing shopper marketing. In fact, it cannot exist without shopper marketing, as it is the basic task of bringing products and services and buyers together to generate sales. Normally, the activities of shopper marketing are organized across different departments, such as marketing, trade marketing, sales, and distribution. Nevertheless, some companies have a department specialized in shopper marketing and when this is so there is often a focus on research, category management and trade marketing.

Category management is often only partially implemented. Cooperation between manufacturers and retailers normally works better on operations, like logistics, where interests are more aligned, than on commercial issues.

The internal positioning of shopper marketing is well reflected in the types of provider of shopper marketing solutions. The continuous development of markets makes it necessary for companies to look to external expertise, so solution providers are usually consultants..

A simple categorization of consultancies can be made along two dimensions. One dimension is the level of solutions provided. The two extremes of that dimension are research-focused companies on the one hand and strategic consulting companies on the other. The other dimension is that of focus, that is, whether they are consulting firms that offer a broad palette of services, or specialists who dedicate themselves to one discipline or one industry. Not included in this simplified categorization is the size of the consultancy, ranging from one person to multi-billion-dollar international consultancies.

Examples of research houses are Nielsen, Kantar, IPSOS and IRI, companies that according to the American Marketing Association (AMA) are among the largest market research companies. These are all companies with an international presence that also offer shopper marketing services focused on insights. Many of these companies also

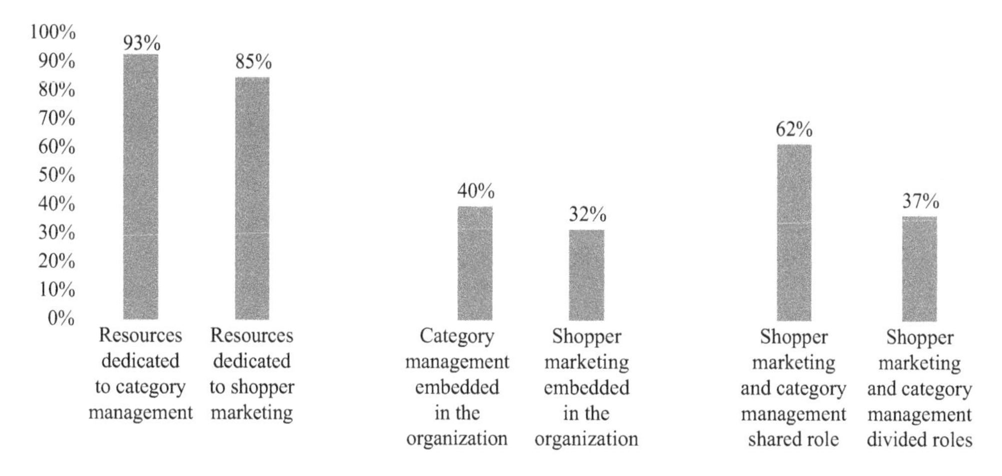

Figure 2.7 Implementation of shopper marketing in company organizations
Percentage of companies that have resources dedicated to category management and shopper marketing, how many have these activities embedded into the organization, and in how many shopper marketing and category management are either a shared or a divided department, across 14 countries in Europe.
Source: ECR, 2015

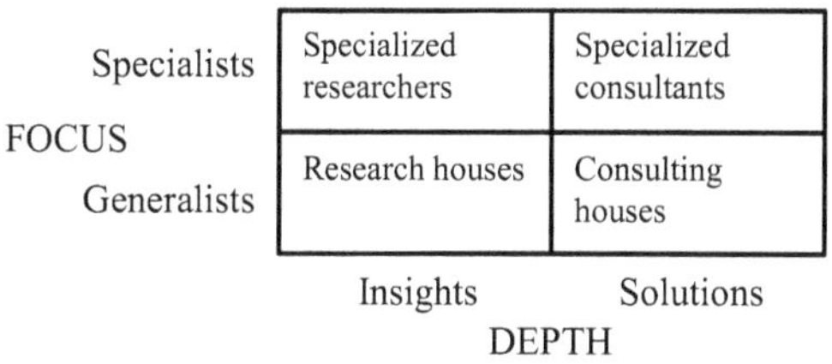

FOCUS	Insights	Solutions
Specialists	Specialized researchers	Specialized consultants
Generalists	Research houses	Consulting houses

DEPTH

Figure 2.8 Categorization of consultancies
Consultancies categorized according to their focus and level of solutions delivered.
Source: Author

want to move into the consulting side, but are partially limited due to their operational model and differences in allocation of the number and level of resources dedicated to projects. Market research companies often have expertise in specific methodologies and technologies.

When it comes to solution providers, there are the classic consultants, such as the big three, McKinsey, Boston Consulting and Bain & Company, as well as the strategic departments of the big four: EY (Ernst & Young), Strategy& (part of PwC) and the consulting departments of KPMG and Deloitte. Additionally, there are many specialized and boutique companies.

Strategic consultancies have gradually put more focus and emphasis on shopper marketing. As an example, McKinsey developed the idea of jointly agreed growth (JAG), which is category management with growth objectives and a strategic touch, and recently changed the name of one of its practices from consumer marketing to consumer and shopper marketing.

Shopper marketing has traditionally focused on shopper insights and in-store activation. This understanding is shared by the shopper marketing definitions of the In-Store Marketing Institute (today the Path to Purchase Institute), GMA/Deloitte, and the Retail Commission on Shopper Marketing.

The In-Store Marketing Institute definition of shopper marketing used to focus on in-store activation:[11]

> The use of strategic insight into the shopper mindset to drive effective marketing and merchandising activity in a specific store environment.

With the change from the In-Store Marketing Institute to the Path to Purchase Institute the definition of shopper marketing has become focused on the shopper journey and the need for cooperation across functions:[12]

> A cross-functional discipline designed to improve business performance by using actionable insights to connect with shoppers and influence behavior anywhere along the path to purchase.

The GMA/Deloitte definition includes the process towards purchase and the importance of brand development:[13]

> The employment of any marketing stimuli, developed based on a deep understanding of shopper behavior, designed to build brand equity, engage the shopper and lead him/her to make a purchase.

The definition of the Retail Commission on Shopper Marketing speaks of shopping experience and the goal of improving the outcome for manufacturer and retailer:[14]

> The use of insights-driven marketing and merchandising initiatives to satisfy the needs of targeted shoppers, enhance the shopping experience, and improve business results and brand equity for retailers and manufacturers.

Shankar in his definition goes further and includes all marketing activities that are related to the shopper and to purchasing:[15]

> The planning and execution of all marketing activities that influence a shopper along, and beyond, the entire path-to-purchase, from the point at which the motivation to shop first emerges through to purchase, consumption, repurchase, and recommendation.

However, shopper marketing clearly also has a strong association with the supply chain, as products and services in order to be purchased have to reach the shopper.[16]

The basic idea of shopper marketing is to ensure the encounter between shoppers and products and services. This implies the right product and service that best meets the needs of the shopper, at the right place and time. From a business standpoint, this means capturing the opportunities in the marketplace by converting shoppers into buyers, and in the longer term building brand equity and loyalty. The definition of shopper marketing in this book is therefore strategic and brings together the important facets of attracting shoppers, as well as securing availability:

> Profitably and sustainably convert shoppers into buyers by maximizing the preference during the purchase process by optimizing value offering, shopping experience, touchpoint management and availability at the right time and place along the shopper journey based on relevant shopper, customer and channel insights through a coherent management of the involved functions.

One of the key points of the above definition is that it views shopper marketing as cross functional. It goes beyond just including the shopper in the marketing strategy.[17] Successful shopper marketing is dependent on an integrated management of shoppers, channels and touchpoints.[18] It also includes the offer, the products and services, as the most important shopper loyalty driver.[19]

To many companies the cross-functional aspect poses an important challenge. The way companies are organized and structured has its roots at the beginning of the last century. Then, the key challenge was internal efficiencies and the focus was less on the market and on marketing. There was, at the time of industrialization, a strong focus on production. In addition, society was less educated and certainly more authoritative. The basic idea was to group similar tasks to gain efficiencies, and then coordinate different departments when bringing the products and services to the market.

Tasks had to be very well defined with clear assignments of responsibilities. This basic concept of organization is still dominant in many companies. Often, there is a logic to this approach, as few people would see the marketing department as responsible for logistics or production. However, these functions are key for a successful marketing strategy and value offering.

Normally, the marketing department is responsible for the relationship with consumers, sales for the relationship with customers, production for manufacturing and logistics for the efficient availability of products and services. Moreover, there are the support functions, such as finance, human resources, legal, etc. As companies become increasingly complex, new departments have developed whose affiliations are not always clear. Is design and innovation part of production or marketing, or is it a department in itself? Is distribution part of logistics or sales? Is trade marketing part of marketing or sales? Different companies solve this in different ways, depending on their specific situation. Some companies are organized in business units by type of customer, e.g. institutional customers and residential customers, or

Table 2.1 Classical organizational theories

CLASSICAL ORGANIZATIONAL THEORIES	
Key principles	*Academics*
• Organizations exist to achieve economic and production objectives • There exists an optimum way to organize based on science • Production can be maximized through specialization and division of labor • People and organizations act in line with rational economic principles	• Taylor: *Principles of Scientific Management* (1947) • Fayol: *Administrative Theory* (1962) • Weber: *Theory of Bureaucracy* (1980)

Classical organizational theories and their key principles.

Source: Shafriz et al., 2011

by product categories. Project organizations have become more frequent, as a way to ensure the interconnection between different departments.

With the objective of connecting shoppers with products and services shopper marketing is by its nature cross functional. Ensuring the availability of the right product and service for a specific consumption occasion for a defined target group at the right time and place, and activated to draw consumers' attention goes across several functions. It includes marketing, sales and logistics and ranges from defining the optimum offering and target groups, to deciding on the appropriate communication strategy, developing and activating the right channels to reach the target group and activate the point of purchase, to ensuring the availability and presentation in the most efficient manner at the defined points of purchase.

Shopper marketing has to ensure that there is coherent management across the functions to ensure that shoppers encounter products and services as profitably for the company as possible. On one side, shoppers need to be directed toward the products and services. On the other hand, the products and services need to be directed toward the shopper.

The touchpoints and the way of leading to the purchase of a product is normally named shopper, customer or consumer journey. In addition, path to purchase is used. In this book, the term route to purchase is introduced. The difference between the journey or path versus the route is the design of a deliberate strategy. Once a company has mapped and understood the shopper journey, it can start designing the strategy to best manage this journey and turn it into the managed route to purchase. In other words, it is the difference between a description of how the shopper arrives at the product and service, and the management of this process to ensure that the shopper arrives at the product and the service in an optimum way for the company.

The management of the route to purchase includes the definition of the product and service suitable for each type of consumption occasion and target group, and the touchpoints involved in managing the purchase process and building awareness and preference until the final selection at the time of purchase. Shopper marketing is no longer only about the store, but before the store, and after the store. In addition, with both e-commerce and digital touchpoints, it is about the point of purchase, wherever it happens, digitally or in a store. Modern shopper marketing needs to be well coordinated with marketing, sales and distribution, and needs to view the shopping process from the perspective of the shopper, rather than organizing and managing it from the inside out, from the perspective of the company. Shopper marketing requires an integrated view and approach.

On the other side of the equation is the challenge of how the products and services should reach the shoppers in the most profitable way possible. Key elements when purchasing are normally variety and choice, availability of the preferred options, service and experience, as well as price and special offers. When shoppers choose the point of purchase, the point of encounter between shopper and product and service, they normally choose the place, both brick and mortar and digital, with the attributes most fitting their needs and expectations. The management of the process to meet these expectations in the most optimal way is referred to as the route to market. In some cases it is also referred to as go to market. It denominates the step from mapping the channel and distribution reality of a market to developing a strategy to meet shopper needs and expectations in the most optimal and profitable way.

Route to market strategies touch important points, such as the management of stores and other points of purchase, including digital ones, the distribution to the points of purchase or directly to shoppers and consumers. Sometimes it includes logistics and warehousing.

Finally, the route to market strategy has to ensure that the right products and services are at the right points of purchase at the right time, and activated in the right way. In addition, it needs to ensure that the money from the purchase flows back to the company.

As an example, having a snack on the way to work or having dinner with friends both cover a need to eat, but the consumption occasions and motivations are very different. Therefore the experience and shopping service looked for are different. Based on needs and expectations, the optimum offer for the expected consumption situation has to be defined and delivered. The task of the route to purchase is to understand these needs and activate the products and services accordingly, and the role of the route to market is to ensure that the products and services are available. Strategic shopper marketing is about connecting the route to purchase with the route to market in line with the defined marketing strategy in terms of consumption occasions, target groups and offering.

When defining where to focus, the key is to understand the market opportunities, as well as the strengths and weaknesses of the company. Different tools have been developed in this area, e.g. SWOT analysis (strengths, weaknesses, opportunities, threats), Porter's value chain analysis, or McKinsey's 7S analysis. In the end, it is about identifying possibilities for competitive differentiation. The strategic point of defining objectives and direction in the case of shopper marketing is referred to as capturing the shoppertunity, i.e. how to generate sales and optimize profits by converting shoppers into buyers.

Strategic shopper marketing has an outside-in perspective. As the shopper is external to the company a good market understanding is key to defining the shoppertunity, as well as aligning the internal processes to capture it. It is crucial to understand the ecosystem in direct contact with the shoppers and their purchase process, e.g. touchpoints, sales channels, distributors, competitors and stakeholders in order to be able to manage it in the most optimal manner. Without a consumer there is no shopper. Understanding the consumer and the consumption process is fundamental to understanding the reason for the purchase and the role of the shopper. Additionally, the influences on the purchase during the shopping journey need to be mapped, as well as the route to market landscape in terms of channels, distributors and other suppliers. Only with a clear understanding can a profitable route to purchase and route to market strategies be designed.

Connecting the route to purchase with the route to market in the new omnichannel reality

During 2018, 69 percent of US adults made an online purchase at least a few times, and 43 percent made an online purchase at least once a month.[20] When starting the shopper journey for online purchases, e-retailers such as Amazon have a clear lead. Forty-four percent of online shoppers start their journey with Amazon, and 33 percent start on search engines such as Google. Large retailers (such as Walmart or Target), brand websites and online marketplaces (eBay or Etsy) have significantly less importance as a shopper journey starting point; just 10 percent, 6 percent and 5 percent of shoppers begin their journeys there, respectively.[21] Groceries are purchased online far less than other categories of goods, such as electronics or books, with important differences between countries. In the USA and Canada, the probability that respondents would buy groceries online in the next year was found to be 15 percent and 8 percent, respectively.[22] In the UK, this probability is 32 percent, and in China, it is 59 percent.[23] Sixty percent of shoppers do research online before they buy in store while 27 percent do research in store before buying online. This is often referred to as webrooming and showrooming. The importance of this omnichannel shopper experience is accentuated by the fact that omnichannel shoppers spend 3.5 times more money than shoppers who use just one channel.[24]

The purchase process has become more complex. In the year 2000, 82 percent of shoppers used one or two touchpoints when purchasing. Fifteen years ago, the average consumer typically used two touchpoints when buying an item. Today 90 percent of customer use three or more touchpoints. With this comes new strategic shopper marketing challenges that need to be managed in the omnichannel environment.[25] Due to ongoing fragmentation and digitalization, shopper journeys are becoming longer, more fragmented and multidirectional, an issue well depicted in Scholz & Friends advertising video on the subject from 2008.[26] Communication and influence is no longer a one-way street, but multidirectional and not under the full control of companies. One of the key drivers of these changes and resulting challenges is technological development. Markets are moving from connected to hyper-connected via artificial intelligence for automatic ordering or voice-activated purchases. Digitalization and automation will continue to influence the route to market value chain. On-demand last-mile delivery through meal delivery solutions, like Uber Eats, have already entered the route to market sphere, as have sharing-economy solutions, like FLEXE for warehouse spaces.

Convenience is becoming more important to shoppers. Originally, convenience in marketing was attributed to products that needed little cognitive decision making; later, it expanded to include convenience channels.[27] Convenience channels, such as 7-Eleven, are defined by their proximity and speed of purchase. Convenience has also entered the purchase process. Solutions such as Uber, cashless stores as tested by Starbucks, or voice ordering through digital assistants such as Alexa, offer increasing convenience to shoppers. Furthermore, direct consumption, on trade channels, are increasing in importance, often driven by increased incomes, with a wide variety of sub-channels such as restaurants, bars and pubs for different consumption needs.

Commercial customers are looking for convenience, too. In Vietnam, MuaCoke, a self-ordering app for retailers, where the type and service of delivery can be chosen, has been introduced. In Sweden, mobile payment methods like Swish are expanding, simplifying the payment process not only for shoppers, but also between suppliers and retailers.

As the concept of convenience develops and goes beyond just products or sales channel proximity, companies need to understand the specific significance it has for shoppers in different categories or for commercial customers. It involves understanding the job to be done and where the key barriers are. Understanding the task at hand can give convenience a new meaning. Examples include convenience shopping at discounters, end-to-end services for the purchase of men's toiletries (e.g. Harry's)[28] or the use of apps in the management of deliveries and warehousing for commercial customers.

As shopper journeys become more complex, there is a shift in focus from sales channels to shoppers. The omnichannel concept depicts an always connected shopper who uses multiple channels for information and purchase. These purchases can take place both online and offline in different channels. Connecting the route to purchase with the route to market means delivering on shopper expectations at the different points of purchase. It implies understanding shopping missions, and thereby the roles of the different touchpoints and points of purchase. The aim is to activate each of these points in the most effective and efficient manner. Developing a seamless shopping experience starts with mapping and understanding the shopper journey. Dependent on the role and importance of each touchpoint along the shopper journey, the resource allocation in terms of investment and content can be prioritized to optimize the conversion of the shoppers. The fragmentation and digitalization of shopper journeys and sales channels have led to more fluid shopper behavior, where shoppers use different types of channels in their search and buying process in an omnichannel approach.[29] As opposed to multichanneling, where channels are managed in parallel, the starting point is the shopper, his needs and the role of the different touchpoints and sales channels, and their interaction. Still, such a strategy needs to be evaluated well, as it can be more costly in fact, and less effective than expected.[30]

Sales channels are facing fragmentation, as well as new challenges from digitalization. Over time, there has been a certain consensus that channels would develop toward a mainly modern trade, big-box environment, but in many parts of the world, like South America, Africa and many countries in Asia, traditional retailing is preeminent. In addition, many chains are developing different formats to better meet shopper needs or, indeed, compete with the traditional channel and service they provide to shoppers.

The concept of the shopper journey is important as it shows that the interaction between the different touchpoints with the brand have a bigger impact on shopper behavior than the individual touchpoints by themselves. It is thus important to optimize the journey experience over the experience of each touchpoint.[31] If the experience at the point of purchase is disappointing, even if a marketing campaign is perfectly designed and developed, building awareness and preference through TV, radio, outdoor and digital media, the journey, as a whole, is sub-optimal.

Shoppers expect a seamless omnichannel shopping experience where they can order and buy from anywhere, anytime. This puts the route to market under pressure to fulfill from anywhere, anytime as well. Customers want to buy online and pick up in a store or at lockers, place orders on cell phones and have purchases delivered at home with the ability to return them. The challenge of omnichannel fulfillment has made logistics a part of shopper marketing.

The increasing expectations for seamlessness and convenience implies that purchase decisions can be taken across the shopper journey through the internet, mobile devices or in store with a variety of fulfillment options. These include click and collect, buy online and return in store, home delivery, showrooming, or just buying in store while receiving offers and promotions through a mobile device. This implies rethinking the supply chain and the role of existing and new players, as well as the use of existing assets, such as the store. Analysis of customer data plays a vital role in better understanding needs and the flow of goods required to be able to optimize these. Examples include how brick-and-mortar retailers use their stores for fulfillment of online orders, the usage of courier, express, parcel (CEP) companies for last-yard delivery, and connecting wholesalers or food delivery agents through ordering apps for a more flexible fulfillment in terms of timing and service. Lately, drones as a fulfillment alternative have gained increased attention.

Shoppers enter the journey with an ideal proposal to satisfy a future consumption or usage situation.[32] In that sense, not only does the journey need to be well managed, but also the offering needs to be in line with the solution the shopper seeks. Taking wine as an example, even the best service and the best food will not cover up the fact that the appropriate wine to accompany the occasion was unavailable. A glass of wine at an informal family dinner compared to a formal dinner party would in most cases trigger different types of solution in terms of wine type and price. In addition, the shopping journey would differ in terms of information touchpoints and ultimately the point of purchase and consumption occasion.[33] A satisfactory shopper experience can only be achieved if a suitable wine is available to accompany the intended consumption occasion.

The availability and presentation of the adequate product and service at the moment of purchase, to convert the shopper into a buyer, also needs to be ensured. Shopper marketing is strongly associated with the supply chain.[34] Only by ensuring that the shopper will end up with the product or service that he has intended to buy to meet the consumption need, and that he has been activated along the journey toward the moment of purchase, and more importantly that he has been activated at the moment of purchase at the point of purchase, will ensure a coherent shopper experience aligned with the brand intent.

Managing points of purchase is complex, as it involves aspects of logistics, as well as of activation, based on the specific role of the shopper and the importance to the company. The question is how to optimize effectiveness in terms of activation and cost to serve across the different sales channels. Management challenges vary between modern trade channels with centralized negotiations and logistics, small independent outlets that need to be managed individually, either directly or through third parties, and digital channels.

For companies to deliver a shopper experience in line with the brand intent in the new omnichannel reality, they need to coherently connect the management of the shopper journey toward a specific product and service, the route to purchase, with the management of this product or service toward the shopper, the route to market.[35]

A more complex shopper journey and increasing expectations on shopping convenience are influencing sales channel structures. As convenience becomes a more important factor, channel roles are blurring. Discount grocer Lidl now offers convenience shopping in its stores in Germany and the UK. With continuous urbanization, rising disposable incomes and smaller families, away from home or immediate consumption (i.e. consumption at the outlet or on the go) is growing. In parallel, chains are consolidating the retail market, looking for growth in the changing channel landscape. The sales channels and points of purchase are the point of conversion of the shopper journey. As shopper journeys have become more complex and the importance of convenience has increased, the role of sales channels and points of purchase is changing. The shopping missions determine the type of point of purchase shoppers are looking for. They give an idea about the current and potential future role of points of purchase and provide an understanding of the ongoing channel blurring and the emergence of new channel formats (e.g. pop-up stores), as well as the interplay between online and offline channels and omnichannel solutions.

Connecting the management of the shopper journey, the route to purchase, with the management of the product and service, the route to market, is a complex endeavor, as in many cases sales channels are not under the direct control of companies, but it is where business to business (B2B) and business to consumer (B2C) or shopper meet. The knowledge set needed to manage the route to market is quite different from the one needed to manage the route to purchase, which makes the internal coordination challenging. Still, as the shopper reality grows more and more complex, different touchpoints and channels cannot be managed apart, as this no longer corresponds to how the shopper operates. To deliver a shopper experience in line with expectations, companies need to connect their route to purchase with their route to market. A challenging task, as the intersection of the route to purchase and the route to market is where different business realities meet, due to the different objectives, shopper vs. channels, and type of management, B2C (or shopper) vs. B2B.

With the new omnichannel reality manufacturers need to adapt their route to purchase and route to market.[36] Manufacturers and retailers are facing the challenge to ensure a seamless shopping experience and manage the complexity of omnichannel fulfillment while minimizing the cost to serve. Eighty-seven percent of retailers agree that omnichannel is critical to their business, but only 8 percent say they have mastered it.[37] Eighty-five percent of fast-moving consumer goods (FMCG) companies have resources dedicated to shopper marketing, which shows that shopper marketing as a concept has reached the mainstream of company reality, especially in the case of consumer goods companies.[38] With the introduction of the concept of the shopper journey, shopper marketing has stepped out of the store to encompass more accurately the reality of today's shoppers and what leads them to buy. The shopper journey is where the shopper is in contact directly or indirectly with the product and service and thus can be influenced by marketing activities to drive preference and ultimately conversion.[39]

Omnichannel strategy implies shifting the emphasis from selling to the point of purchase to focusing on supporting the point of purchase to activate and sell to shoppers.[40] The development of an omnichannel context encourages companies to focus less on sales and order taking and more on advising clients on how best to develop their businesses, transitioning the role of sales from selling to giving advice on developing business. To stay ahead in the new omnichannel reality, manufacturers must reevaluate the role of sales. The goal is not to focus on sell-in, but to partner with retail and other players to activate shoppers and focus on the sell-out. This implies not seeing retailers and intermediaries as the end customer, but as part of the system to reach the shopper. By understanding the role of retailers and intermediaries within the shopper journey and how to activate the shopper, clear plans can be developed to trigger conversion. Companies such as spirits manufacturer Diageo are talking about route to consumer, connecting the route to purchase and the route to market, integrating sales and marketing to better activate the shopper and consumer in line with their brand strategies. The sales function of the future will be more closely integrated with shopper marketing internally, and partner with commercial customers to better serve the common shopper.

Notes

1 (Crawford, 2012) and (Schneider & Rau, 2009)
2 (Stengel, 2011)
3 (Cadent Consulting Group, 2020)
4 (GMA, 2011), (ECR Europe, emnos & The Partnering Group, 2011), (Huskins & Goldring, 2009), and (Harris, 2010)
5 (Hillesland, 2013)
6 (Pauwels et al., 2002)
7 (Sommer, 2010), (Sansolo, 2010), and (Dellaert et al., 2008)
8 (Silveira & Marreiros, 2014)
9 (Basuroy et al., 2001)
10 (Desforges & Anthony, 2013)
11 (In-Store Marketing Institute, 2009)
12 (Consumergoods.com, 2019)
13 (GMA/Deloitte, 2007)
14 (Retail Commission on Shopper Marketing, 2010)
15 (Shankar, 2011)
16 (Flint et al., 2014)
17 (Nitzberg, 2012)
18 (Shankar et al., 2011), (Fam et al., 2011)
19 (Millward Brown, 2008)
20 (NPR, 2019)
21 (NPR, 2019)
22 (PwC, 2019)
23 (PwC, 2019)

24 (Wood, 2018)
25 (Clarke, 2018)
26 (Scholz and Friends, 2008)
27 (Kaufman, 2015)
28 (Harry's, 2019)
29 (Verhoef et al., 2015)
30 (Reagan, 2017)
31 (Maechler et al., 2016)
32 (Stilley et al., 2010)
33 (Hall, Lockskin & O'Mahoney, 2001)
34 (Flint et al., 2014)
35 (Krentzel, 2018a)
36 (Krentzel, 2019a)
37 (Hook, 2015)
38 (ECR, 2015)
39 (Shankar, 2011)
40 (Lapoule & Colla, 2016)

3 The route to purchase

Without a consumer there is no shopper. Defining the route to purchase strategy starts with a consumption need state and building a coherent shopper activation throughout the different touchpoints until a shopper becomes a buyer and uses the products and services.

The majority of the shopper marketing effort lies in the process leading up to the conversion of shopper to buyer. Consumption need states are the starting point of shopper marketing programs. Shoppers seek solutions to future intended consumption occasions. Consumption need states describe the basic need, the occasion of usage, the motivation for specific solutions, and thereby the potential alternatives available to shoppers. They define the competitive playing field and the competitive position, as well as the opportunities for solutions within adjacent and complementary categories, products and services. Consumption need states are the basis for competitive strategies within the field of shopper marketing. Shopper attitudes are key to explaining shopper behavior and are the basis for activation strategies. The involvement, the importance of the purchase, the level of planning, the intent to purchase, shopping missions, the reason to purchase and the attributes looked for at points of purchase are the key pillars that define activation strategies. The shopper journey, the path from consumption need states to conversion and usage has become more iterative and non-linear with more touchpoints, often outside the direct control of manufacturers. Understanding the role, importance and interaction between touchpoints is key to prioritizing the activation to best convert shoppers into buyers and maximize the return on the shopper marketing investment.

Consumption need states as catalysts of shopper behavior

Without the consumer, there is no shopper. Consumers consume at consumption occasions. To fulfill the needs of a specific consumption occasion the most suitable products and services need to be planned for, encountered and purchased. Shoppers purchase to solve the needs of intended future consumption at specific occasions. In that sense a shopper does not primarily look for a specific brand, product and service, but for a solution along specific criteria for an intended consumption occasion. It can be a practical solution, such as to satisfy hunger, thirst or transport, or it can be solutions to satisfy more intangible needs, such as transferring signs of status or identity. In these cases the product, service and brand can play a more important role in the hierarchy of solutions. Marx already spoke of products as fetishes, in which the basic need is not the focus, but how the brand, product and service creates a need that otherwise did not exist.[1] In that setting the brand has a key role. Marketing has either to understand the needs of consumers, or create or adapt needs to create demand. This is referred to as latent needs. The role of shopper marketing is less in developing, adapting or creating latent needs. Consumer needs and the associated consumption occasions are the starting point for shopper marketing. Consumption need states can be understood as the combination of the needs of consumers combined with the motivation to select specific solutions. Understanding these in combination with understanding attitudes and the shopper journey is the basis to develop the route to purchase strategy.

The consumption need states describe the solution the shopper needs to look for, and the range of alternatives available, e.g. the range of products and services to meet the aforementioned needs. The definition of consumption need states helps in mapping and understanding the competitive position of a company, and how adequate its products and services are to meet the specific consumption need state targeted. This approach is consumption and solution oriented, rather than the more traditional category and product-oriented view of understanding the market. For example, the category of coffee or the drivers of consumption could be analyzed. Looking at the drivers of consumption, different consumption occasions are mapped with their corresponding consumption need states. One occasion could be breakfast, for which different solutions could be considered, e.g. tea, hot chocolate, juices. Together with the motivation behind selecting a solution and the occasion of the consumption, the consumption need states are defined. Consumption need states are the drivers for purchase, why shoppers buy.

Consumption need states are analyzed across three key areas, the needs, the solutions and the competition set in terms of brands, products and services. To delimit the consumption need states, normally the four dimensions of consumer needs, motivations, the occasion of usage and the potential solutions, i.e. brands, products and services, are evaluated.

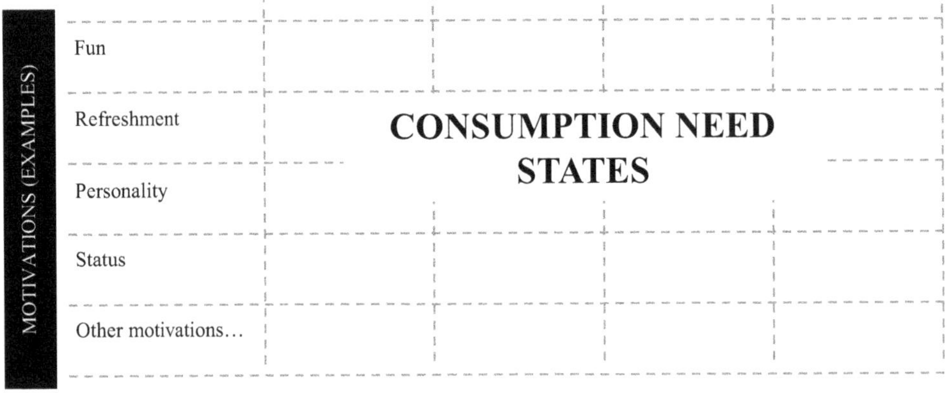

Figure 3.1 Consumption need states
Illustration of consumption need states based on occasions or situations of usage and the motivations for the selection of alcoholic beverages.
Source: Author

Motivation comes from the Latin word *movere* and describes the process, the direction and strength of an individual's behavior in meeting his needs. The basic discussion in motivation has been between behaviorism, based on Skinner's ideas,[2] i.e. the reinforcement of behavior through operative conditioning, and its application in Bandura's social learning theory [3]. One of the best-known theories is Maslow's theory of the hierarchy of the five basic needs (physiological, safety, love and belonging, esteem, self-actualization), in which the satisfaction of one level of needs makes the individual move to satisfy the next level.[4] Based on Maslow's theory, Alderfer showed with his existence, relatedness, growth (ERG) theory that more than one level of needs could be operational at the same time.[5] Herzberg showed with his work-related two-factor theory that there were hygiene factors, whose absence produce dissatisfactions, but do not motivate, and motivators that produce positive satisfaction.[6] Related to the idea of different types of motivators McGregor developed the idea of the authoritarian theory X and the participative theory Y leadership styles. In theory X workers are not motivated and need to be controlled, while under theory Y workers are motivated to achieve. Successful leadership should strive for the latter approach.[7] Steven Reiss divided motivation into intrinsic, where individuals are motivated by the task or potential rewards, and extrinsic motivation, where individuals are motivated by compensation or by avoiding sanctions.[8] Other work-related theories include goal-setting theories,[9] in which the goals themselves are part of the motivation process, or equity theory, in which individuals seek a balance between effort and reward.[10] McClelland, based on Henry Murray's[11] personality theory, showed that there are three types of motivators, which are a result of culture and personality: achievement, affiliation and power. To McClelland the interaction of these three motivators correlate with the development of society.[12] Vroom does not see behavior as solely driven by needs but, dependent on the expected outcome, alternative ways to act are evaluated.[13]

Many of the theories have been developed for the workplace and are centered on how to motivate people in organizations to improve performance. Nevertheless, they can also be useful for shopper marketing. Purchases are made to find the best solution to satisfy consumption needs. To best meet these needs, the motivations that drive the preferred solution to a specific need have to be understood. The idea of different levels and types of need helps to better understand the behavior of consumers and shoppers. A product and service can satisfy basic needs, e.g. hunger or thirst, but to understand the preferences for specific brands, needs and motivators like togetherness, affiliation, recognition or self-fulfillment and status play an important role. A product and service can satisfy more than one level of needs at the same time and the selection of a specific alternative over another depends on the expected result in terms of best meeting the need.

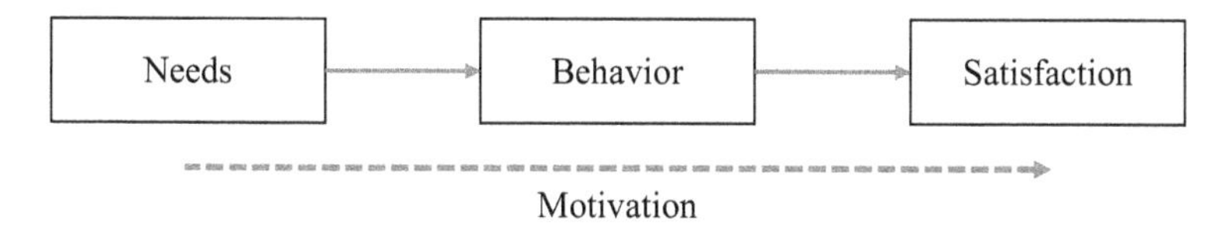

Figure 3.2 Motivation as a concept of goal orientation
Motivation as a process to move toward satisfying needs.
Source: Author

In order to fully map the consumption need state we have to understand not only needs and motivations, but also the situation, the occasion in which the product and service will be used. The usage situation, also denominated the occasion, is a way to segment consumers on their real usage behavior. The idea is that this behavior best explains the consumer needs that ultimately are to be satisfied by the shopper.[14] Unlike other consumer-oriented segmentation methods a consumer can belong to several segments depending on the situation in usage-driven segmentations. This gives the consumer a multidimensional rather than mono-dimensional profile typical of more classical segmentations in where each consumer is assigned to one segment. Incorporating situational influences on behavior is based on the field theory according to which behavior can only be understood in relation to its environment.[15] Different studies show that situation-based segmentations better predict consumer behavior than profile-based segmentations.[16] Additionally, an understanding of the combination of a consumer description and usage situation produces better insights into product and service selection.[17] A good shopper understanding is therefore dependent on a good understanding of the occasions of consumption, or the situation of usage.[18] The intended consumption occasion, together with the motivations, influence the selection of brands, products and services.[19] Through understanding the consumption occasions and motivations, the preference for brands, products and services can be understood, and thereby the purchase process from the identification of a need to the purchase can be analyzed.[20] This approach helps to categorize and link consumers and products and services for the intended situation of usage, i.e. consumption occasion.[21] Segmentation by consumption occasions has proven to be fruitful and relevant for brand positioning and advertising strategies.[22] The intended consumption occasion not only predicts the brands, products and services preferred, but it also gives insights into why specific solutions are preferred.[23]

In combination with the motivators of purchase the consumption occasions give a good insight into the drivers of the purchase, e.g. the why, for whom and when. Each purchase

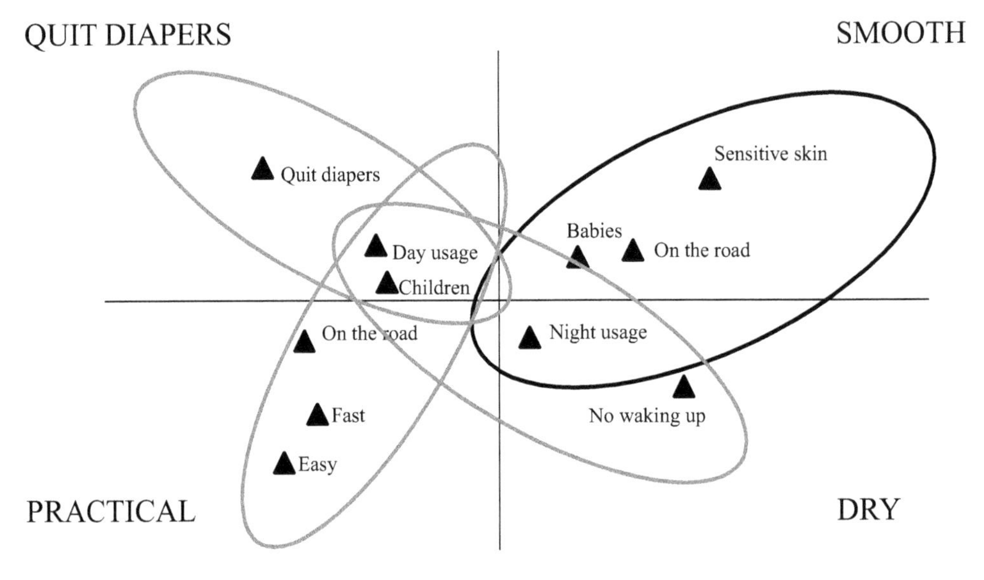

Figure 3.3 Correspondence map for diapers (occasions, motivations and type of solution) Illustration of diaper purchase drivers in Scandinavia and possible solutions.
Source: Author

driver has its appropriate solution in terms of products and services. For example, in the case of soft drinks, a large bottle would be more suitable for an occasion at home with friends. On the other hand, for immediate consumption occasions, e.g. on a hot day, a small, refrigerated bottle would be more suitable as a solution.

Understanding the purchase drivers and the possible solutions is the basis to develop the consumption need states map, and how to activate the same. The occasions define what type of solution is sought and the motivations why, and on that basis, an activation strategy can be designed in terms of solution and message.

The analysis of the consumption need states is not only the starting point to understanding the shopper. It also represents the shopper view in terms of the adequacy of the offer as well as the opportunities to expand the offer vs. other categories and manufacturers. For example, to evaluate the opportunities for expanding the market of current usage, similar occasions and motivations of other categories can be analyzed. Thus, a brand in the beer category could enlarge its playing field outside the beer category, and could enter into competition in categories covering similar motivations and occasions.

Thus, competition is no longer defined by the product, service or category, but rather by the needs that the product and service satisfy. This view enlarges the competitive setting and opportunities for the manufacturer. A market is ultimately defined by the needs of consumers and the willingness of shoppers to buy products and services to satisfy those needs. A classic example is the typewriters and the need to manage texts as efficiently as possible. Handwritten texts are time-consuming and difficult to copy. An important aid was the development of typewriters, which were initially mechanical. Building typewriters was a mechanical craft. A very successful company in that category was the Swedish company Facit, which expanded successfully internationally with an aggressive marketing strategy in the 1960s and early 1970s. The focus was on mechanical typewriters, which was the heart of the company. In the 1970s the first electronic typewriters were introduced, which were more efficient and could manage texts better and within just a few years, their pricing became competitive as well. This was the beginning of the digital era, when companies like IBM began to develop computers that eventually would replace other text management tools. Facit's focus on the product and not on understanding the users' needs, which was not a product, but a solution, ultimately led to the company's bankruptcy.[24] Clearly, this was not only due to misinterpreting needs, but also a poor understanding of technological change.

A company can redefine the playing field, such as in the soft drink category, where leaders like Coca-Cola look at criteria like share of throat. This indicator includes all beverages consumed, including non-commercial beverages, to understand the total potential market. Within this total potential market, the growth objectives are set for within and outside the current product category.

The telecommunications industry occasionally adopts an approach to understanding the daily behavior of residential and business users in order to analyze needs for which telecommunications services can be developed. In a mixture of technical possibilities and user needs new offers are developed. Initially, cell phones were used primarily for calls and SMS. Today, they are mainly used for chatting, social networks, entertainment and information, anytime and anywhere.

Consumption need states map out the needs, motivations and potential solutions for consumers and initiates the process of shopping. It is the basis to understanding what type of offer should be directed toward which consumption need state, the attractiveness of that consumption need state, the competitive position and how it should be activated along the shopper journey to convert the shopper into a buyer.

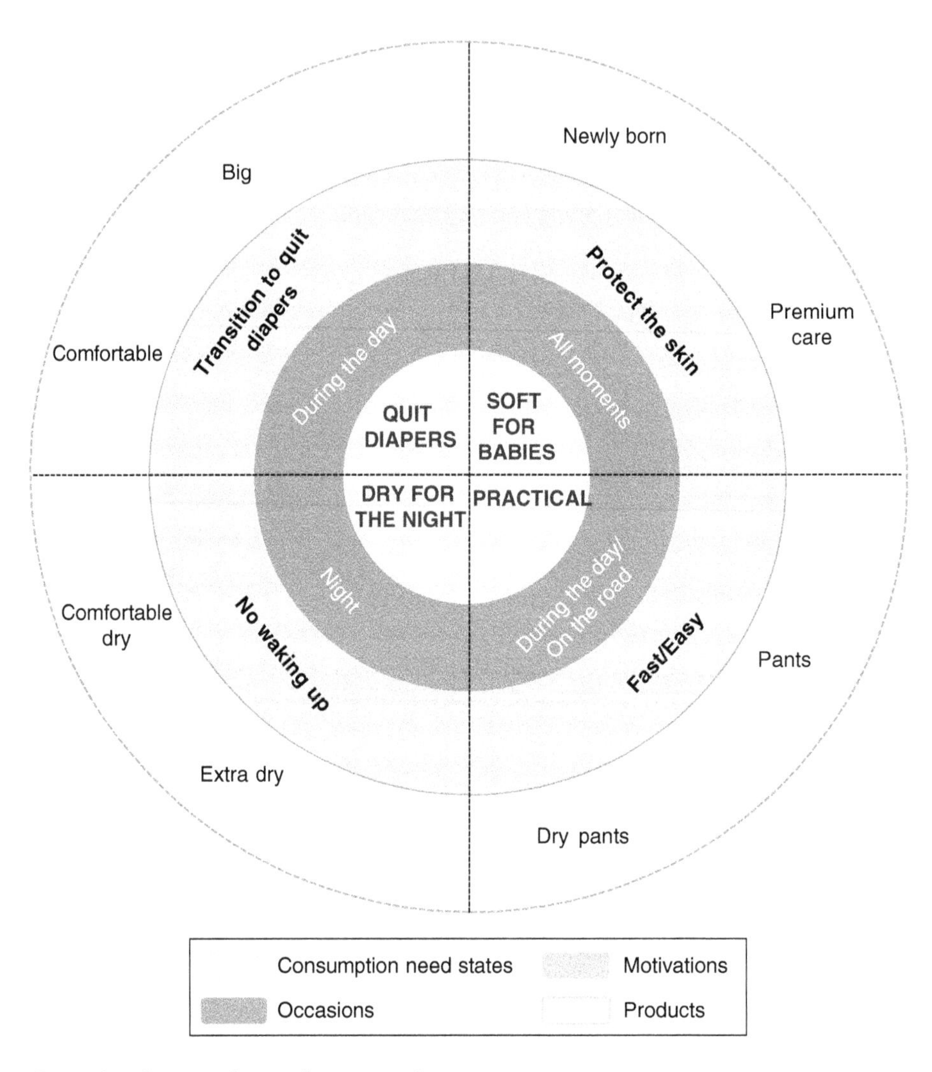

Figure 3.4 Consumption need state mapping

Illustration of a consumer need state mapping for the category of diapers in Scandinavia based on occasions, motivations and products.

Source: Author

Shopper attitudes

Introduction

Attitudes are key to explaining buying behavior.[25] They describe the predisposition of an individual to react in a consistent way to an object, a person, an institution or an incidence.[26] That predisposition is the attitude, the positive or negative feeling toward a behavior or goal.[27] A distinction can be made between cognitive (thinking), affective (feeling) and conative (acting) components of attitude.[28]

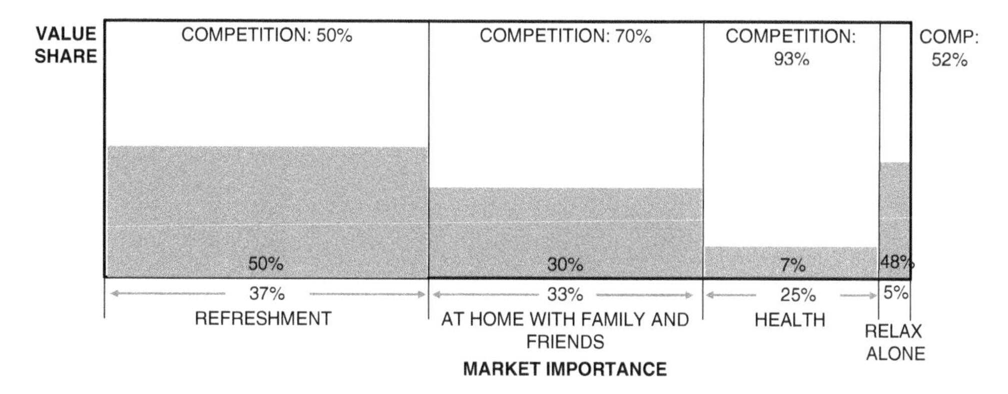

Figure 3.5 Competitive position by consumption need state

Example of beverages in Eastern Europe. In the horizontal dimension is the importance of the market and the importance of each consumption need state. On the vertical axis is the market share of the main manufacturers within each consumption need state. The total area of each consumption need state shows the competitive position of the manufacturers, as well as the opportunity for growth.

Source: Author

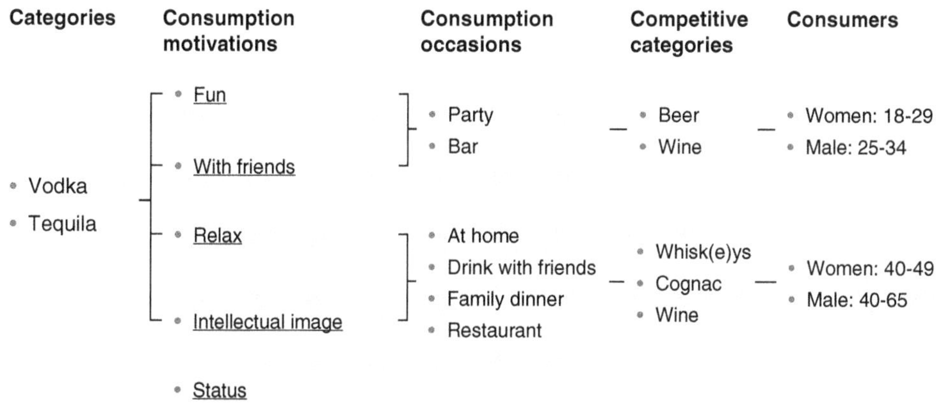

Categories	Consumption motivations	Consumption occasions	Competitive categories	Consumers
• Vodka • Tequila	• Fun • With friends	• Party • Bar	• Beer • Wine	• Women: 18-29 • Male: 25-34
	• Relax • Intellectual image	• At home • Drink with friends • Family dinner • Restaurant	• Whisk(e)ys • Cognac • Wine	• Women: 40-49 • Male: 40-65
	• Status			

Figure 3.6 Motivations and occasions for adjacent categories

Example of alcoholic beverages. Analysis of motivations and occasions of consumption of alternative/adjacent categories.

Source: Author

Attitude is not an observable construct, but attitudes must be deduced from the shopper's behavior.[29] That attitude-based behavioral predisposition of the shopper defines the way the shopper will inform himself and ultimately purchase a product and service. The attitude is the framework for the behavior of the shopper toward a specific potential purchase. Three dimensions of attitude can be distinguished in shopper marketing: involvement, planning and the shopping mission. This order of types of attitude also describes their internal hierarchy. The level of involvement influences planning, with a higher level of involvement usually implying more planning. In addition, a higher level of planning usually means a more organized shopping mission.

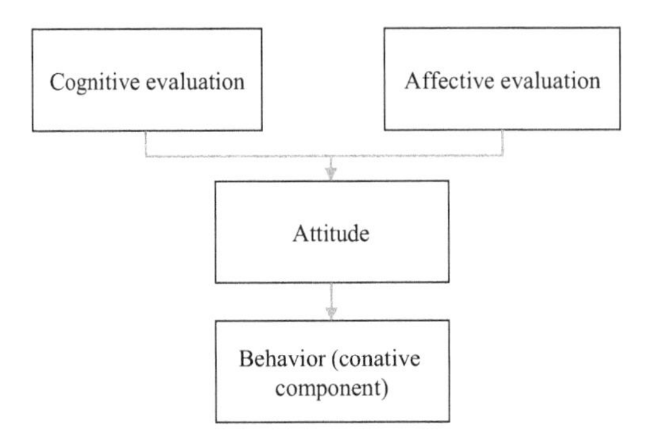

Figure 3.7 Components of attitudes
Cognitive and affective evaluation of an object or situation influences the attitude toward that object or situation, and leads to action, the conative component.
Source: Kuβ & Tomczak, 2007

Figure 3.8 Dimensions of attitude in shopper marketing
Dimensions of attitude in shopper marketing and their hierarchy of influence. The involvement influences the level of planning, which influences how the purchase is organized, i.e. the shopping mission.
Source: Author

Involvement

Involvement generally describes the importance of a purchase to the shopper. The challenge is to define in what sense a purchase is important. One possibility is to see it as a cost in terms of the value of an erroneous purchase. Simplistically, it could be put as the price in relative terms of a product and service. The more expensive they are, the higher the involvement. Therefore, there are approaches that seek to lower the risk of a purchase for the shopper through product tests or exchange policies. Another aspect of cost is the complexity associated with rectifying a purchase decision. One example are contracts, e.g. mobile or internet products and services. These contracts are for a certain period, i.e. when the contract is signed it is difficult to change, or changing it is associated with a certain cost. Therefore, it is a decision that has to be made with care. Other important costs of purchasing decisions are social costs. The chosen product and service has to work in the specific social environment of the shopper and consumer. It can be linked to the occasion of purchase or usage, with fashion or status. Involvement could be defined as the risk of failure and, therefore, there are different types of risk of a wrong decision or purchase: financial, complexity of change, or social cost. In addition, there is a dimension that is not the cost of failure; it is the emotional involvement, the identification with the product or brand. A good example is Apple. Clearly, the dimensions of involvement types can be interrelated: clothing can be associated with an important investment, or the change of a contractual supplier is not only complex, but can also be expensive. The social cost of an inexpensive product can be high, such as fashion accessories or gifts.

The concept of involvement in marketing was initiated with the measurement of involvement with advertisements.[30] The concept has its origin in social psychology, specifically in the approach of social judgement-involvement (commitment to social judgements) to explain attitudes and changes in the same.[31] There are three dimensions to this: acceptance, rejection and commitment.[32] The impetus to change an attitude lies in the discrepancy between the message a person conveys and his real position. The concept of ego-involvement explains the involvement of a person with a social issue and it is at its highest when a topic is intrinsically important, i.e. a person identifies with or is committed to the topic.[33] Sociopsychologists have investigated involvement in relation to persuasiveness in communication,[34] but in marketing the use has been broader. Research has focused on involvement in products,[35] personal involvement,[36] purchase involvement,[37] purchase decision involvement, involvement with brands,[38] involvement and tasks,[39] involvement with specific topics,[40] involvement and service,[41] involvement and advertisements.[42] Further, associations between involvement and perceived risk of purchase and the change of brands,[43] the type of product,[44] the purchase decision,[45] or a task or event[46] with services,[47] with advertisements and with the processing of messages[48] have been analyzed.

There is not one definition and measurement of involvement, but different approaches, from one-dimensional to multidimensional.[49] One important definition of involvement is the ability to generate excitement with a specific object (goal-directed arousal) and two types of motives govern this: cognitive motives related to the cost–benefit or the function, and affective motives related to symbolic dimensions, such as status and self-esteem.[50] Involvement can be seen as a mediator of behavior or as behavior itself.[51] When understanding involvement as a behavioral mediator the difference between general and situational involvement needs to be considered.[52] General long-term involvement describes a relationship with a category that is manifested by the search for extensive information, brand awareness and a possible commitment to specific brands. It is defined as the level of psychological connection between an individual and an object, a product, a brand or an idea.[53] Situational involvement is defined as a situation of temporary concern with an objective raised by a motive, such as perceived risk.[54] It describes a shopper's involvement in the specific purchase situation, and when that situation has passed the involvement also disappears.[55] In situational involvement, the behavior may manifest itself in attention, price sensitivity or awareness of brand differences.[56] For situational involvement the situation itself, i.e. the shopping mission, has an influence. For example, during an emergency shopping mission the level of involvement with the brand is lower than during a regular shopping mission.[57] Type of shopping mission and brand importance influence the level of situational involvement during the purchase, e.g. routine vs. emergency purchase, or when buying a gift.[58] General involvement can be transformed into situational involvement during the purchase, but situational involvement cannot be transformed into general involvement.[59]

A more expensive product, such as a car or a new fashion product, normally triggers a higher level of information search, and drives general involvement. An example of a situational involvement could be diapers. This is an important product for parents of small children, but perhaps does not generate much attention before the purchase. However, during

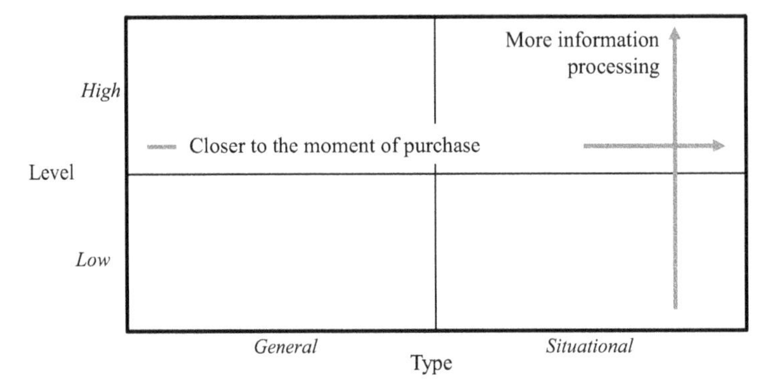

Figure 3.9 Type and level of involvement
Involvement matrix differentiated by level and type (general and situational).
Source: Author

the purchase, when comparing products, specific attributes may very well be important to the shopper, leading to in-depth evaluation of the potential alternatives. Activation, presentation, price or promotions can have a big impact on the purchase of situational involvement products and services.

General involvement often does not end with the purchase. Many times shoppers and consumers look for arguments for the choice made, to rationalize their decision and lower possible discrepancies due to the uncertainty of knowing whether the decision was the right one.[60]

To correctly activate products and services the involvement type and its drivers need to be evaluated. In cases of high involvement, the underlying drivers need to be understood. For example, if the driver is about the financial risk, there have to be arguments to lower it for the shopper, e.g. through product tests and exchange policies. If the involvement is driven by social considerations, the brand, product and service need to be in line with social expectations and positioned adequately. In terms of emotional drivers the brand, e.g. Apple, plays a key role.

When the involvement is low, brands, products and services need to draw attention, along the shopper journey, but specifically at the moment of purchase. The same is true for situational involvement.

For products and services with general involvement, the shopper journeys are usually longer and more complex with more points of contact and more need to lower the potential dissonance after the purchase.

Purchase planning

Purchase planning is the decision to purchase a product and service in the future. The dominant model for explaining behavioral intent and understanding purchase planning is the theory of planned behavior.[61] The stronger the intention, the higher the likelihood that an individual will act, especially if the individual has control over the act as such.[62] In addition, external factors influence whether or not an act is carried out, depending on the actual or perceived availability of the necessary resources, such as money, time or capacity.[63]

Scarcity of time can reduce both planned and unplanned purchases.[64] Frequent shoppers and customers, who are more familiar with the design of a point of purchase, make fewer unplanned purchases.[65] The key in the theory of planned behavior is the subjective norm, which describes the social environment in which the individual acts, his opinion about the expected future action and his perception if a specific action is accepted and reaffirmed.[66] Obstacles, internal and external, e.g. money and time, are interpreted subjectively.[67] The perception of the impact of the potential intended action influences the behavior. Closer to the purchase possible negative aspects about the purchase gain in importance.[68] Studies show an association between intention and behavior in grocery shopping,[69] customer retention,[70] technology acceptance,[71] mobile marketing and e-commerce.[72]

The theory of planned behavior can predict observable behavior, but it does not show the process of transforming intention into action.[73] Neither does it explicitly include spontaneous impulse behavior when there is no prior intention to act.[74] However, past behavior is a strong predictive factor of future behavior, especially spontaneous behavior, repeated or under time pressure.[75] Shoppers adapt their purchase process, choice of brands and volumes to their experience with the point of purchase.[76]

There is a clear distinction between planned and impulse purchases. Normally, there is a correlation between the involvement level and the planning. The higher the involvement the higher the planning. Buying real estate, which normally has a high involvement due to its financial and social implications (location, size, type), is normally well planned and prepared, with financing calculations and in-depth evaluations of different factors. A purchase of cookies or other snacks on the way to work or school is a purchase with a lower involvement. It may have a high situational involvement during the purchase situation, and may have a high or low level of planning. If it is a routine purchase, in which a snack and the same brand are bought frequently, then it would be a planned purchase, but of low involvement. It can also be an impulse purchase where the shopper sees a product that he or she craves and therefore buys. In the end, the risk of failure is very small and new products can be tested, repeatedly. Although there is some planning, preparation is minimal. Clearly, there are cases with high involvement and a high level of planning where there is a last-minute

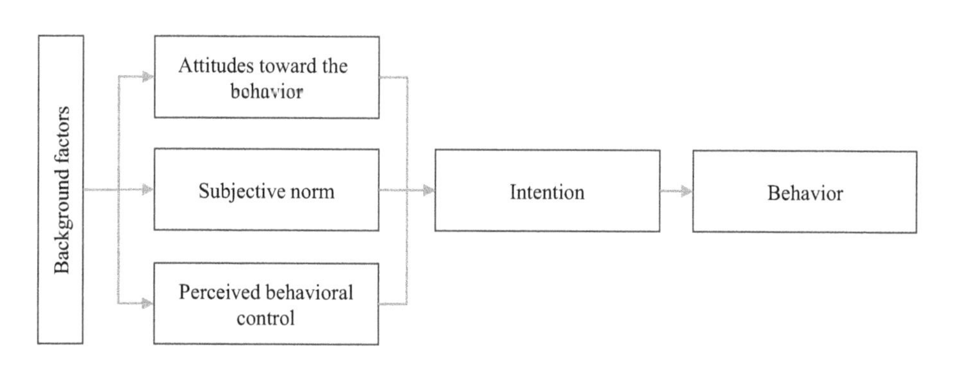

Figure 3.10 The theory of planned behavior

Behavior is associated with the intention to act, as well as the attitude toward the intention, the behavior, and the subjective norm (describing the individual's social environment and opinion about the intended behavior), as well as the perceived control over the intended behavior. In addition, different background factors influence attitude, norm and perceived control.

Source: Based on Ajzen, 2005

change of plans caused by triggers or information at the time of purchase that were not known before. For example, a car salesperson might offer a better deal on a model that the shopper prefers but would otherwise have been beyond his financial budget. It does not have to be a direct discount, but can be an offer of attributes that improve the cost of ownership. In the case of a car, these could be a warranty, maintenance, extras, or a color or sound system upgrade, for example. In this situation, the purchase and type of product were planned, and due to additional information, there was a change to the planning in terms of the product type, but not the category as such.

The flexibility of the planning depends on the level of involvement and preparation. The example of real estate is normally a case of almost complete planning, with some room for price negotiation, while in the case of a car purchase more attributes can be added to the decision set. Although the purchase of cookies can be planned, it can most probably be quite flexible to new offers and brands.

Two key aspects of planning are the timing of the purchase, and what is being planned. The closer to the purchase, more and more dimensions may be planned, but also the opposite is possible. A shopper may desire a specific product and service, and then, while evaluating different dimensions and attributes, decides on an alternative.

The dimensions being planned can be quite general and refer to the solution to the consumption need state in broad terms. For example, going to the store with the general plan to shop for the family dinner. A more specific planning could be to cook an Italian dinner. In addition, if more planned, a detailed list of the ingredients could have been prepared. Also, the shopper can have an idea of the budget for the dinner. This budget can be related to the total purchase or to specific categories.

The shopper can plan the solution, category, brand or a specific product and service, and write it down in his mental or real shopping list. The level of planning depends on the detail of attributes being planned. Depending on what was planned there are different implications on the activation, and if the solution in general, the category, brands or specific products and services have to be activated. The planning drives the decision process and guides the activation logic within the shopper journey. The planning process and the activation begin before the point of purchase and have to be managed throughout the shopper journey. Often, closer to the purchase the decision triggers become more related to price and promotions.

With high involvement products and services, managing the planning process usually becomes more complex, as the shopper and the consumer are more informed and use more touchpoints. Manufacturers will try to increase the involvement with their products and services to include them in the planning process and decision set of the shopper. The more the touchpoints are outside the control or influence of the manufacturer the more challenging the task becomes.

The more planned different aspects of the purchase are, the more organized the shopping mission. Buying real estate will rarely be an emergency shopping mission, while this could very well be the case when preparing dinner, e.g. if an important ingredient is missing.

Shopping missions

Shopping missions are often used to explain the difference between consumer and shopper marketing. While consumers have a reason to consume, shoppers have a reason to purchase. The reason to purchase is driven by the reason to consume. At the beginning, the concept of the shopping mission was a means to understand purchasing in brick-and-mortar stores. As a result, shopper marketing was focused on inside the store. As the sales channel landscape

Figure 3.11 Black box model of the relationship between needs and shopping missions
Traditional view of shopper marketing focused on shopping missions.
Source: Author

has become more complex, the understanding of the purchase process between consumer marketing and sales and distribution has gained more focus. Today, in an omnichannel reality the focus of shopper marketing has moved out of the store to include what happens before and after the purchase. Moreover, with digital sales, the point of purchase is more than just the store. It is vital to understand the different touchpoints, and the key touchpoint is the point of conversion, the point of purchase, and the reason for selecting this point, i.e. the shopping mission.

Traditionally, shopper marketing focused much on shopping missions. Shopping missions were used to understand the reason to buy to fulfill a need. What happened in between was a black box.

Modern approaches to shopper marketing include the touchpoints from consumption needs to shopping missions.

Shoppers and consumers are not only passively influenced through the different touchpoints; they actively seek information and interact with these touchpoints. Different touchpoints have different roles and importance in the decision process of the shopper.

More touchpoints make the shopper journey more complex. At the same time, it offers more possibilities to be in dialogue with the consumer and the shopper. One example is the airline industry. Most bookings are made online today and there are websites with price comparisons and destination information. The same applies to rental vehicles. This drives efficiencies and transparency, especially on prices. Another example is computers. With the evolution of the industry, as well as the possibility of information online, consumers and shoppers have become more knowledgeable. For retailers it is costly to hold large stocks of a wide range of products. In many cases, the personal computer business has developed into a click-and-collect business, i.e. the order is made online and then picked up in a brick-and-mortar store. With multiple touchpoints, omnichannel solutions, and a variety of points of purchase there are not only shopping missions to consider, but also touchpoint missions. Touchpoint missions describe why shoppers use different touchpoints, e.g. to be informed or share opinions. The challenge is to manage the different touchpoints and points of purchase to develop the route to purchase strategy.

The idea of shopping missions is that each mission will generate a different purchasing behavior and the need for a different activation strategy. The shopping mission details the solution the shopper will look for to satisfy the consumption need state. Further, depending on the shopping mission, the shopper will look for specific attributes of the point of purchase. The mix of attributes describing the point of purchase defines its role to the shopper. The consumption need state together with the shopping mission define the attributes in terms of types of products and services and points of purchase the shopper will target. With this understanding, as well as an understanding of the involvement and the level of planning, the offer and the activation can be aligned with shopper needs at each shopping situation.

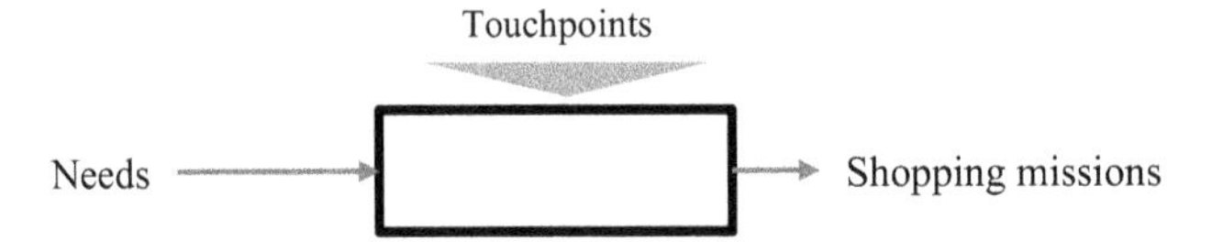

Figure 3.12 Model connecting needs and shopping missions through touchpoints
Touchpoints as a point of connection between needs and shopping missions.
Source: Author

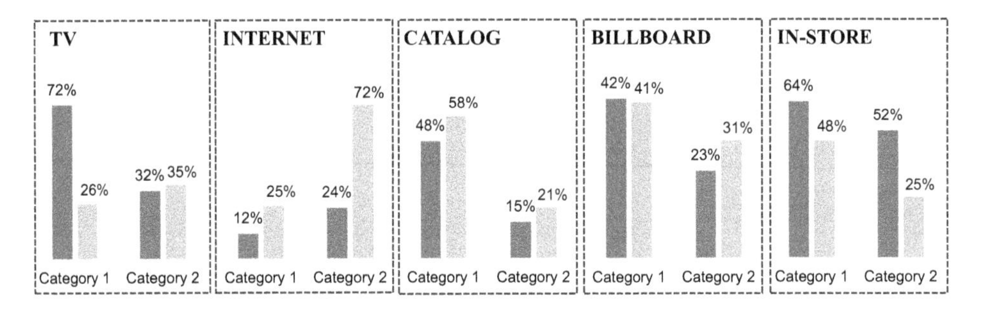

Figure 3.13 Reach and importance of different touchpoints
Reach (dark grey) and importance (light grey) of different touchpoints of two different categories.
Source: Author

In grocery shopping there are three main shopping missions often referred to: stock up, replenishment and urgency. In the stock-up mission, the shopper normally buys larger amounts, looks for lower prices and therefore usually browses for larger packages and special offers. The replenishment shopping mission is about purchases of specific products that need to be restocked before the next stock-up purchase. Urgent shopping missions describe situations where a specific product is needed almost immediately, e.g. an ingredient that is missing while preparing dinner or having guests. From stock-up to urgency, shopping missions are normally associated with more to less planning, and more proximity to the point of purchase, or speed of delivery, as well as less price sensitivity.

The concept of shopping missions was developed originally for the grocery category and modern trade. The concept is useful for other categories, but needs to be adapted to the reality of each category.

Both shopping and touchpoint missions need to be analyzed and understood to develop the optimal activation strategy along the shopper journey. By analyzing the drivers of the touchpoints and shopping missions, the activation strategy can be detailed and the competitive position assessed. For touchpoint missions looking for information, manufacturer and retailer websites or reviews are often used, while for giving and sharing opinions social media, as modern word of mouth (WOM), are more frequently used. Understanding the drivers of touchpoint and shopping missions helps to understand the priorities for the offering and activation at the touchpoints and points of purchase.

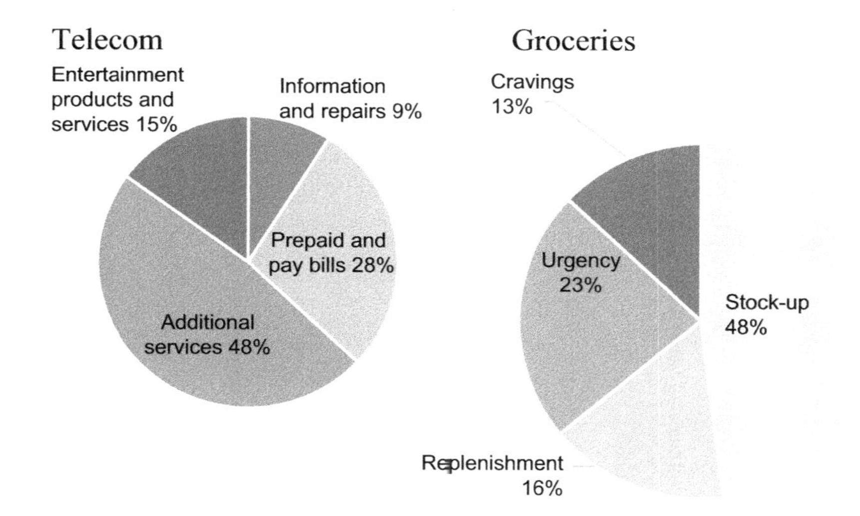

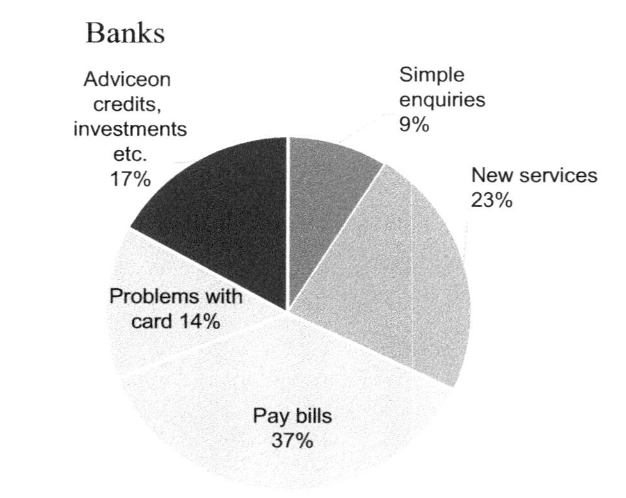

Figure 3.14 Shopping missions of different industries
Examples of shopping missions for telecommunications, groceries and bank services.
Source: Author

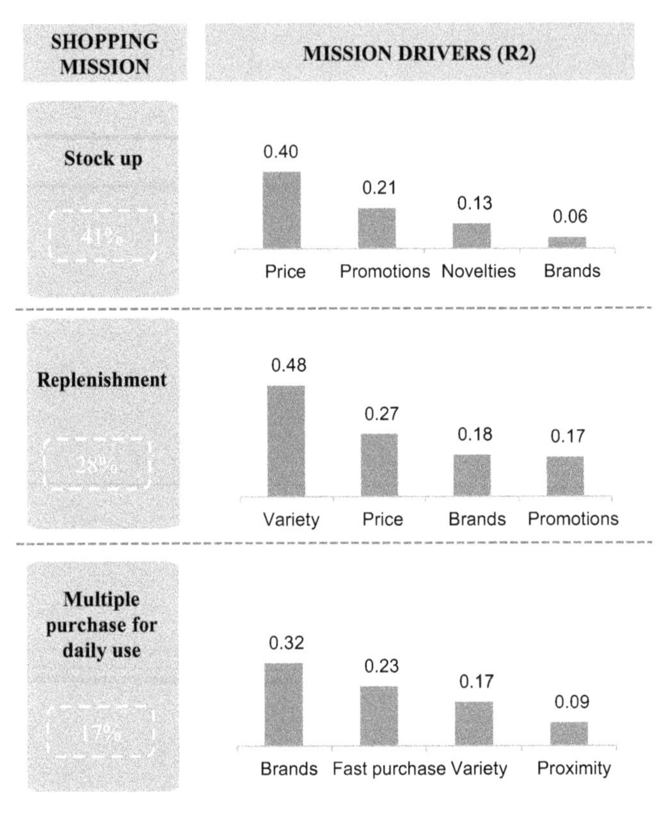

Figure 3.15 Attribute importance by shopping mission
Importance of attributes by type of grocery shopping mission. Correlation for searched attributes of different missions measured in R2.
Source: Author

The attributes associated with each mission, and the importance of the missions by point of purchase is the basis for defining the offering and activation strategy by group of points of purchase and sales channels.

The shopper journey

From touchpoints to shopper journeys

The route to purchase is the management of the shopper journey in the interest of the manufacturer.

Developing a route to purchase strategy based on the shopper journey starts with understanding the different touchpoints between the shopper and the potential solutions to the consumption need states with the goal of understanding the drivers of conversion. To understand the differences in the use of touchpoints, their role and importance, as well as the competitive position by touchpoint, it is interesting to look at the touchpoints of the category and the products and services of the manufacturer.

The touchpoints between manufacturers and shoppers have changed profoundly in the last two decades. Traditionally, companies divide between above the line (ATL) and below the line (BTL) activation. This division refers to their position in the profit and loss statement. Above are the expenses related to the brand and consumer marketing activities, such as television, radio and press. Below are the expenses associated with sales and the activation of brands, products and services in the different sales channels to activate shoppers at the time of the purchase. This division is clearly based on the idea of departments and aligned with how the profit and loss and the costs of a company are traditionally structured. It also reflects the understanding of marketing as developing the awareness and preference on the one hand, and the activation and conversion at the point of purchase on the other hand. This view is deterministic to some extent and based on a clear idea of a marketing funnel from awareness, interest, consideration, evaluation and purchase. The basic idea is to move the consumer and shopper from one point to the next closer to the purchase. In such a view, each touchpoint is separate to the next, and an interaction between steps and touchpoints is not considered.

The experience from customer service management and loyalty programs shows that the sum of the performance at each touchpoint does not automatically result in a high satisfaction level. It is enough for the performance at one touchpoint, or the communication between two touchpoints, to be poor to result in low customer satisfaction. Therefore, the interaction of the touchpoints needs to be considered. The challenge is not to optimize each touchpoint, but rather to understand their role and interaction, and optimize the route through the shopper journey.[77] Tracking and evaluating the role of the different touchpoints and their interrelationship in the increasingly complex environment of multi-touchpoint and omnichannel shopper journeys is something with which many brands are struggling.[78]

Above the line and below the line have been complemented by a through the line (TTL) view with a more integrative perspective managing the interconnection of touchpoints from the initial activation toward the purchase. An example could be a mass media consumer promotion with clear interaction with other media channels on more information and activation, e.g. coupons, in paper or digital, to purchase the product in a specific channel or chain, where the product is being fittingly activated.

As the number of media channels and touchpoints are increasing, the interaction between them increases as well, making the more classical touchpoint and marketing funnel model obsolete. The new models for shopper journeys are more iterative and non-linear.[79] Winning or optimizing each touchpoint is not the goal, but understanding the journey and the role of the different touchpoints, how they interact and what the decision process is.[80] The shopper is influenced long before the purchase, for planned, as well as unplanned purchases.[81] With digital touchpoints, their number and their influence on the shopper before he arrives at the point of purchase becomes more important.[82]

The shopper journey neither starts at the point of purchase, traditionally a store, nor does it end with the purchase. The term "moment of truth" was introduced to describe the encounter between shopper and product and service. It describes the importance of meeting shopper expectations and ensuring the conversion from shopper to buyer in a competitive environment. This moment of truth is often called the first moment of truth. There is a zero moment of truth (ZMOT) as well, which takes place before the purchase. It includes the touchpoints of searching for a solution to a consumption need state before purchasing a product and service. The ZMOT idea was developed by Google to establish the importance of being present throughout the different touchpoints, especially the digital ones, up to the moment of purchase. The second moment of truth is when the product and service is used and evaluated.[83]

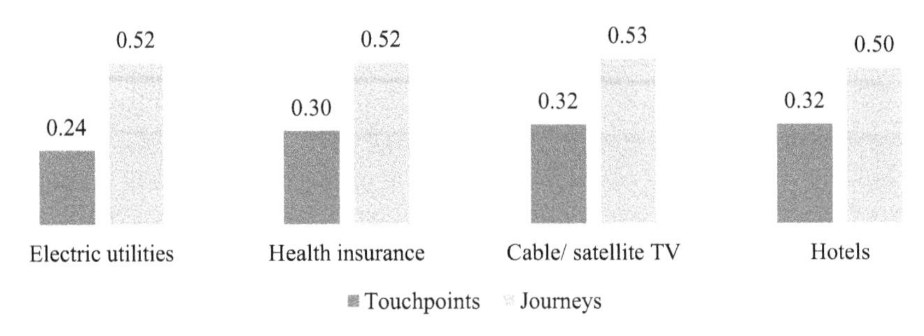

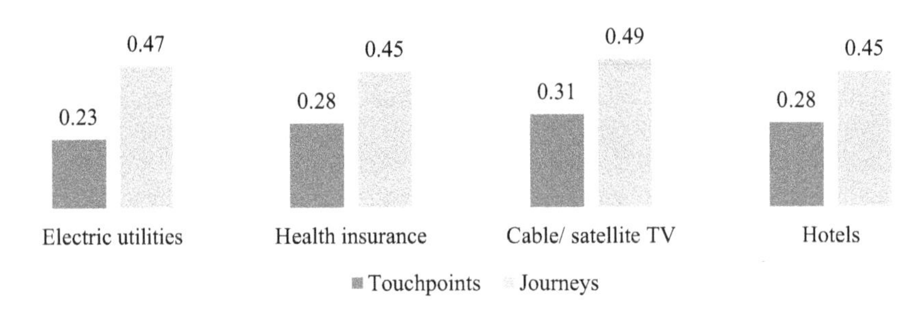

Figure 3.16 Comparison of the correlation of touchpoints vs. shopper journeys in relation to customer satisfaction and willingness to recommend

Level of association measured through the regression R2 coefficient through a multiple regression model between touchpoints vs. shopper journey and satisfaction and willingness to recommend.

Source: (Maechler et al., 2016)

The shopper journey starts before and goes beyond the point of purchase. Shoppers do not buy specific products and services, they buy solutions to the consumption need states, and only if these are satisfied will the product and service be beneficial to the consumer and the shopper.[84]

Shopper journeys need to be analyzed together with shopper attitudes and their impact on shopper behavior. Next to the solution sought for a specific consumption need state the attitudes toward the purchase, in terms of the involvement with the purchase, the level of planning and the shopping mission, define the behavior of the shopper. Depending on these attitudes, the activation and conversion strategy has to be adapted.

The starting point of a shopper journey is the consumption need and future intended usage, and the awareness of possible solutions. Attitudes in terms of involvement, planning and shopping missions influence the shopper journey. This influences the shopper in selecting the most appropriate point of purchase as a function of his consumption and shopping needs. The process of searching, selecting and buying is related to the attributes of the point of purchase and the shopping experience. With the acquisition of the product or service the consumption need state can be satisfied, i.e. the consumption or usage of the products and services. The experience with the selected solution influences the future preference and relation in terms of loyalty, recommendation and advocacy. During the entire shopper journey

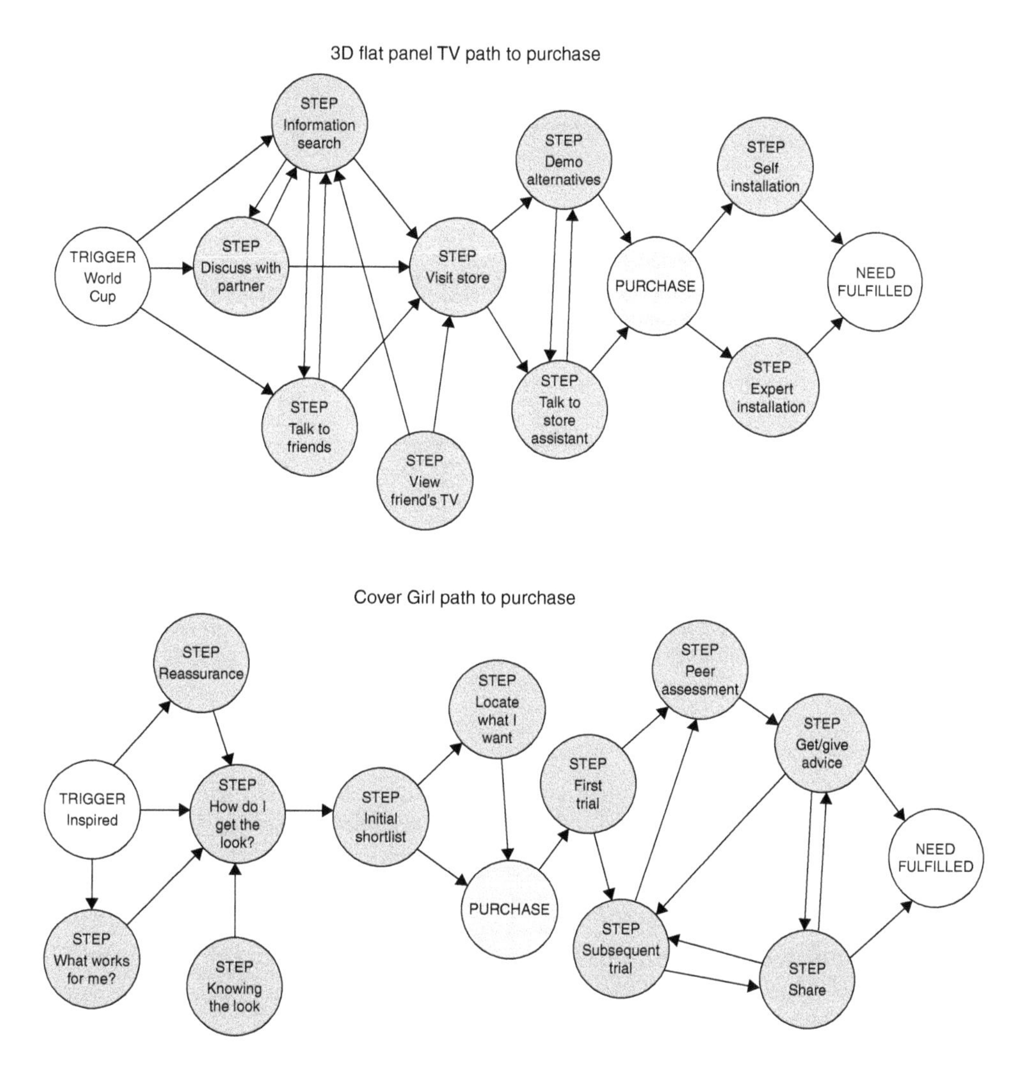

Figure 3.17 Comparison of shopper journeys for television sets and cosmetics
Example of two shopper journeys, one for television sets and one for cosmetics.
Source: Based on Dodd, 2011

process, there are different touchpoints, including social platforms. The process is influenced by the social reality of shoppers, e.g. sociodemographic characteristics and the level of digitalization.

The consumer of products and services is the target of consumer marketing. The objective of consumer marketing is to initiate, secure and increase consumption through developing awareness, preferences and loyalty for brands, products and services. To develop the need, preference and willingness to pay for products and services at a price higher than the cost to serve is the basis for each profitable company. To achieve this there needs to be a purchase. Without the act of purchase, there is no consumption. And there is no need for purchasing if there is no intention of consumption. Many times the buyer and the user, the shopper and

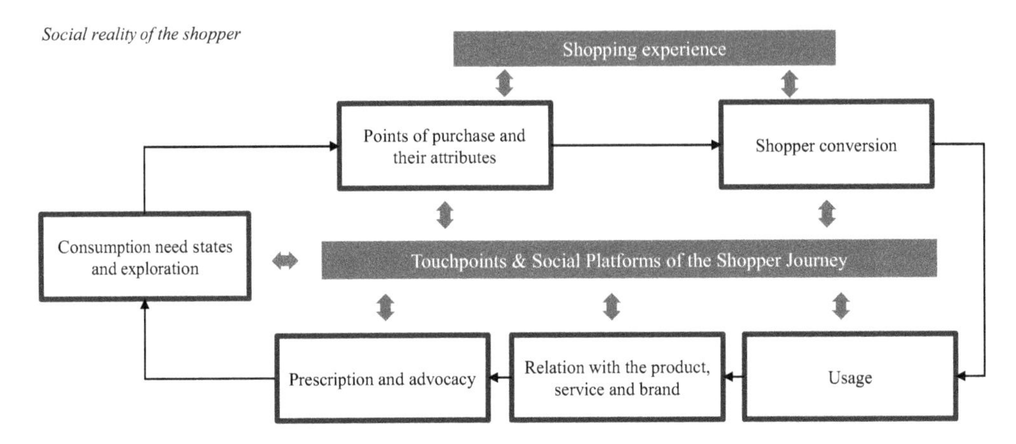

Figure 3.18 Shopper journey framework
Key phases of the shopper journey from the consumer need states to the use and evaluation of the product and service. The consumption need states generate the shopping trip and choice of point of purchase in line with the shopping mission. The conversion from shopper to buyer takes place at the point of purchase with the influence of the shopping experience. Through the use of the product and service, as well as through the different touchpoints and social platforms, a relation to the brand, product, and service is developed which influences recommendations and advocacy. This again influences the initial considered set of solutions of the consumption need states.
Source: Author

the consumer are identical. Here there are important differences between categories and situations. For example, with cosmetics, the consumer and the shopper are the same people in more than 90 percent of cases. The same applies to beer in direct consumption situations, in on-trade channels, e.g. bars, pubs, restaurants etc. In the case of groceries, the situation is usually different. The shopper and the purchasing process connect consumer marketing with the moment of product and service selection, i.e. the availability and presentation of products and services at the point of purchase.

Broadly speaking, consumer marketing is focused on developing awareness and preference for products and services, while shopper marketing focuses on purchasing, product and service selection. These are two separate processes, and even if the consumer and shopper are the same person, the attitude as a consumer and as a shopper is different. As a consumer, there is a preference, as a shopper there is a multidimensional decision on preference, consumption occasion, availability and price. Therefore, the objectives of consumer marketing and shopper marketing differ. Consumer marketing is often aspirational, describing and identifying what consumers would like, often with an emotional component. In many cases the people associated with a brand, product and service are different from the consumer.

Shopper marketing, on the other hand, has to focus on the people who will actually buy the products and services to meet their specific needs. While consumer marketing triggers engagement with consumers, shopper marketing triggers needs more aligned with the reality of the shoppers, in terms of usage and price, but also in terms of availability.

In the B2B environment an important distinction is made between the user and the chooser. The purchase decision is made in the intersection between these two. The user is

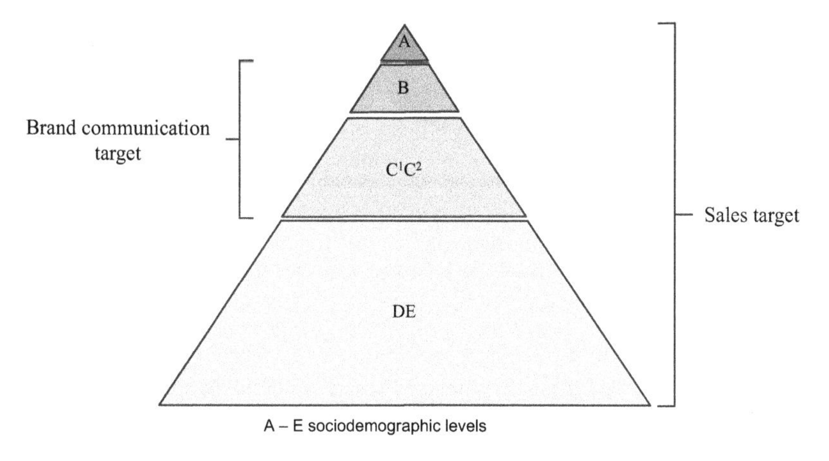

Figure 3.19 Brand communication and sales targets
Example of brand communication and sales targets in Africa in relation to socioeconomic levels.
Source: Author

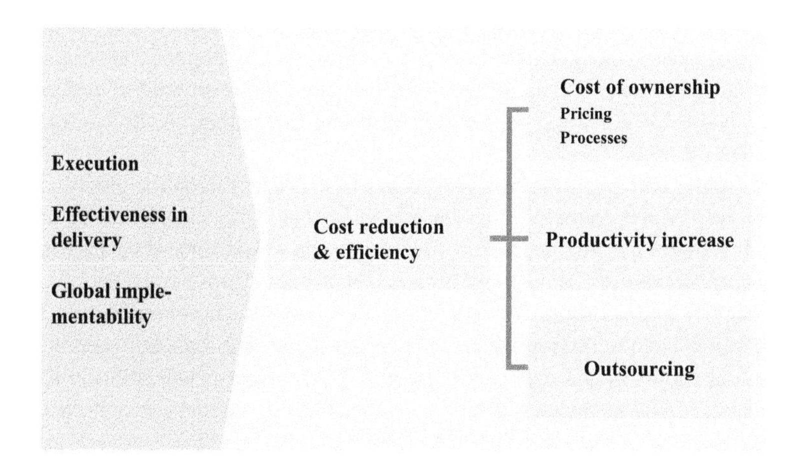

Figure 3.20 Cost of ownership
Example of evaluation criteria for products and services in the B2B field, in this case for the telecommunications industry in Western Europe.
Source: Author

the one who has to define the needs and the basic criteria to evaluate the product and service. Based on this the chooser can evaluate the different alternatives and select the best that satisfies both the needs of the user and the economic criteria of the chooser. The economic criteria are not reduced to just price, but also include the cost to serve, the quality and the service. For example, the price of a machine may be lower if it does not include service or maintenance, but depending on the need for service or maintenance, it may be that the lower priced machine is more expensive in the end than the other, where service and maintenance are included in the price.

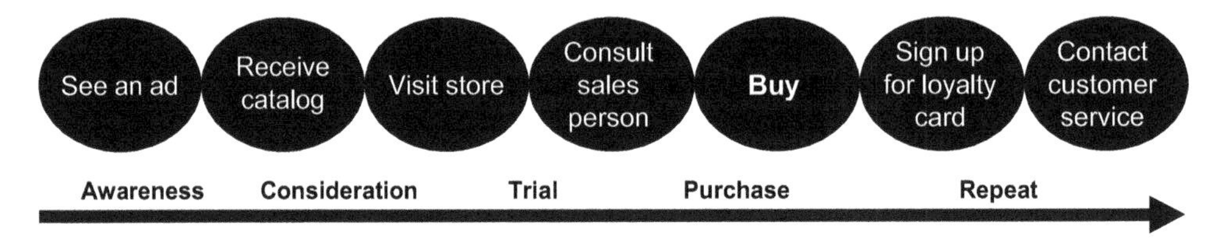

Figure 3.21 Traditional shopper journey in retail
Linear shopper journey to receive information, be informed, test, buy and evaluate the purchase.
Source: Bastistich, 2013

The concept of cost of ownership is very useful to better understand the B2C sphere. One example is low-cost flights in Europe. The best-known low-cost European airline is Ryanair. The price of a ticket is usually cheaper than that of other airlines. However, the price only shows the face value that the buyer sees directly, and not the total cost. The total cost of travel can be in line with that of other airlines. Ryanair often works with smaller and more distant airports, because they are cheaper and for each service, such as luggage, food etc., travelers have to pay extra. If all costs are added up the total cost of the flight, such as the ticket, transportation, luggage, additional time etc., often becomes considerably less attractive. Therefore, the cost of ownership varies dependent on how the different dimensions of a product and a service are evaluated at a certain point. It is therefore important to understand that the decision drivers that activate shoppers are different depending on the occasion of the purchase.

To activate the shopper and lead him through the purchase process from the identification of the consumption need states to the purchase needs, this same process needs to be understood and analyzed. Without a need, awareness, preference and availability at an appropriate price and cost of ownership there will be no purchase. The process from needs identification to purchase, the shopper journey, describes the interaction between the brand, product and service and the shopper. The interaction takes place across the touchpoints between brands, products, services and shoppers and drives the selection of the appropriate solution for the shopper depending on his or her needs in terms of consumption need state and purchase situation.

The route to purchase is the management of the shopper journey in the interest of the company to drive preference and purchase in favor of its own products and services. In other words, it is the strategy to manage the shopper throughout the shopper journey in favor of the company and its brands, products and services. Traditionally, the shopper journey was relatively simple and the main information sources were through classical media, like TV, radio and newspapers, and at the retail store.

Today, shoppers are informed through a multitude of media channels and buy in different sales channels, depending on the consumption need state and purchase situation. A shopper journey today is not linear and has more touchpoints.

For such a shopper journey it is clearly more complex to develop a route to purchase strategy. The management of the route to purchase is the management of the shopper toward the product or service to connect with the route to market, which has to ensure that the product and service is available at the right place, time and activated in line with the shopper expectations. The route to purchase connects the marketing intent with the route to market strategy.

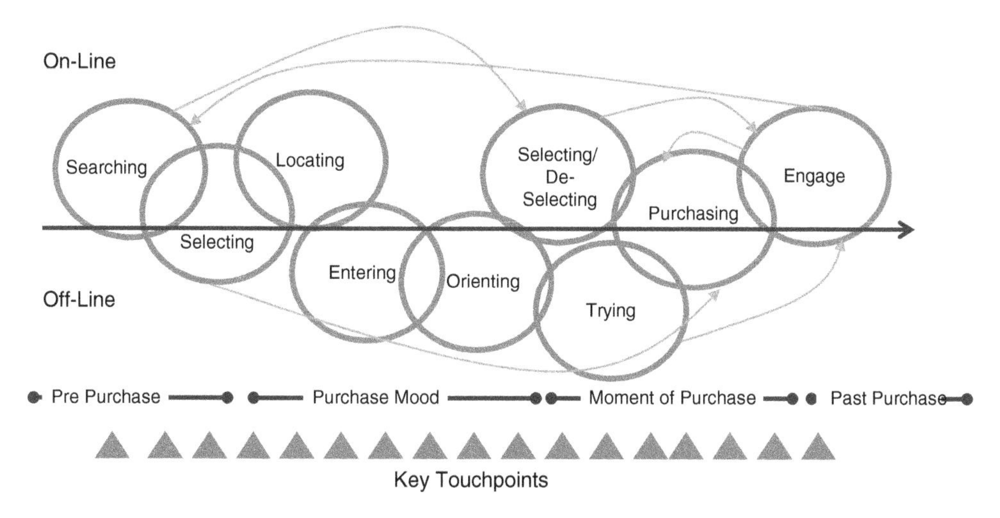

Figure 3.22 Shopper journey for personal care products
Shopper journey for personal care products in Western Europe.
Source: Author

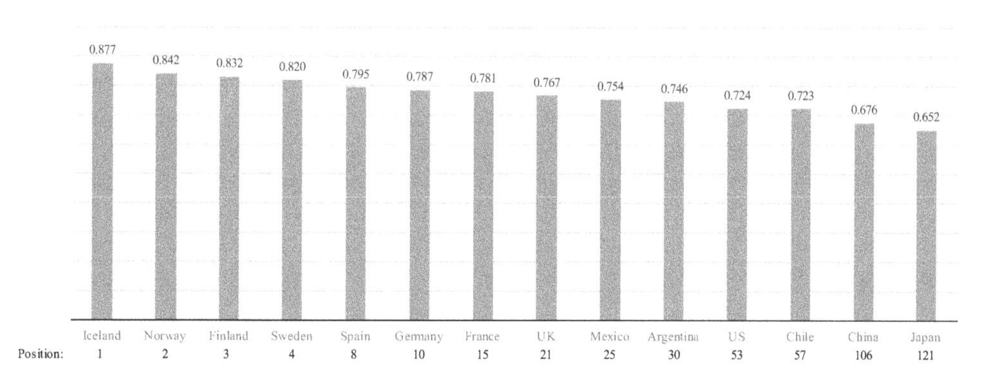

Figure 3.23 Global Gender Gap Index 2020
Level of gender equality in 2020.
Source: World Economic Forum 2019

Shopper journeys are local

Consumer marketing strategies of international companies often have a strong global component, but the closer to the moment of purchase, the more important the local specifics of a market become. Shopper marketing therefore needs to have a local focus in design, and even more in the phase of implementation.

The sociopolitical environment can differ significantly between countries and regions and has an important impact on purchasing behavior. In more traditional societies, the responsibility for grocery shopping often remains with housewives, while in countries with a higher degree of gender equality the responsibility for shopping is more evenly distributed between the genders. In addition, the incidence of single households differs between societies.

Economic differences, not only between segments of the population, but also between countries and regions, influence shopper marketing approaches. The economic differences of countries imply differences in the understanding of shoppers, their segmentation and the strategies needed to reach those segments. In the telecommunications industry, as an example, segmentation in developed countries is often based on lifestyle, while in emerging countries segmentation by income levels can be more useful.

In such different markets, the needs of segments are different, as are the ways in which people buy and the points of purchase are structured. In addition, the role of digital touchpoints and e-commerce differs.

The shopper journey and how the shopper arrives at the product and service depends on the category, but also on the reason for the purchase, the consumption occasion, as well as the involvement, the importance of the purchase, and the information necessary for the purchase decision.

Shopper marketing is ultimately a local challenge, depending on the sociopolitical environment, the economic situation, the market structure and the supply and use of technological solutions. The strategy to activate shoppers and deliver the products and services to the shopper needs to be based on local specifics, even if the brand strategy and its positioning are global.

Shopper to buyer conversion

Conversion is when the shopper decides to buy a product and service and becomes a buyer. On average a very small share of shoppers become buyers of a specific product and service. In the case of shoppers in brick-and-mortar stores, 2.5 percent represent 80 percent of the sales of specific brands in consumer goods categories.[85] The conversion process could be viewed from a transaction cost analysis perspective.[86] It is a concept from microeconomics, but can be transferred to explain the relationship between shopper and supplier.[87] The transaction cost is the subjective evaluation of the opportunity cost by the shopper and consumer.[88] This includes costs of the entire shopping process, from information seeking, finding products and services, as well as the cost of the product and service itself, and costs of maintenance and so on.[89] It is not only the price, but the associated costs that are evaluated.

As the shopper journey grows longer with more touchpoints, the possibilities to influence the shopper expand. Shopper management becomes more complex, as many touchpoints are not directly managed or cannot be fully influenced by the company, especially with touchpoints initiated by shoppers and consumers or dependent on direct shopper and consumer feedback.[90] More and more touchpoints are through cell phones that most shoppers and consumers continuously have at hand, enabling a communication beyond the package and the activation at the point of purchase.[91] Through digital touchpoints, the retail and points of purchase can come to the shopper, and not, as traditionally, the other way around.[92] Moreover, information becomes more attuned with their needs.[93] Word of mouth communication is a non-commercial, informal, person-to-person communication.[94] The information that the shopper receives through word-of-mouth communication reduces the perceived risk of the purchase.[95] Therefore, WOM has a positive impact on sales, making social platforms an important challenge for companies to consider in their shopper marketing approaches.[96]

The conversion process transcends the departments of marketing, sales and trade marketing. Shopper marketing has to integrate different areas to successfully activate

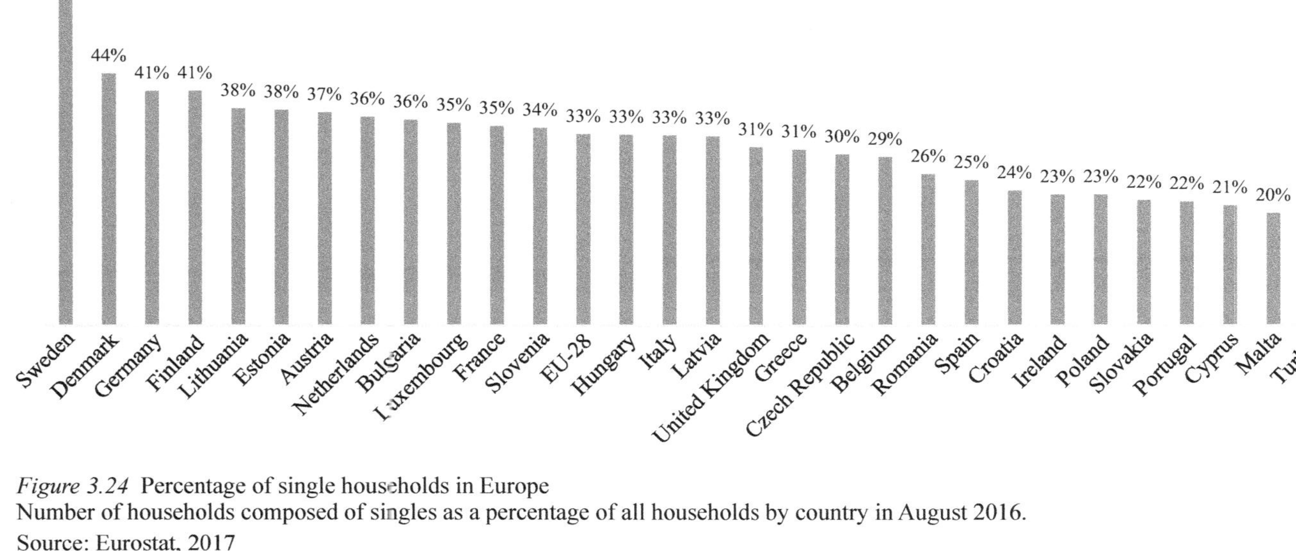

Figure 3.24 Percentage of single households in Europe
Number of households composed of singles as a percentage of all households by country in August 2016.
Source: Eurostat, 2017

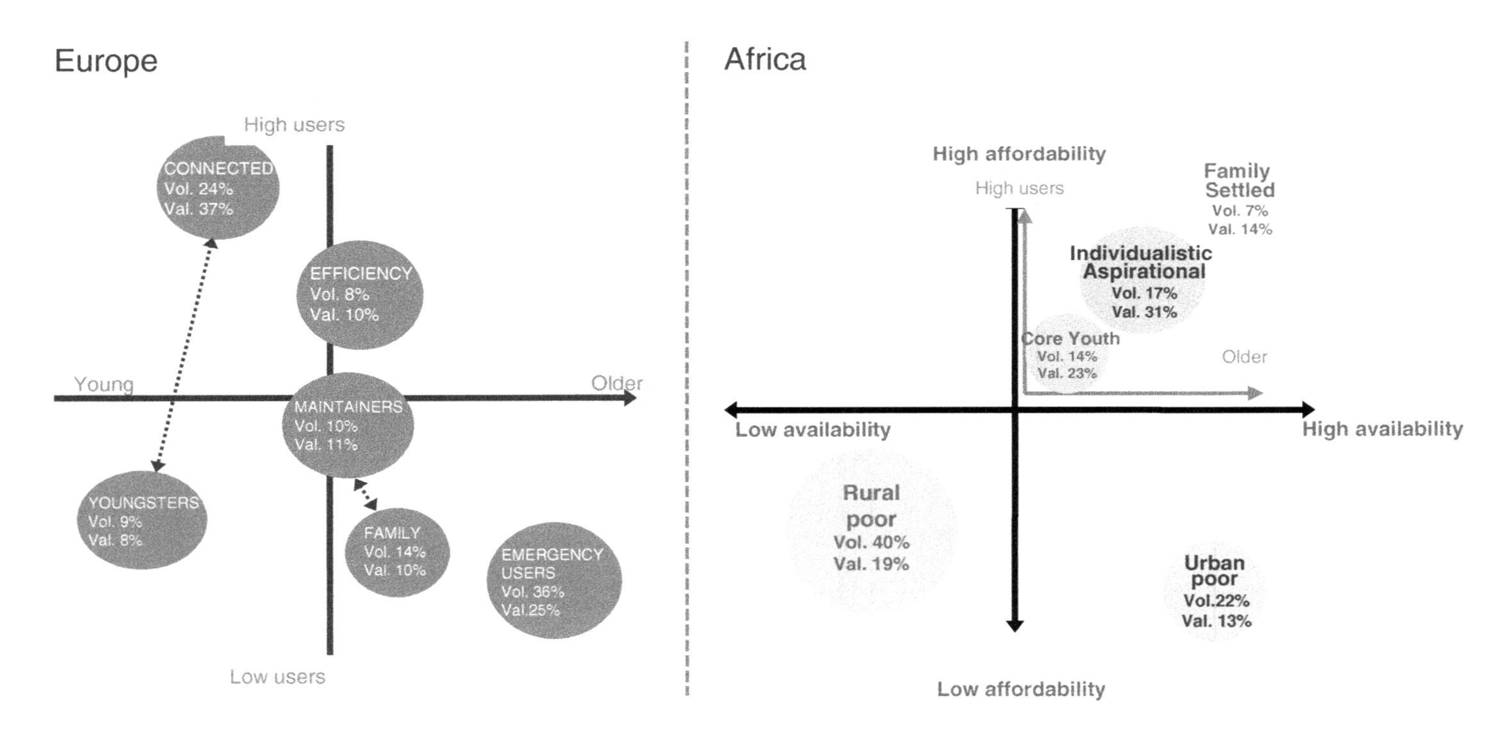

Figure 3.25 Segmentation of users of cell phones in Europe and Africa

Comparison of a cell phone market segmentation in Western Europe and Africa. In Western Europe, the main differentiation criteria were level of usage and age, while in Africa the main differentiators were the level of income and availability. For the high income segment a Western Europe sub-segmentation was used.

Source: Author

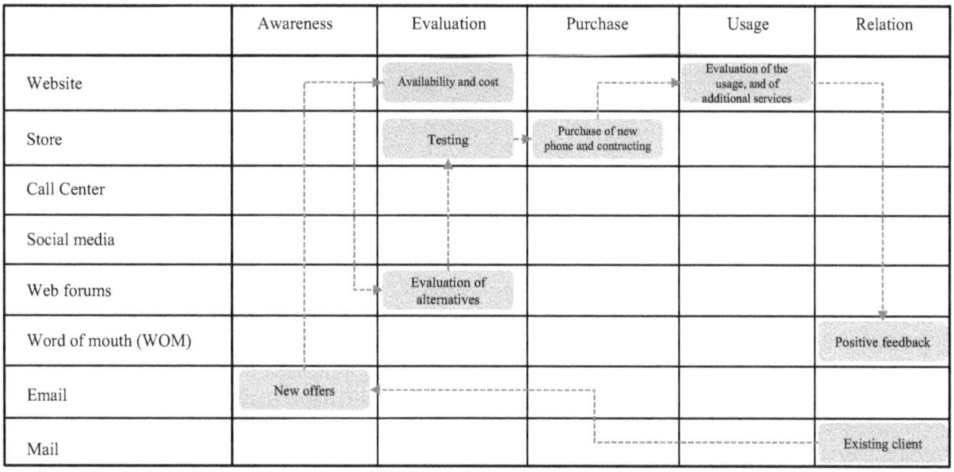

	Awareness	Evaluation	Purchase	Usage	Relation
Website		Availability and cost		Evaluation of the usage, and of additional services	
Store		Testing	Purchase of new phone and contracting		
Call Center					
Social media					
Web forums		Evaluation of alternatives			
Word of mouth (WOM)					Positive feedback
Email	New offers				
Mail					Existing client

Figure 3.26 Shopper journey in the mobile telecom industry in Western Europe
Example of a shopper journey in Western Europe for cell phone renewal and service of an existing customer.
Source: Author

	Awareness	Evaluation	Purchase	Usage	Relation
Store		Testing	Purchase of new phone and contracting		
Call Center		Available phones and cost			
Social media				Evaluation of the usage	Positive feedback
Word of mouth (WOM)	New offers				Existing client

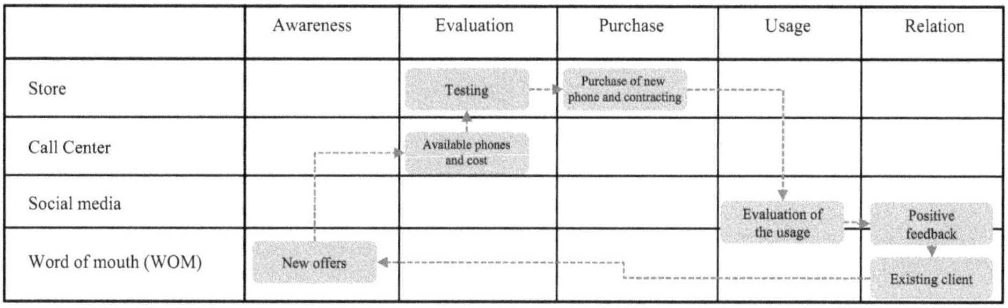

Figure 3.27 Shopper journey in the mobile telecom industry in Africa
Example of a shopper journey in Africa of cell phone renewal and service of an existing customer.
Source: Author

shoppers along the shopper journey and its touchpoints. Consumer marketing has to develop the right offer for the right consumption need state and target group, while sales and distribution need to ensure that the offer is available and activated in the right sales channels and points of purchase in an effective and efficient manner. Shopper marketing has to align and connect coherently the different activities to manage the process from the consumption need state to the profitable conversion at the point of purchase. This includes the complexity of integrating a B2C view with a B2B understanding and management of retailers and partners, such as distributors. In addition, the step from consumer to shopper and their different perspectives need to be managed.

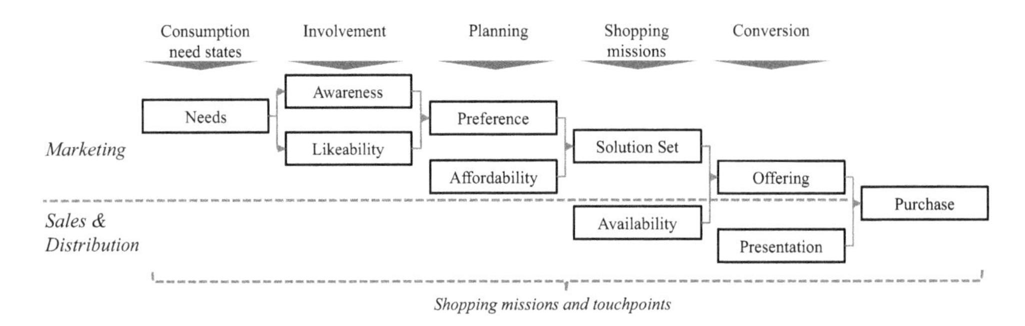

Figure 3.28 Overview of the shopper conversion process
The conversion process begins with the consumption need state and leads to an evaluation of alternatives depending on the awareness and liking of these alternatives. Awareness and liking leads to the preferences and combined with their affordability the relevant decision set is defined. The availability of the solution set results in the offer, and the relevant shopper activation leads to the purchase of the product and service.
Source: Author

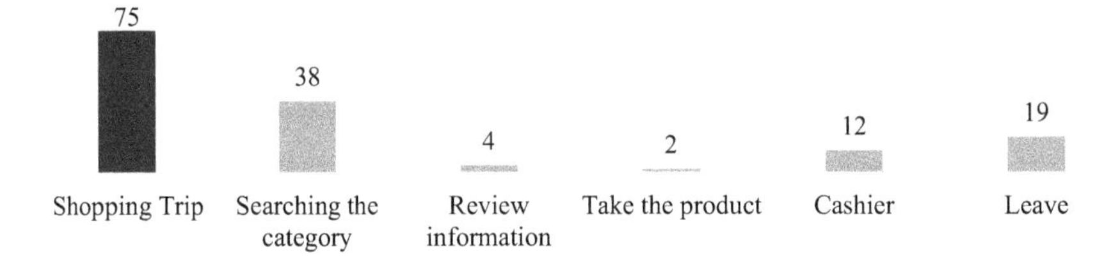

Figure 3.29 Moment of purchase
Example of the moment of purchase for beers in South America in a traditional brick-and-mortar store for immediate consumption. The length of the entire purchase trip is 75 seconds. 38 seconds are used to find the category, 4 seconds to review the information at the category, 2 seconds to take the chosen product, 12 seconds at the cashier, and 19 seconds to leave the store.
Source: Author

Consumers and shoppers can be identical, but in many cases, the shopper is distinct from the consumer. Marketing needs to develop a preference for its products and services, both for consumers and shoppers. This preference is based on the awareness and positive likeability of the products and services. The more important the product or service, or the more importance that can be built, the higher the involvement with the products and services. However, to enter the relevant solution set for the shopper and become part of the purchase planning the products and services need to be affordable. The right presentation of the offer will lead to a successful conversion and purchase, as long as there is not a better competitive alternative along the conversion process. The conversion from shopping to buying mode at the point of purchase can be short. Much of the shopper marketing effort lies in the process leading up to the final conversion.

Depending on the final conversion challenges, the manufacturer has to adapt his tactics at the point of purchase in terms of information, promotions, support material (including clicks for additional information at digital points of purchase) and promotions, but also strategically in terms of brand, price, product format and services. The effectiveness of different

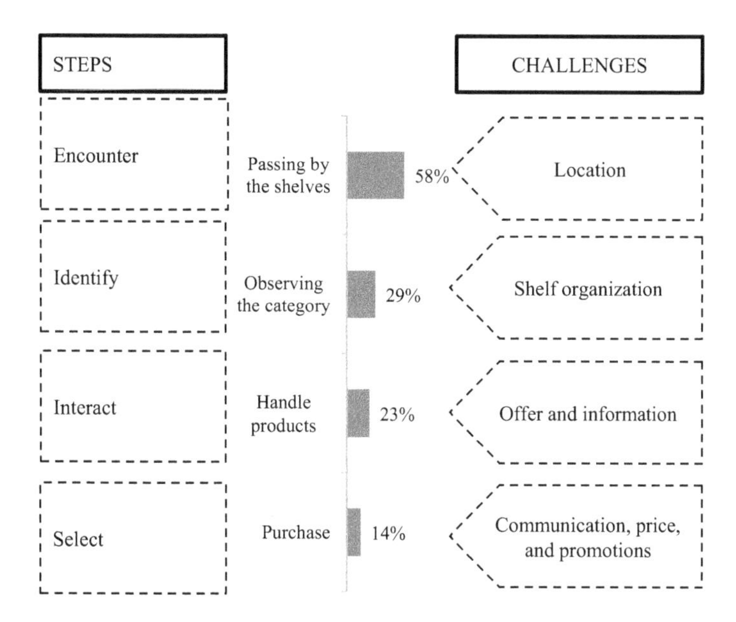

Figure 3.30 Shopper conversion funnel
Example of a shopper conversion funnel and corresponding challenges: 58% of shoppers who entered the store passed by the shelf, 29% observed the category, 23% interacted with the products and 14% made a purchase.
Source: Author

purchase drivers in terms of conversion power depend on the product and service, the consumer need states, the shopper attitudes, the activation along the shopper journey and the type of point of purchase.[97] The conversion power of different purchase drivers also differ by shopper segment.[98]

With higher levels of planning shoppers are more likely to purchase.[99] The presence of friends and family during the shopping trip influence the purchase decision,[100] as well as price sensitivity.[101] Shoppers buy more products and spend more money when accompanied.[102] The shopping environment and the price structure affect the purchasing behavior.[103] The shopping behavior is influenced by the location of the store,[104] how products[105] and shelves[106] are organized, colors[107] in the store, the position of the product on the shelf,[108] and audio-visual effects.[109] In addition, the assortment of goods,[110] a spacious environment, smells and other elements have an important role in influencing shopping behavior.[111] Still, even if activation increases sales, the longer term impact on the brand image is not conclusive.[112]

Route to purchase strategy design

Strategy is about prioritization, deciding how to best use scarce resources and deciding what not to do. Depending on the shopper journey, the challenge is to prioritize the right touchpoints and define the right level of investment to best manage the shopper toward the conversion.

The starting point in developing any route to purchase strategy is to understand the consumption need states and the associated purchase process. The development of the route

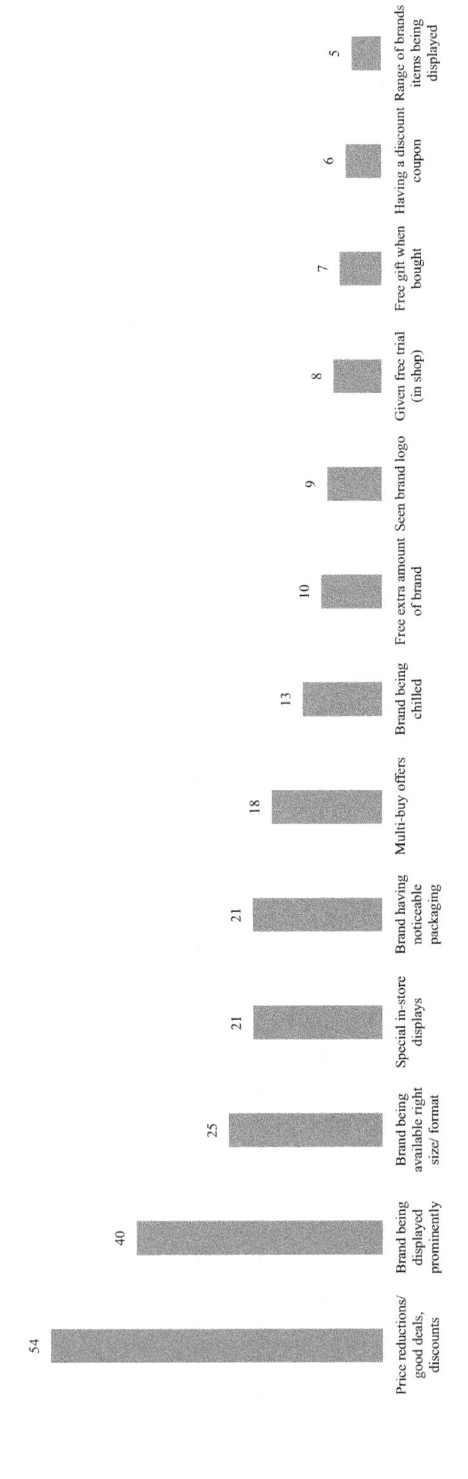

Figure 3.31 Power score of in-store shopper conversion drivers
Example of in-store purchase drivers and their conversion power.
Source: Millward Brown, 2008

to purchase strategy depends on where the company will compete, i.e. which is the target consumption need state(s). This determines the competitive environment, as well as the shopper behavior. For example, in the airline industry, if the targeted consumption need state is business travel or economy family travel, the implications will be different in terms of shopper behavior, and how to design the route to purchase strategy.

When the consumption need states and where the company will compete has been defined, the competitive position within the consumption need state, and specifically the category, in terms of shopper penetration of the category and the market share of the manufacturer's products and services, has to be evaluated to understand the overall strategic challenges.

Understanding the consumption need states and the competitive position also gives important feedback for the development of products and services, as well as the positioning of brands. This is not a task that normally falls within the confines of shopper marketing. Still, shopper marketing has an important role to provide insights to ensure that there is an adequate offering in line with the strategic positioning and the shopper marketing challenge at hand.

After understanding the competitive challenge, the attitudes of the shoppers need to be mapped. Crossing the involvement with the level of planning gives insights into the activation priorities. In situations with high involvement, the purchase process needs to be supported with adequate information along the shopping journey. When the involvement is low, the challenge is more to draw attention at the moment of conversion. The level of planning influences where the focus of the activation should be, before the purchase or during the shopping trip, closer to the moment of conversion.

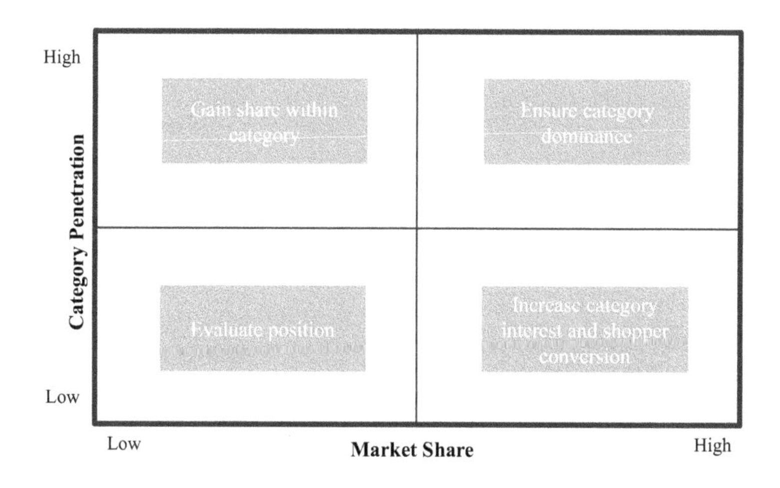

Figure 3.32 Shopper penetration and market share matrix

The vertical dimension shows the shopper penetration, i.e. the percentage of shoppers buying the category. The horizontal dimension shows the market share of the manufacturer's products and services within the category. In the upper left cell many shoppers buy the category, and the challenge of the manufacturer is to gain market share within the category. In the lower left cell, few shoppers buy the category, and the manufacturer needs to evaluate the possibility and potential attractiveness of the position. In the right lower cell, the challenge is to increase the interest and conversion of the category. In the upper right cell, the challenge is to continue to ensure dominance. Obviously, positions of low penetration and market share can be attractive, if the value and the margins are profitable.

Source: Author

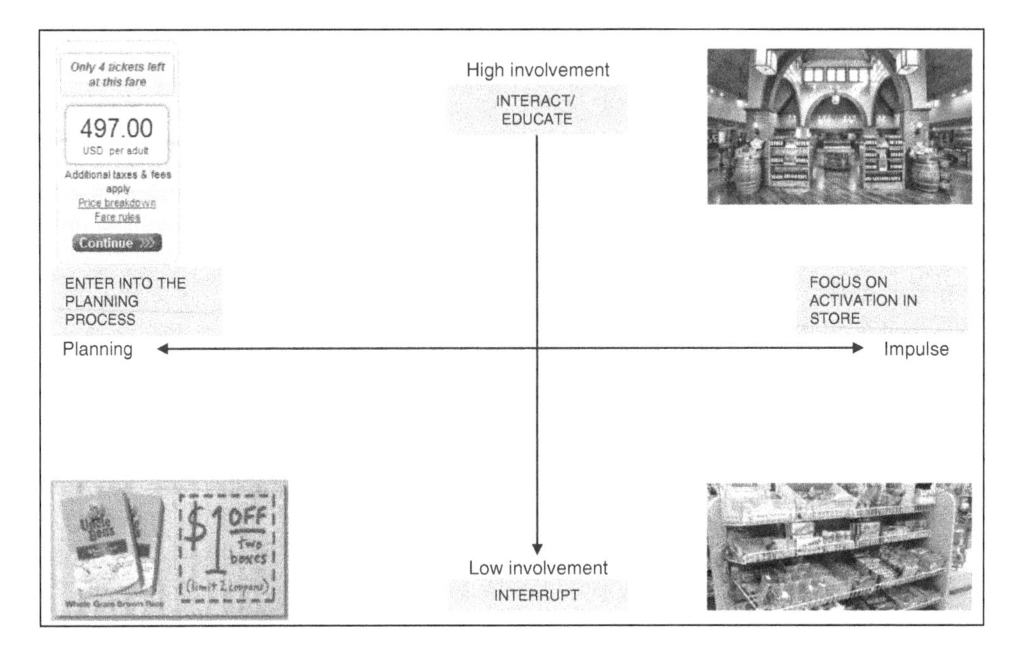

Figure 3.33 Involvement and planning matrix

The vertical dimension shows the involvement level and the horizontal dimension the level of planning. The upper left cell shows high involvement and planning, and demands interaction, information and education along the various touchpoints of the shopper journey. The upper right cell shows high involvement, and low specific planning, which demands interaction, information and education close to the moment of purchase. The lower left cell describes low involvement and high planning. In this situation, the different touchpoints need to be managed with interruptive messages to draw attention and build preference. The lower right cell describes a situation with impulse buying and low involvement, which demands interruption and attention building through activation close to the moment of purchase.

Source: Author

Mapping the touchpoints along the shopper journey, and understanding their importance and role is the basis for prioritizing them in terms of management and investment.

Touchpoints can be divided into touchpoints that lead to a purchase and those that drive the conversion at the moment of the purchase. In an omnichannel environment, there is not just one point of purchase, but several across different channels. Orders and purchases can be done on a mobile device, through the internet, or in a brick-and-mortar store. Not only do the number of touchpoints increase, but they can have a double role of supplying information and building preference to drive the actual purchase, as well as being a point of purchase. Not all touchpoints can be addressed with the same focus, but investments in them need to be prioritized to optimize conversion and relationship building. The role and importance of the different touchpoints need to be understood to develop the optimal shopper marketing program and route to purchase strategy. The prioritized touchpoints need to be understood in terms of their role to the shopper and activated accordingly. That is why it is necessary to understand with which touchpoints and with which investments the effect is optimal.

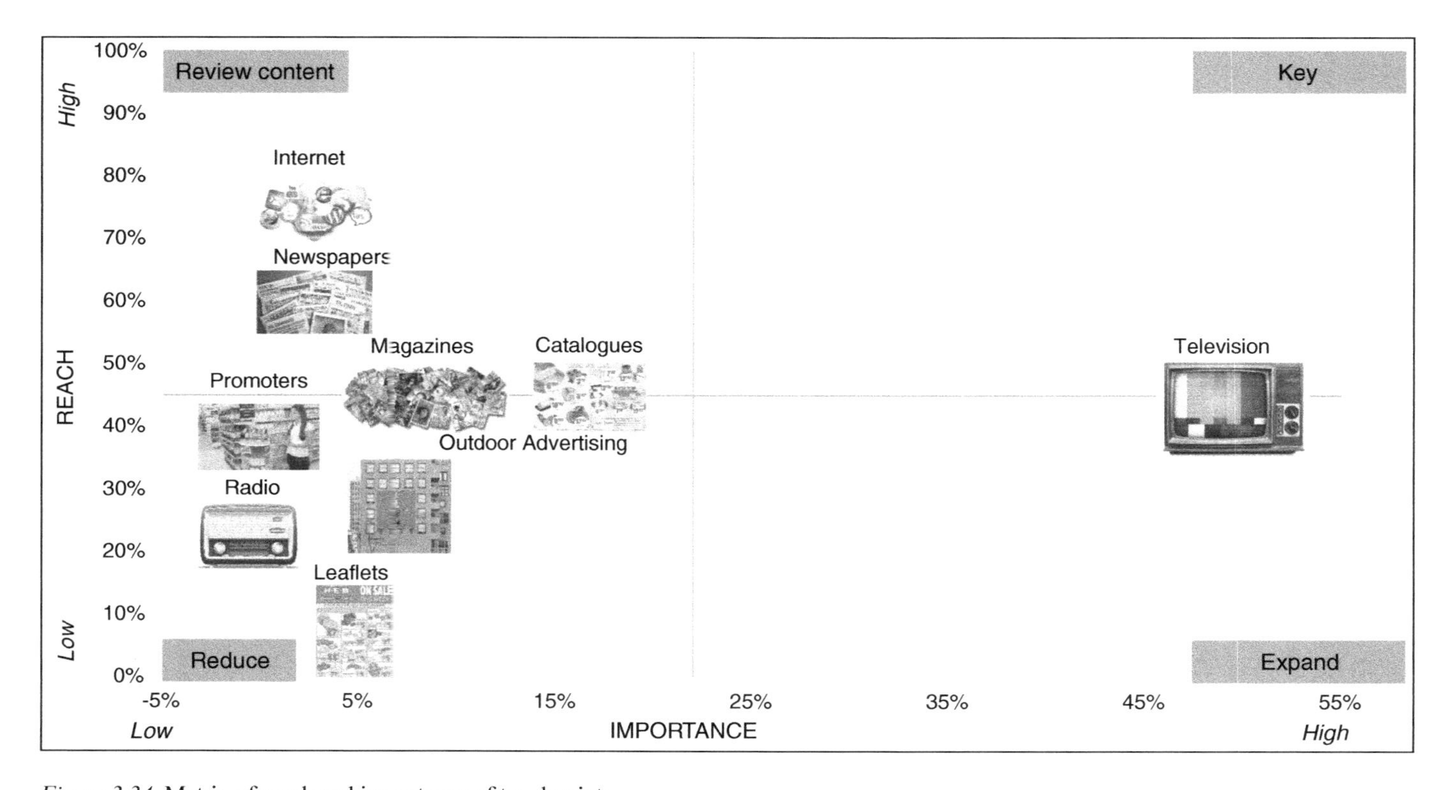

Figure 3.34 Matrix of reach and importance of touchpoints
The vertical dimension depicts the reach of the touchpoints by percentage of shoppers. The horizontal dimension shows the importance in terms of percentage of shoppers that associated an important influence of the touchpoint on their final purchase decision.
Source: Author

The key is to understand the missions of the prioritized touchpoints to activate them in line with their role. In addition, the type of activation has to be evaluated to ensure the optimum investment by touchpoint. The return on investment (ROI) of the shopper activation program and the route to purchase strategy needs to be calculated and optimized in terms of the conversion effect and the sales and margins generated. Caution is required when calculating the ROI of marketing program investments as often longer-term impacts on customer loyalty and brand image are difficult to quantify. This is a challenge often discussed in relation to promotions and price discounts; they can be conducive of short-term sales, but have a small or even contrary effect in the longer term.

Defining the target consumption need states, understanding the strategic challenges, mapping the shopper attitudes and the touchpoints along the shopper journey, and prioritizing the touchpoints in line with their roles and ROI all form basis for developing the route to purchase strategy. The route to purchase strategy can be built upon existing shopper journeys, but can also imply developing new touchpoints and changing the shopper journey in line with the strategic shopper activation interests of the company. Examples are online solutions, such as Dell or Amazon, or streaming in the music and movie industry, that have fundamentally changed traditional shopper journeys.

A clear and coherent message across the route to purchase is key to building trust with consumers and shoppers. The challenge is not only the route to purchase, but also the linkage

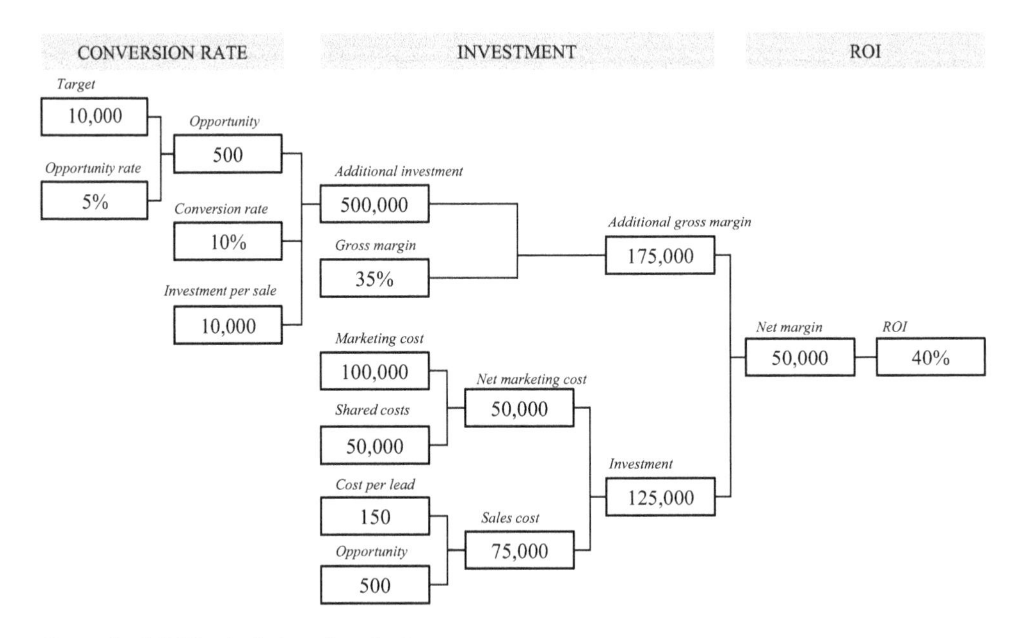

Figure 3.35 ROI calculation of marketing programs

Example of a ROI calculation of a marketing program. The conversion value is calculated based on the shopper target, the relevant opportunity, expected conversion rate, and sales per conversion. The investment is calculated as the marketing cost to activate the priority touchpoints minus the costs shared with other programs or partners, and the variable specific cost per lead opportunity. The profit of the program is the additional margin generated minus the marketing program cost. The ROI is the profit of the program as a percentage of the program investment.

Source: Lenskold Group, 2017

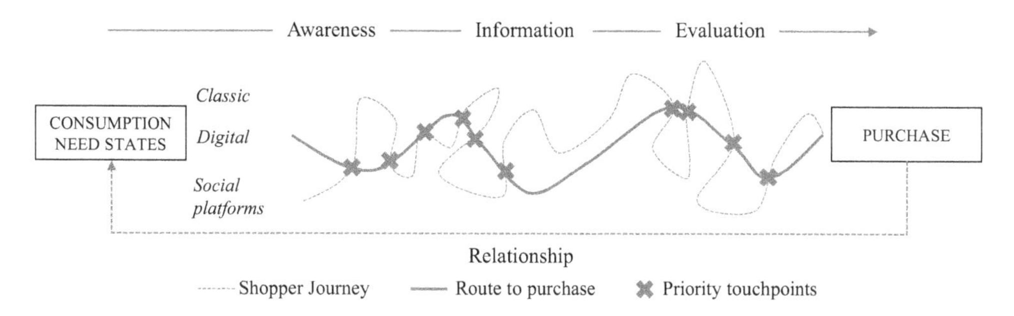

Figure 3.36 From shopper journey to route to purchase strategy
Representation of the development of a route to purchase strategy. From consumption need states, shopper journey and role of touchpoints mapping and prioritization, in terms of awareness building, information, and offer evaluation touchpoints, to the purchase, and the influence of the experience on the initial consumption need state.
Source: Author

with the route to market. Products and services need to be available at the right points of purchase for the targeted consumption need states, and in line with the touchpoints activated. An example of building coherent route to purchase and route to market strategies is the TOP model (target – occasion – place). Specific consumers are the target for a specific occasion of usage, and the products and services are available in points of purchase aligned with the target consumers and consumption occasions.

Another example is Coca-Cola and its Motor program to ensure a 360-degree coherent activation approach. The program connects the different touchpoints of the shopper journey according to the media channel and shopper conversion funnel, from ATL, out of home, in the store, until the product package, and the role of each touchpoint in the shopper activation journey. Hereby, the route to purchase strategy becomes linked with the route to market, at least when it comes to the place of purchase. For example, for their program in Thailand Coca-Cola won the silver Ogilvy Award shopper marketing award. In Thailand, Coca-Cola was facing stagnant growth and loss of leadership in the soft drink category in the main sales channel, the traditional trade. With a coherent shopper marketing program Coca-Cola was able to turn around the situation. The program included the management of different media from outside to inside the point of purchase, until the packaging of the product itself.[113]

The design of the route to purchase strategy is key to managing scarce resources to optimize the shopper conversion along the shopper journey in line with the positioning within the consumption need states and the strategic objectives.

The route to purchase strategy can actively change the initial shopper journey to achieve strategic advantages. For example, the banking sector and Fintech has radically changed the shopper journey and opened the market to new digital only competitors, e.g. N26 from Germany. Dell is another example of a company that changed the competitive dynamics in the PC market through a digital marketing and sales process. These examples of change in the banking and computer industries describe radical changes to the commercial value chain, not only in the route to purchase, but also in the route to market.

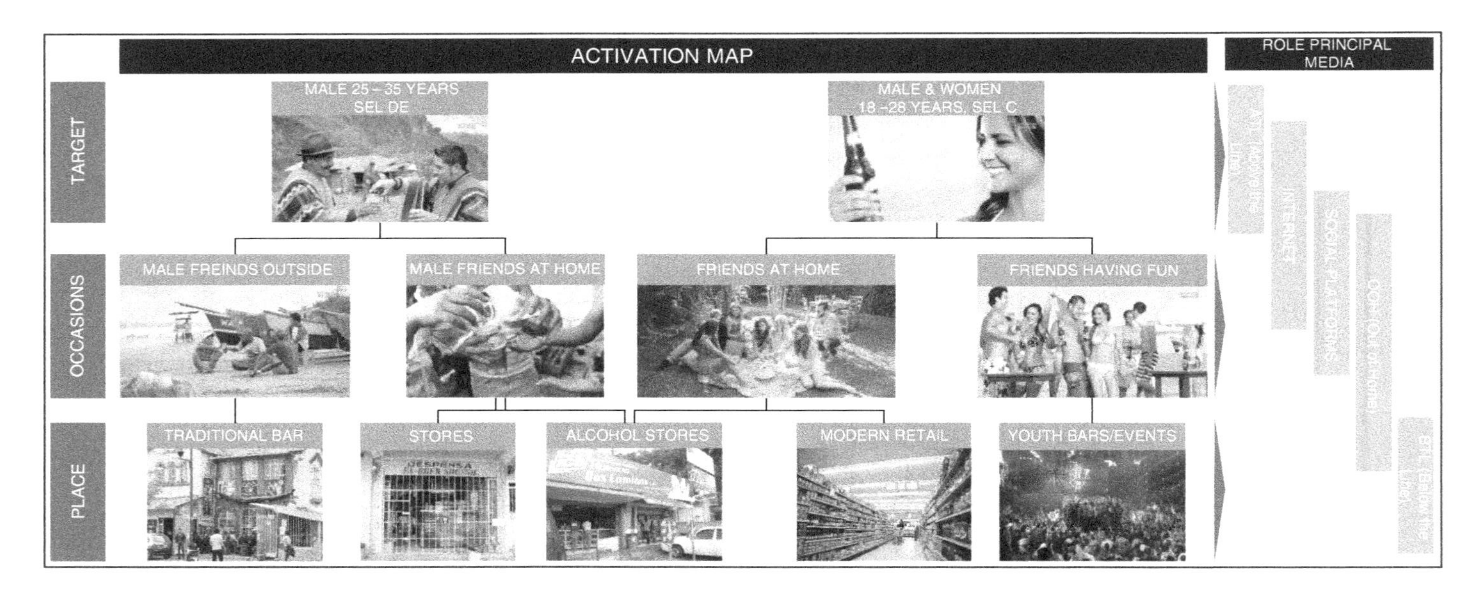

Figure 3.37 TOP activation scheme for beer in South America

Example of TOP (target – occasion – place) model for activation strategy for the beer category in South America.

Source: Author

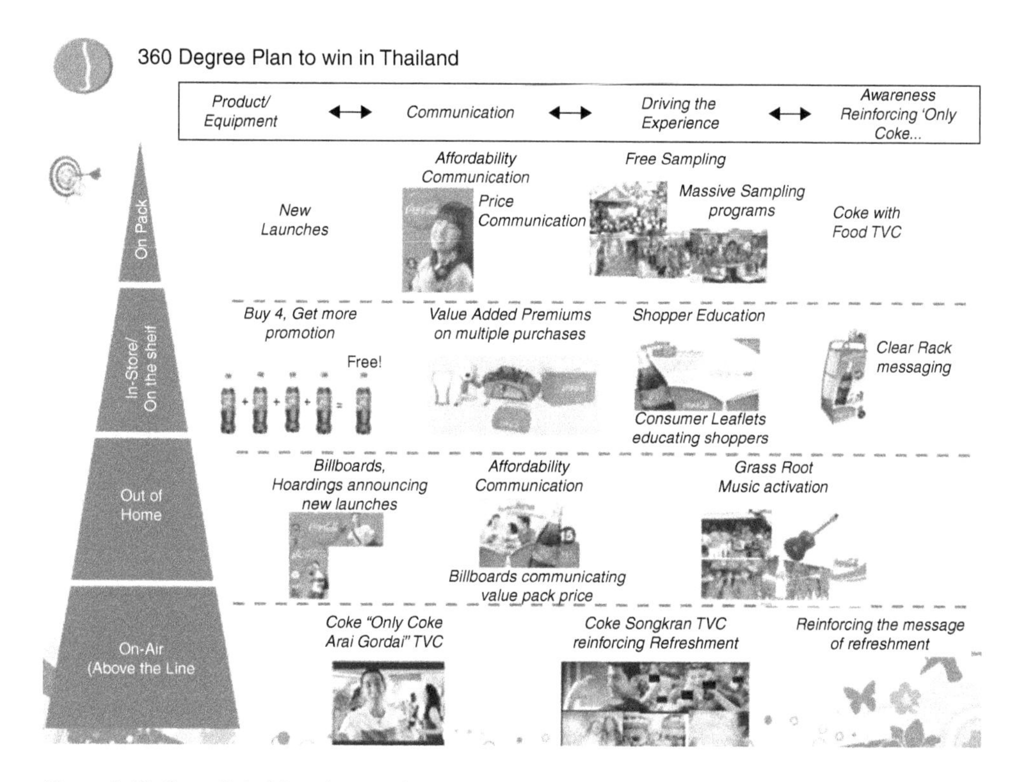

Figure 3.38 Coca-Cola Motoring to win program in Thailand
Silver shopper marketing award winner of David Ogilvy Awards. Motor of Coca-Cola is a shopper marketing design and implementation initiative.
Source: Coca-Cola, 2008

Notes

1 (Marx et al., 1970)
2 (Skinner & Schlinger, 2015)
3 (Bandura, 1977)
4 (Maslow & Ribé, 2012)
5 (Alderfer, 1972)
6 (Herzberg, 1974)
7 (McGregor & Cutcher-Gershenfield, 2008)
8 (Reiss & Bootzin, 1985)
9 (Locke & Latham, 2013)
10 (Adams, 1963)
11 (Murray, 2008)
12 (McClelland, 2016)
13 (Vroom & Jago, 1988)
14 (Kotler & Armstrong, 2014) and (Kotler et al., 2007)
15 (Lewin, 1936)

16 (Belk, 1975), (Dickson, 1982), and (Sandell, 1968)
17 (Green & Rao, 1972), (Belk, 1974a; 1974b), (Srivastava et al., 1978), and (Srivastava, 1980)
18 (Stanton & Bonner, 1980)
19 (Hall et al., 2001a; 2001b)
20 (Haley, 1968), (Dickson, 1982), and (Stanton & Bonner, 1980)
21 (Gehrt & Shim, 2003),and (Srivastava et al., 1978)
22 (Dubow, 1992)
23 (van Kenhove et al., 1999) and (Zidda et al., 2008)
24 (Pettersson, 2003)
25 (Lord et al., 2004) and (Cohen & Reed II, 2006)
26 (Berekoven et al., 2006)
27 (Venkatesh et al., 2003)
28 (Berekoven et al., 2006) and (Hammann & Erichson, 2006)
29 (Ajzen, 2005)
30 (Krugman, 1966)
31 (Sherif & Sargent, 1947), (Sherif et al., 1965) and (Sherif & Sherif, 1967)
32 (Sherif et al., 1965)
33 (Freedman, 1964), (Sherif et al., 1965) and (O'Keefe, 1990)
34 (Sherif & Sherif, 1967) and (Laaksonen, 1994), (Bloch, 1981)
35 (Bloch, 1981) and (Michaelidou & Dibb, 2006) and (Zaichkowsky, 1985)
36 (Slama & Tashchian, 1985)
37 (Mittal, 1989)
38 (Kirmani et al., 1999)
39 (Tyebjee, 1979)
40 (Petty & Cacioppo, 1981)
41 (Ganesh et al., 2000)
42 (Zaichkowsky, 1985)
43 (Dholakia, 1997), (Dholakia, 2001), (Greenwald & Leavitt, 1984), (Kinley et al., 1999), (Lockshin et al., 1997), (Muncy, 1990), (Petty & Cacioppo, 1981), (Quester & Lim, 2003), (Venkatraman, 1988), (Worrington & Shim, 2000), (Zaichkowsky, 1994) and (Vaughn, 1980)
44 (Kapferer & Laurent, 1985), (Kapferer & Laurent, 1993), (Michaelidou & Dibb, 2006), (Rahtz & Moore, 1989), (Zaichkowsky, 1985) and (Zaichkowsky, 1994)
45 (Mittal & Lee, 1989), (Slama & Tashchian, 1985) and (Smith & Bristor, 1994)
46 (Flynn & Goldsmith, 1993), (Goldsmith & Emmert, 1991), (Mittal & Lee, 1987), (Mittal & Lee, 1989), (Neelamegham & Jain, 1999), (Speed & Thompson, 2000) and (Tyebjee, 1979)
47 (Keaveney & Parthasarathy, 2001)
48 (Andrews et al., 1990), (Laczniak & Muehling, 1989), (Mitchell, 1979), (Petty & Cacioppo, 1981), (Vaughn, 1986), (Zaichkowsky, 1994) and (Greenwald & Leavitt, 1984)
49 (Michaelidou & Dibb, 2008)
50 (Park & Mittal, 1985) and (Michaelidou & Dibb, 2008)
51 (Laaksonen, 1994)
52 (Houston & Rothschild, 1978), (Rothschild, 1979) and (Richins & Bloch, 1986)
53 (Bloch, 1981), (Celsi & Olson, 1988), (Hupfer & Gardner, 1971) and (Lastovicka & Gardner, 1979)
54 (Dholakia, 1997)
55 (Mittal, 1989)
56 (Kassarjian, 1981), (Stone, 1984) and (Bloch, 1981)
57 (Mittal & Lee, 1989)
58 (Kinley et al., 1999), (Lockshin et al., 1997) and (Mittal, 1989)
59 (Kapferer & Laurent, 1985) and (Richins & Bloch, 1986)

60 (Anderson, 1973), (Peyton et al., 2003), (Olson & Dover, 1979), (Festinger, 1957) and (Hovland et al., 1957)
61 (Krueger Jr. & Brazael, 1994)
62 (Ajzen, 1991) and (Jonas & Doll, 1996)
63 (Ajzen, 1991)
64 (Nicholls et al., 1997)
65 (Iyer, 1989) and (Park et al., 1989)
66 (Pavlou & Flygenson, 2006)
67 (Bamberg et al., 2003)
68 (Jonas & Doll, 1996)
69 (Shaw et al., 2000), (Shaw & Shiu, 2003) and (Smith et al., 2008)
70 (Braunstein et al., 2005)
71 (Pavlou & Flygenson, 2006), (Legris et al., 2003), (Venkatesh et al., 2003) and (Taylor & Todd, 1995)
72 (Walter & Reutterer, 2009)
73 (Kendzierski, 1990)
74 (Jonas & Doll, 1996)
75 (Orbell et al., 1997), (Albarracín & Wyer, 2000), (Soman, 2001), (Kidwell & Jewell, 2003) and (Kidwell & Jewell, 2008)
76 (Ebling, 2008)
77 (Maechler et al., 2016)
78 (Bylykbashi, 2015)
79 (ECR Europe, emnos & The Partnering Group, 2011)
80 (Maechler et al., 2016)
81 (Bell et al., 2011)
82 (Elkin, 2001)
83 (Löfgren, 2005) and (Grönros, 2000)
84 (Berry et al., 2002)
85 (Pointer Media Network & CMO Council, 2008)
86 (Williamson et al., 1991)
87 (Klingenberg, 2000)
88 (Kaas & Fischer, 1992)
89 (Kreller, 2000)
90 (Future exploration network, 2008)
91 (GS1, 2008)
92 (Shankar et al., 2010)
93 (Kumar et al., 2007) and (Ahrens & Dressler, 2011)
94 (Harris-Walker, 2001)
95 (Bansal & Voyer, 2000), (Murray, 1991) and (Ho & Chung, 2007)
96 (Liu, 2006), (Swan & Oliver, 1989) and (Ho & Chung, 2007)
97 (Parsons & Thompson, 2009)
98 (Odekerken-Schröder et al., 2003)
99 (Engel et al., 1995), (Kollat & Willet, 1967) and (Holbrook & Hirschman, 1982)
100 (Beardon et al., 1989)
101 (Wakefield & Inman, 2003)
102 (Nicholls et al., 1994)
103 (Krämer, 2010)
104 (Babin & Babin, 2001)
105 (Simonson & Winer, 1992)
106 (Kumar & Leone, 1988)

107 (Bellizi & Hite, 1992)
108 (Hitt, 1996)
109 (Alpert & Alpert, 1990) and (Bruner, 1990)
110 (Stassen et al., 1999)
111 (Koelemeijer & Oppewal, 1999) and (Bone & Ellen, 1999)
112 (Lutzky, 2007)
113 (Coca-Cola, 2008)

4 The route to market

The route to market is the path of goods and services to the shopper and the flow of money from shopper back to the company. The key role of the route to market is to ensure the implementation of brand, product and service strategies at the point of purchase in the most profitable manner. Without the availability of products and services at the right place and time, there is no shopper conversion and no sale. The point of purchase is the meeting point between shoppers and products and services. Points of purchase are segmented by their role to the shopper, their importance and their cooperation pattern. The route to market strategy needs to optimize effectiveness and cost efficiency of developing a competitive position, sales and order taking, and operations that ensure that products, services, equipment and materials are present at the right place and time. Points of purchase belong to three main sales channels: traditional or fragmented; modern, organized or consolidated; and e-commerce channels. Traditional sales channels have less bargaining power, but are complex to manage due to their often low individual sales in numerous outlets. Modern channels require a key account and collaboration approach, like category management, ECR, and jointly agreed growth (JAG). E-commerce means sales generated by connected activities, such as websites, mobile devices, and applications, and covers channels like websites, online retailers, and brokerage platforms, e.g. marketplaces, affiliates, social media, and search engines. Analytics and search engine optimization (SEO) are key. E-commerce adds a new cost-to-serve challenge by incorporating the last yard delivery, e.g. goods and returns directly to and from shoppers, into the route to market cost. The emergence of omnichannel, the interaction between different sales channels, has increased the complexity of the route to market management.

Introduction

Route to market can be defined as the path of goods from manufacturer to shopper and the flow of money from the shopper to the manufacturer.

The economic changes from an economy of scarcity to an economy of oversupply, fragmentation of media and sales channels, and more critical shoppers has made the management of the route to market more challenging.

The development from a traditional sales channel into a multichannel and now omnichannel reality has increased the complexity of channel management. This includes understanding the role of sales channels, their interaction, and how to optimize investment and resource allocation in terms of channel support and management. There are differences in the way traditional, modern and digital sales channels work, and therefore how they need to be activated.

The key role of the route to market strategy is to ensure the implementation of the brand, product and service strategy, to ensure the encounter with the shopper at the right place and time. The opportunity detected in the route to purchase to generate preference, usage and sales of brands, products and services has to be implemented by the route to market by ensuring the encounter with the shopper through availability and activation, while optimizing profitability. If the cost of developing a sales channel surpasses the sales opportunity, new ways of selling need to be developed to optimize sales and investments.

With the digital revolution the route to market has gone from realizing brand, product and service strategies to, at times, becoming the strategy itself. Examples are Facebook, WhatsApp, Instagram or YouTube. Here the consumer and shopper have emerged from being mere users and buyers to become producers of content to be shared and presented. At times, with a sufficient audience and likes, the users become brands themselves and influencers build preference for specific brands, products and services. New channels open the possibility of reaching consumers and shoppers in new ways, and change the rules of the game, not only in how to sell, but what to sell. Examples are MPESA in Kenya (the transfer of money through cell phones) or the possibility of obtaining medical and veterinary services in remote areas through cell phones. Other services bring more transparency to the market, e.g. through price comparison internet sites for products and services. Before, price information for travel was accessed mainly through travel agencies, but can now be done by shoppers directly. The internet channel, both for information and buying has fundamentally changed the travel industry.

The development of a route to market strategy is often something organic, which develops over time and depends on the development of sales channels, distribution systems and competition. A company's route to market is something that is adapting, continually changing, due to influences external to the company. One classical example is Coca-Cola. Founded in 1892, its key product was and still is the beverage Coca-Cola. When Coca-Cola was founded, the predominant sales channels were what we today call traditional sales channels. A key differentiation can be made between home and immediate consumption. Home consumption is normally served through grocery stores, and immediate consumption through outlets, like restaurants and cafés. Immediate consumption is of course also possible in grocery stores, if a product is bought, e.g. during a shopping trip, for immediate consumption or almost immediate consumption directly after the visit to the store. A key challenge that Coca-Cola faced at the beginning was the availability and competitive position in store of its products. Pepsi was founded just one year after the Coca-Cola Company in 1893. A high level of availability, i.e. penetration of potential sales outlets, and adequate activation of the same, would not only have been difficult to organize and manage in a centralized manner, but very costly, as well. It would have required a high level of investment at the outset of the founding of the company. Coca-Cola, as well as Pepsi, developed a bottling system, leaving investment and control of local markets to local entrepreneurs. In many countries and territories, the strategy was to collaborate with existing strong companies in non-competitive categories, but with strong control and knowledge of the local market, and well-developed customer relationships. Logical allies in many countries were beer companies and with different strategies depending on the situation of the local market. For example, in Germany, which has a multitude of local breweries, Coca-Cola worked with many different local bottlers and breweries to ensure local reach and dominance. On the other hand, in Scandinavia, where the brewery business was consolidated relatively early, Coca-Cola worked with just a few national companies. In northern Germany, in Hamburg, bottling rights were given not to a brewery, but rather to the famous boxer and world champion Max Schmelling, a person of immense popularity in Germany. Coca-Cola has followed a "glocal" strategy, even before the word was used in academic research in the 1990s to describe multinational companies with global strategies adapted to the specific local situations and challenges. Coca-Cola was, and still is, responsible for consumer marketing, and the bottler for the sales channel management, distribution and production. As sales channels and shopper marketing have evolved the clear division between consumer and sales has become less clear and has affected the way the Coca-Cola system is working. The growth and increasing importance of the modern sales channel, dominated by national and international retail chains, has limited the negotiating power of local, regional or even national bottlers. Retail chains are more than mere distributors of goods that implement manufacturer strategies in their outlets. They are marketers themselves, with their target shoppers, market positioning, marketing, loyalty programs and own brands, as well as being a marketing channel for manufacturers. As retail chains grew in importance "power wars" between retailers and leading manufacturers unfolded. The main argument was about who was more important in developing the market and generating sales. Did brands generate traffic in stores, or did retail chains, due to their size and appeal to shoppers, ensure distribution and sales of brands, products and services of the manufacturers? Who is more important, the consumer or the shopper? The power wars even led to the delisting of brands and products by retail chains, or to lower promotional and activation initiatives by manufacturers at certain retailers. The importance of retailers has been one of the reasons that has forced manufacturers to focus more on shoppers. As modern retailers grew in importance, Coca-Cola had to develop key account management approaches. Key account management is difficult on a regional level, and national and international solutions were and are necessary. Managing big retailers also goes beyond just sales, and includes shopper marketing initiatives. In Germany, Coca-Cola introduced an overlayer organization to coordinate and manage national retailers across the different bottler territories. However, it is not only the sales channel reality that has been changing and consolidating, the same is true of the intermediary market, distributors and wholesalers. In order to gain efficiencies in production, distribution and bargaining power the idea of key bottlers (anchor bottlers) developed. These are very large, multinational bottlers, focused on the products of the Coca-Cola Company. They also sell complementary products to offer a complete portfolio to consumers, shoppers and retailers. Still, the bottler system and the cooperation with retailers and distributors can lead to opposing interests, especially when it comes to product innovation and introduction. While innovation is key from a marketing perspective, it can be less interesting for an independent sales arm, if bigger sales and profits can be generated with already successful products that need little investment in activation.

The development of category management and ECR was a response to the ongoing power struggle between retailers and manufacturers. Over the years, retail has gained in power, but the development of digital and e-commerce with the emergence of e-tailers, and the possibility for manufacturers to sell directly to shoppers is affecting the current power situation.

To ensure a successful route to market strategy it needs to be well linked with the route to purchase strategy to ensure shared interests and integration of the different activities, either between different departments, or, as in the case of Coca-Cola, between different stakeholders. In addition, across different sales channels and intermediaries there are different route to market alternatives to reach the objectives set out in the route to purchase strategy.

Linking and aligning the route to purchase and the route to market into a coherent strategy starts with a clear understanding of the consumption need states to be served. In developing the route to market strategy the point of purchase is key as the point of encounter of the shopper and the brand, product or service. It is where the route to purchase is linked to the route to market, and it is where the conversion from shopper to buyer takes place. The objective of the route to purchase strategy is to influence the shopper in the interest of the company, while the route to market strategy is about managing the point of purchase and availability to ensure shopper preference through sales, distribution and warehousing, with the right organizational structure and control systems in place. In the case of indirect selling models, where the point of purchase is not under the ownership or direct control of the manufacturer, the route to market strategy needs to manage intermediaries in a systems approach to ensure the availability of products and services. The shopper embarks on his shopping trip with a mental proposal of a solution to the intended consumption need state, obviously with some flexibility.[1] The offer available at the point of purchase has a direct impact on the selection of products and services.[2] Availability can be divided into products that are not available at the point of purchase, out of stock, or out of shelf, implying that the product and service is theoretically available at the point of purchase, but not accessible to the shopper. When products and services are not accessible, this is usually due to poor point of purchase management. In the case of brick-and-mortar stores, this would imply poor management of shelves and store activation. If products and services are not available, they cannot be bought. This not only has implications on sales, but on the shopping experience as well. Effective management of the point of purchase and good cooperation with the retailer has an important positive impact on product and service availability.[3] This impact is true for brick-and-mortar stores, as well as for digital points of purchase.[4] The impact of missing products and services at the point of purchase is moderated by favorable shopper attitudes, price and loyalty towards both the point of purchase and the preferred brand.[5] There are cultural differences in how shoppers react to availability issues.[6] There are important situational factors at the point of purchase that influence shopper decision and spending, with some differences between categories.[7] In the case of brick-and-mortar stores, different stimuli influence the buying behavior of shoppers both outside and inside the store.[8] The shopping environment[9] and sensory stimuli influence the shopper preference for specific points of purchase.[10] Music has a strong impact on the purchase intentions of shoppers.[11] A well-designed, exciting and innovative shopping environment can have a positive impact on the purchase intention, but depending on the design, the experience can also turn negative.[12] In the case of digital sales channels, the design and type of interaction have a direct impact on the willingness to buy online.[13] Employees in brick-and-mortar stores play an important role when it comes to shopper loyalty with the point of purchase.[14] The advice and support given need to be congruent with the expectations of the shopper.[15] Brands influence the image of points of purchase and therefore coherency between positioning and messages from before purchase to the point of purchase is key.[16] Moreover, the image of brick-and-mortar stores influences shopping behavior.[17]

Points of purchase and sales channels

The point of purchase is the meeting point between the product and service and the shopper; it is where the conversion from shopper to buyer takes place. For the shopper, the point of purchase is the place to satisfy the needs generated by the intended consumption need states. The choice of type of point of purchase depends on the attributes the shopper looks for that best meet the needs at the specific purchase situation. These attributes can be price level, service level, payment methods, proximity, etc. The sales channel reality is continuously changing. A change that comes from the interaction of economic, societal, technological and infrastructure development, shopper behavior, channel investments and new business models. Infrastructure change and the dispersion of car ownership are the basis for the big box retail business model. With increasing disposable incomes, consumer credits and credit cards, in connection with more spare time and decreasing prices due to improving productivity rates and low-cost manufacturing, shopping has soared and has developed into a pastime activity. With higher quotas of women in employment, the need for extended service hours has grown, as well as the need for pre-processed solutions and immediate consumption occasions. With less time, convenience solutions become more important. Digital supports convenience in information seeking, as well as in the purchase, delivery and pick-up process.

One of the most important influences on the sales channels has been the technological development and above all the internet. This has given companies the possibility of personalizing a service, although it has also complicated the supply chain by incorporating the last yard to the shopper into the route to market system. In parallel, activities that have traditionally been performed by companies are being outsourced to the consumer and shopper to increase convenience, but also to decrease costs and prices. One example is the Swedish furniture manufacturer IKEA, which has outsourced the assembly of its furniture to the shopper in exchange for lower prices. Internet banking has led to the closure of branches and customers are increasingly being served through the internet. Services, like account information, and transfers are performed by the customers themselves. Buying computers is increasingly done through the internet. Often different types of computers are not available in stores and have to be purchased over the internet. The shopper has to inform himself and

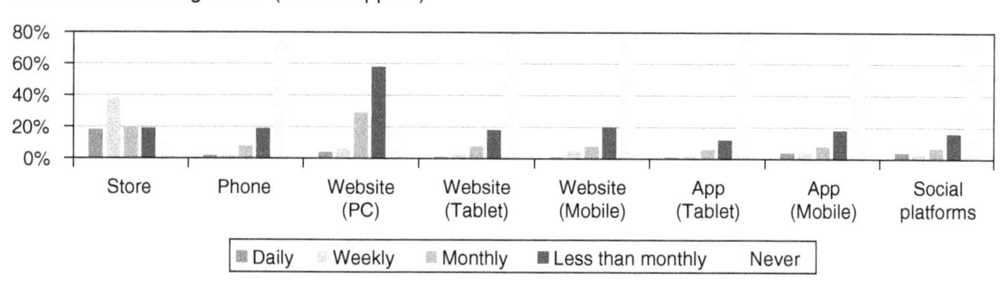

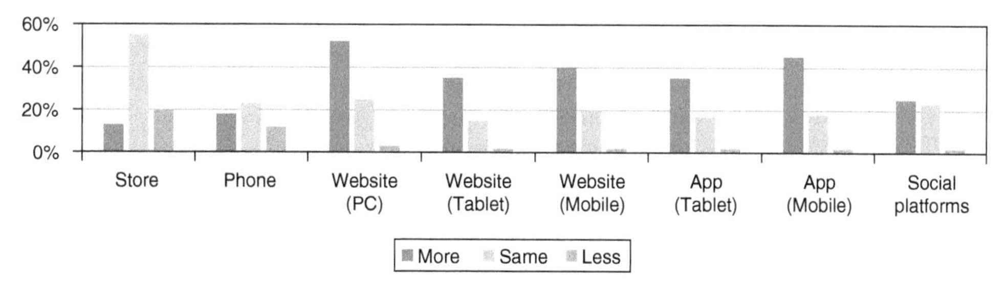

Figure 4.1 Evolution of sales channels
Frequency of use of sales channels in Spain, 2017 and expected future use.
Source: Minsait, 2017

become knowledgeable about the category. Depending on the category, the importance and role of the internet differs. The internet not only lowers costs for manufacturers and retailers, it is also a tool to improve shopper loyalty and increase the sales share with each shopper.

In retail, much of the competition between players has been through offers, promotions and activation. One result has been that shoppers jump between retailers to catch the best offers and thereby reduce the overall cost of their shopping basket. With e-commerce the share of purchase by shopper can be increased. As there is often a minimum purchase to make the internet order worthwhile in terms of delivery cost or time investment there is an incentive for bigger orders.

As sales channels have evolved, the management of them has changed. Broadly, the channel landscape has changed from a single-channel, through multichannel, to an omnichannel environment. In short, a single-channel environment is the predominance of one type of outlet, normally traditional outlets. The multichannel environment describes the parallel existence of different channels that compete, e.g. modern and traditional trade, but also e-commerce, while omnichannel describes the interaction between sales channels with complementary roles to the shopper.

The growth of modern retail was seen as a threat by many manufacturers, as well as by the traditional trade. The same occurred with the growth of internet e-commerce, which additionally was seen as a threat by modern retailers. The emergence of modern and e-commerce retail are the two major changes to the point of purchase reality. They have often been seen as a threat to margins and brand equity by manufacturers, even if they multiply the opportunity to reach shoppers efficiently.

Traditional channels, although more complex to manage, have less bargaining power and thus exert less influence on the margins of manufacturers. Important challenges with the traditional channels are product and service availability and the dependence of intermediaries to reach the point of purchase. With the growth of modern retail, their bargaining power grew, leading to important conflicts of interest between manufacturers and retailers. In addition, channel conflicts grew. The differences in bargaining power led to discrepancies of pricing in different channels, and between channels and distributors, leading to cross-channel purchase, i.e. small outlets buying from other sales channels instead of buying through distributors or directly from the manufacturer. To solve channel conflicts channel management evolved with specific offerings and activations by channel. Still, market regulation and shopper knowledge limit these approaches, as discriminatory customer treatment is prohibited. The perceived differences between the offering by sales channel type are not always important enough to incite specific shopper behavior by channel. For retail, carving out the role and developing the shopper experience has become key to staying competitive and relevant to the shopper.

Channel development has been viewed with some determinism. The view has been that the traditional channel landscape will develop into mainly modern big box retailing. There is a certain correlation between economic development and the development of modern retailing. At the same time, economic development is associated with the growth of immediate consumption, e.g. restaurants and cafés, a channel that is normally fragmented with fewer chains. Still, in some countries the occurrence of chains in immediate consumption is relatively high, e.g. in the USA and UK. There are also countries, e.g. Peru, where traditional channels are growing with economic development.[18] In many countries, traditional channels are still very important and there are few signs of their disappearance.

Many manufacturers have organized themselves following the idea of multichannel management with departments for modern retail, traditional channels and now e-commerce. With

Webrooming Vs. Showrooming

Webrooming
- Browsing online and buying in-store
- Six in ten webroomers have showroomed

Showrooming
- Browsing in-store and buying online
- Nearly nine in ten showroomers have webroomed

% of webroomers and showroomers by age

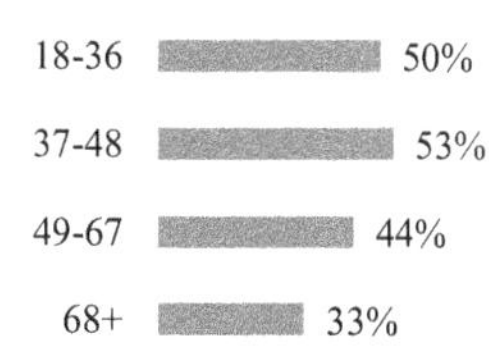

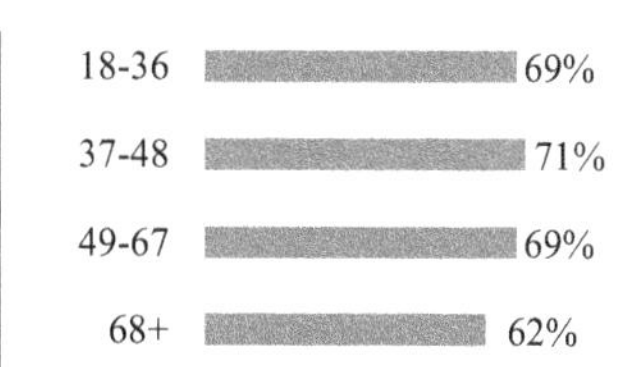

% of webroomers and showroomers by gender

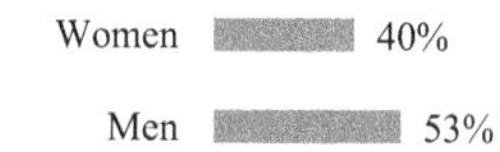

Figure 4.2 Webrooming and showrooming
Webrooming is when shoppers browse the internet to then purchase in brick-and-mortar stores, while showrooming is the opposite: shoppers browsing stores to then purchase online.
Source: Bolsalea, 2019

the internet the perspective has somewhat changed. From viewing which sales channels the company can use to reach the shopper, the view has gradually turned toward which sales channels the shopper uses and prefers to reach the products and services of the manufacturer. The starting point of the omnichannel perspective is the shopper and his or her needs. These needs range from receiving and exchanging information, buying, and changing and returning goods. The shopper seeks to satisfy a consumption need state in the best manner. The sales channel is not an objective in itself but a tool to satisfy a consumption need state. The attributes that best meet shopper needs for the specific purchase situation will define the point of purchase the shopper will prefer. Sales channels can interact during the purchase process, e.g. click and collect solutions, showrooming and webrooming.

Points of purchase have multiple roles, especially as points of information and of purchase. Christmas 2015 is seen as the breakthrough of omnichannel shopping in the UK. Internet shopping boomed without sales in brick-and-mortar channels falling. The shoppers did not decide between channels, but used them in a complementary way.

There are different ways to categorize points of purchase to define their roles to the shopper in the purchase process.

The simplest categorization is the distinction between direct and indirect sales channels. In direct sales channels shoppers purchase products and services directly from the company. The choice of sales channel strategy is dependent on its effectiveness in reaching and activating target shoppers and its efficiency in optimizing profits. Direct sales strategies will therefore be associated with more complex products and services, high sales values, the

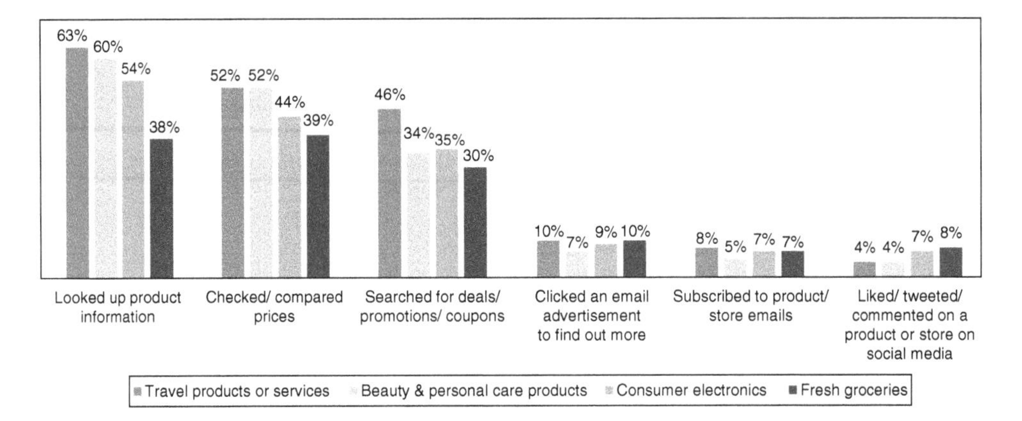

Figure 4.3 Omnichannel behavior
Global top and bottom online shopping activities for selected categories. Information gathering and deal seeking is mainly done online.
Source: Nielsen, Q4 2015

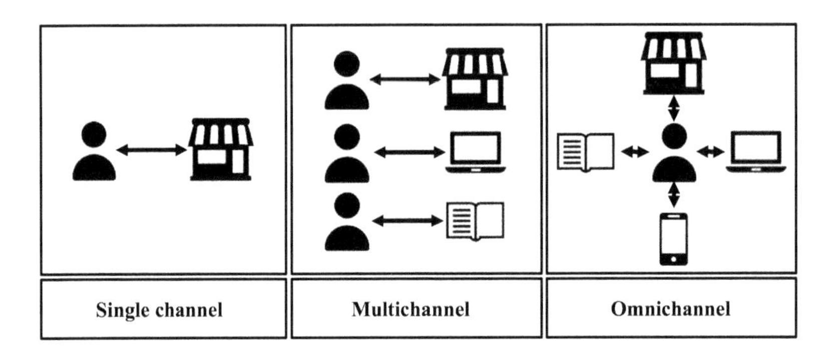

Figure 4.4 Single, multichannel, omnichannel
Multichannel is the parallel use of different channels for different shopper experiences and differentiated offers. Omnichannel is the complimentary use of different channels to optimize a coherent shopper experience.
Source: Wordpress, 2017

importance to further the brand image and shopper experience, or when direct sales can be more cost efficient, as in some cases with e-commerce and telephone selling, such as banks and communication operators.

Reach is closely related to direct and indirect sales channels. Direct channels do not normally have the same reach as indirect mass channels, such as retailers. The more mass-oriented the channel, and the more the variety of categories, the less able the channel to offer tailor-made solutions or provide specific expertise. With the spread of the internet, shoppers can seek information and expertise, and in an omnichannel mode combine high information abilities with potential price advantages of mass channels.

Another distinction is between digital and brick-and-mortar sales channels. In brick-and-mortar channels the shopper can normally encounter the product and service and evaluate them with his or her senses. In digital channels this is not possible from the outset. E-commerce companies and retailers therefore often allow for generous return policies. Digital channels have revolutionized the route to market in industries such as travel, banking and retailing.

Size of the sales channel is an important dimension as it defines the potential of shopper reach. Modern retail makes it possible to reach a large number of shoppers, including shoppers who did not plan to buy that specific category, brand, product or service when entering the point of purchase. Before the rise of the modern retail, manufacturers needed to manage a multitude of individual traditional stores, either directly or through distributors. The emergence of big box retailing has changed shopping habits, as has the development of e-tailers. Big box stores started as supermarkets, and then developed into hypermarkets and department stores. This development was possible because more and more people had cars, and shoppers could reach stores further away and could carry more products. These new formats changed the entire industry in terms of behavior, supply and the relationship between manufacturers and retail. With the revival of urban lifestyles, as well as the interaction between e-tailers with brick-and-mortar stores, smaller stores are now increasing in importance.

Associated with size and reach is the emergence of retail chains. Retail chains can comprise several formats, from convenience, supermarket, hypermarket, to e-retail, and different levels of reach, from regional, to national and international. Many retail chains started as purchasing cooperations to counterbalance the negotiating power of manufacturers. Some belonged to shoppers to ensure favorable end prices, while others cooperated to improve their margins. Size does not only imply increased negotiating power, but also information power, both in terms of market offer, prices and margins, and in shopper insights. Manufacturers will normally be more focused on consumers and consumption occasions, while the focus of retailers are shoppers and the shopping basket. In addition, within the shopping basket each category and brand have their specific role. It could include building traffic, being a destination product, driving margins or generating complementary purchases. The different views on categories, brands, products and services between manufacturers and retailers are inherently conflictive, and has led to the development of collaborative programs, such as ECR, to smooth and solve these conflicts.

There is a correlation between economic development and the evolution of modern retail, approximated through the square meter of retail space per inhabitant. Digitalization and the search for convenience due to new urban lifestyles is challenging this development.

When it comes to traditional brick-and-mortar stores, they are very important in many markets, and, even with continuous economic development, they will most probably stay important for a long time. Traditional channels often give a different service than modern retail, ranging from opening hours, proximity, and services offered. Modern or organized retail is increasingly entering this part of the market, as market expansion opportunities in the big box environment are stagnating.

The emergence of the digital channel has fundamentally changed the game. Amazon and Alibaba are clear examples, but also direct-to-consumer sales, adopted by the likes of Dell, or by subscription models such as Harry's, are changing shopping.

Another categorization of channels is based on the behavior of the consumer and the shopper. The distinction is between channels of direct and indirect consumption. Indirect consumption is when products and services are purchased, but consumed at a later stage and at a different location, e.g. at home. Direct or immediate consumption is when products and services are consumed immediately during or after the purchase, and normally at the

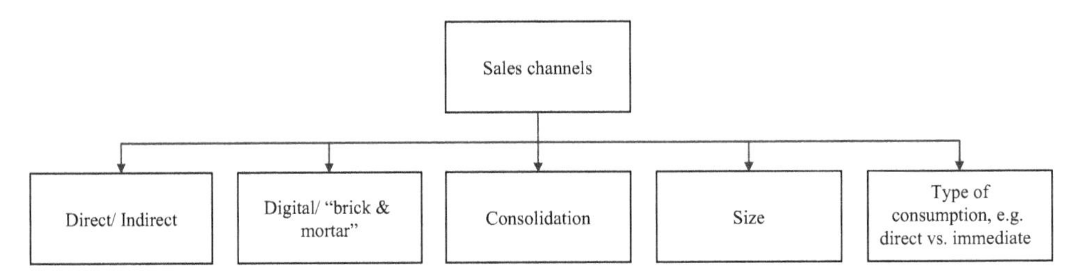

Figure 4.5 Categorization of sales channels
Ways to categorize sales channels.
Source: Author

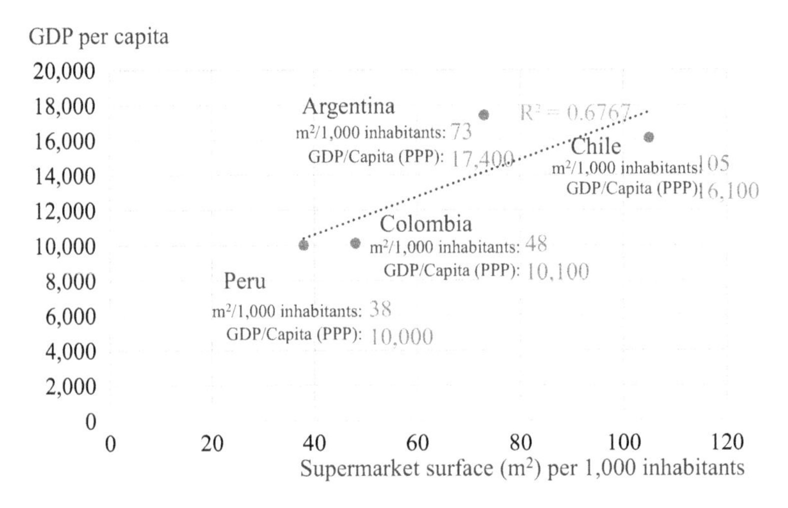

Figure 4.6 Relationship between economic development and modern retail
Correlation between GDP per capita in purchasing power parity and the importance of modern retail channel in Argentina, Peru, Colombia and Chile in 2011 in square meters (m^2) of retail space per thousand inhabitants.
Source: Central Intelligence Agency, n.d.; Author

same location where they were purchased. These are often channels like restaurants and cafés, and often include categories like meals and beverages. Other denominations for these type of channel are on-trade, immediate consumption or HoReCa (hotel, restaurants, cafés). Indirect channels, especially for groceries, are often denominated at home and off-trade. In immediate and direct consumption channels, purchase and consumption are interrelated and often the shopper and the consumer are the same, although this does not need to be the case, e.g. eating out with family or friends. The success of sales channels is due to two main dimensions: meeting shopper needs, and providing marketing and operational advantages for manufacturers and suppliers. For example, the products of the clothing company H&M are found only in their own stores, and although there could be an interesting opportunity in selling through other points of purchase, this would be against the chosen route to market strategy. There are also important changes over time, as in the travel industry.

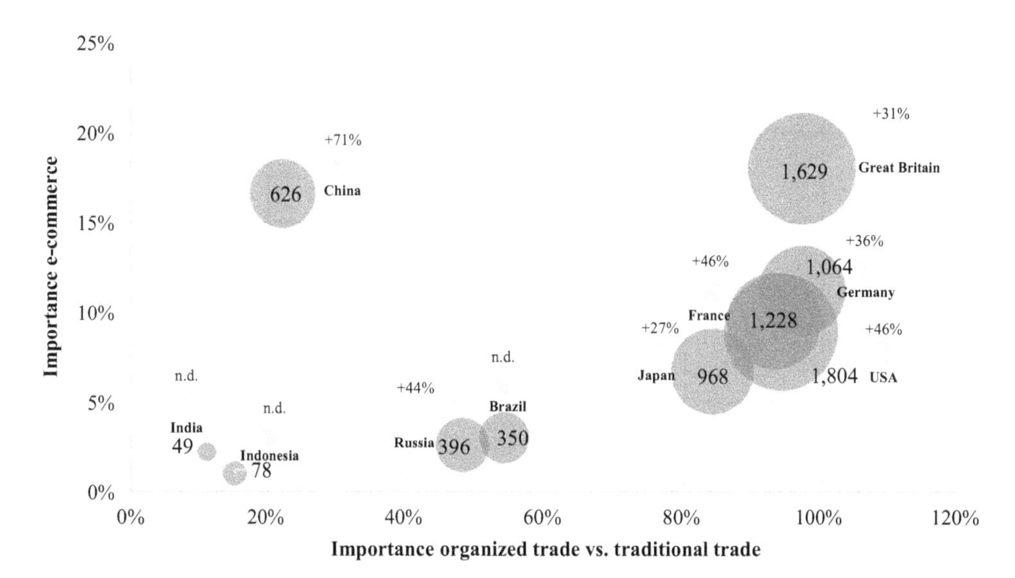

Figure 4.7 Channel structure of the ten leading economies by GDP
Importance of modern trade compared with traditional trade on the horizontal axis, the importance of e-commerce to shopper retail spending on the vertical axis of the ten biggest economies in GDP in USD in 2018. The size of the bubble reflects the average e-commerce spending in USD in 2018. The percentage over the arrows shows the expected e-commerce growth between 2018 and 2023 (n.d. is no data available).
Source: Author

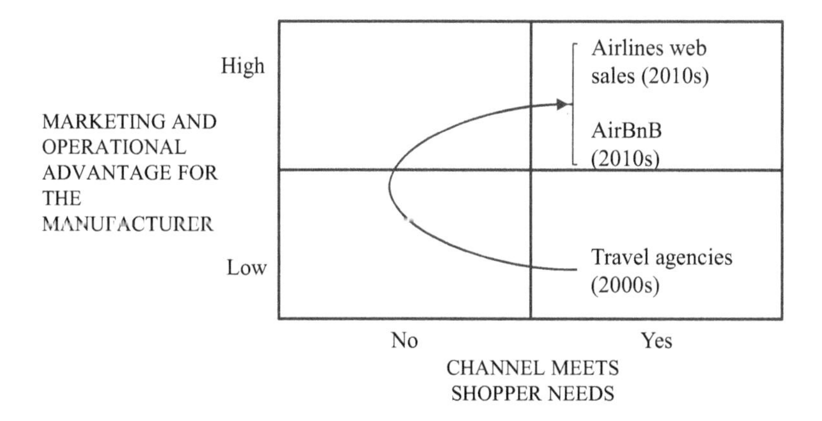

Figure 4.8 Sales channel relevance
Sales channel relevance matrix based on whether the channel has a marketing and operational advantage for the manufacturer, whether the channel meets the needs of shoppers and how it changes over time. Example from the travel industry.
Source: Author

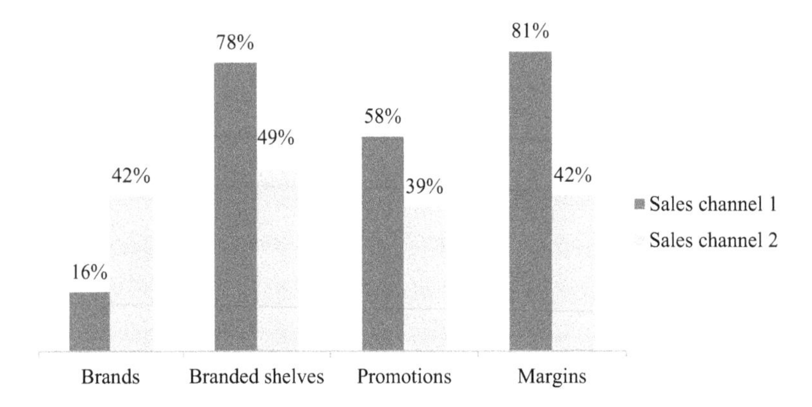

Figure 4.9 Selection criteria of sales channels to list products and services
Importance of listing criteria of different sales channels of points of purchase.
Source: Author

The route to market can be the company strategy itself, as in the example of Airbnb, which has built a business model around the internet channel. In the example of travel, it is clear that there has been a development of sales channel usage, moving from travel agencies to internet sales. Much of the discussion has traditionally been about channel conflict, first between traditional and modern retail channels, and then with e-tail. With the emergence of the more shopper-oriented omnichannel view, the complementarity of channels to serve the shopper has moved into the center of the discussion. With the development of sales channels, their role has also changed, from merely a distribution arm for manufacturers to reach consumers and shoppers to become a marketing platform in their own right.

To reach target consumers the right shoppers have to be activated in the channels they frequent to satisfy the consumption need states. To build preference the different touchpoints toward the point of purchase need to be managed, and the right point of purchase with the attributes that meet shopper needs have to be selected, managed and activated. Furthermore, the interrelationship and multiple roles of points of purchase in an omnichannel approach need to be coordinated. With very strong brands and purchases with a high involvement, shoppers will take the initiative to encounter the brands, products and services they prefer. However, for the majority of purchases the involvement and the brand preference are not that high, and the solution set is open to alternatives.

The description of the retail landscape gives insights into how different sales channels need to be managed, while the role of the point of purchase to the shopper gives insights into how it needs to be activated to convert shoppers into buyers.

Management of the point of purchase and sales channels

Introduction

There are two main challenges when managing the point of purchase, the level of control and the dispersion or number of points of purchase.

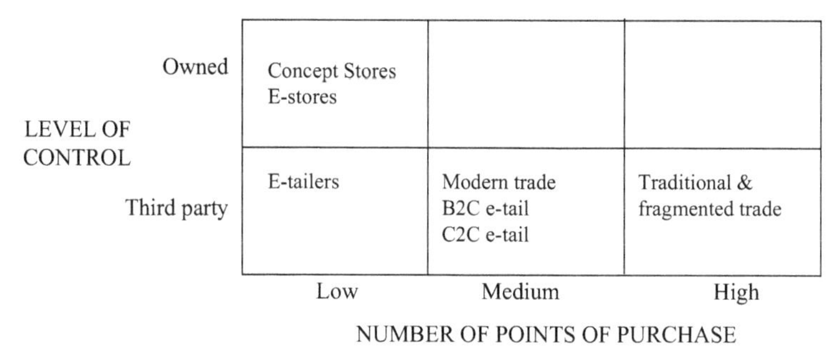

Figure 4.10 Control and dispersion-level matrix of sales channels
Matrix of the channel management challenge in terms of level of control and number of points of purchase. Owned points of purchase, like concept and e-stores, have a high level of control but are small in number. Third-party stores come with less control. E-tailers have few points of purchase, while modern retail normally has a higher number, all with high sales per point of purchase. Traditional and fragmented trade, and e-commerce, either re-sellers or consumer to consumer are more numerous and with fewer sales per point of purchase.

Source: Author

In the case of a high level of control of the points of purchase, the shopper marketing strategy can be fully implemented, and the point of purchase becomes, in the best case, a seamless extension. Where the level of control is low, a specific sales function will be necessary to handle and manage the points of purchase, either directly or through third parties as distributors, or both. Depending on the level of consolidation, key account management or individual point of purchase approaches are necessary. In the case of numerous points of purchase with low individual sales, distributors are often employed. These distributors are key accounts themselves and need to be managed as such. There are also mixed systems where specific tasks are divided among the manufacturer, a distributor and other third-party organizations, e.g. merchandising companies.

Own points of purchase, both brick and mortar and digital, are simpler to activate, as they are under the full control of the brand, product and service owner, even more so in the case of concept stores such as Apple, Nike and Adidas. The more stores, the more complicated to keep up sound implementation, monitoring and control of their outlets.

Franchise and partner points of purchase are a specific challenge. There are partner stores for strong brands, e.g. Apple, and there are franchise businesses, e.g. 7-Eleven stores. There are clear criteria for activation and presentation, but the relationship is defined by a contract and the control of the activation is indirect. The stronger the negotiating power the more concessions a business partner will be able to secure. Partner and franchise solutions are an important way to increase presence while lowering costs and investments.

Managing and activating points of purchase can be summarized in three key activities: development of the competitive position at the point of purchase; sales and order-taking activities; and operations in terms of ensuring that products, services, equipment and materials are present at the right time and place. Depending on the consolidation of the customer, activities can be more or less centralized, and depending on the agreement, the activities can be allocated to either the manufacturer or the retailer.

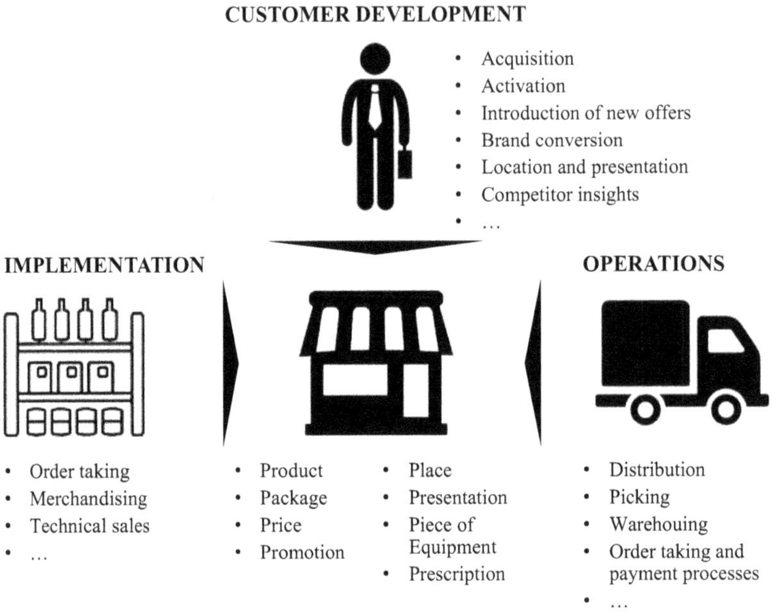

CUSTOMER DEVELOPMENT

- Acquisition
- Activation
- Introduction of new offers
- Brand conversion
- Location and presentation
- Competitor insights
- ...

IMPLEMENTATION

- Order taking
- Merchandising
- Technical sales
- ...

- Product
- Package
- Price
- Promotion

- Place
- Presentation
- Piece of Equipment
- Prescription

OPERATIONS

- Distribution
- Picking
- Warehouing
- Order taking and payment processes
- ...

Figure 4.11 Activities in managing brick-and-mortar points of purchase
Key point of purchase management activities to ensure activation in line with commercial objectives.
Source: Author

Traditional and fragmented sales channels

In traditional sales channels, the challenge is how to ensure the activation across a multitude of independent points of purchase of different sub-channels, roles and importance in terms of sales and image.

When it comes to the management and the economics of individual points of purchase of retail chains the same logic as for traditional and fragmented trade can be applied. The traditional sales channel consists of a multitude of sub-channels.

Activating each store effectively is normally beyond the reach of many manufacturers for reasons of cost, investment, resources or complexity, given the low value of each point of purchase itself. A first step is to group the points of purchase according to criteria, such as their role and importance, to define activation and investment priorities. There are three main dimensions to segment points of purchase: the role for the shopper, the attractiveness in terms of potential sales, and the attitude in the cooperation with suppliers to activate shoppers and generate sales. It is not only about the type of investments in shopper activation, but also about optimizing the level and length of the investment, not sub-optimizing shopper activation and loyalty initiatives.[19]

By understanding the concentration curve, investment can be directed toward the most important points of purchase. Additionally, by evaluating the attitude of the point of purchase in implementing brand, product and service strategies, investment in activation can be optimized. Based on the analysis shopper activation programs can be designed by segment and tier of points of purchase.

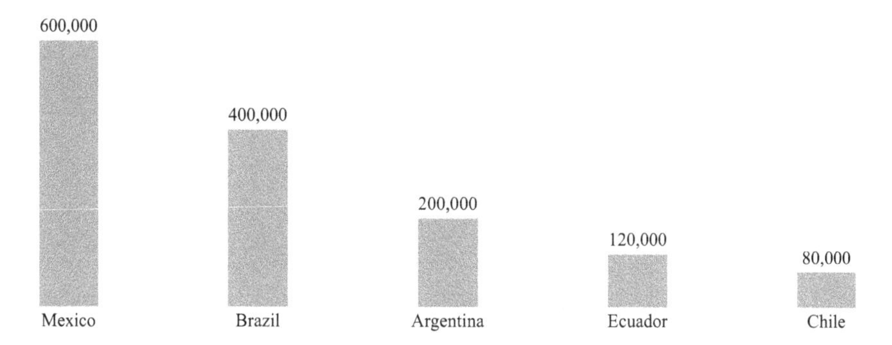

Figure 4.12 Number of points of purchase in the traditional sales channel in some Latin American markets

Number of points of purchase in the traditional sales channel in Mexico, Brazil, Argentina, Ecuador and Chile.

Source: Author, based on information from Euromonitor, The Coca-Cola Retailing Council Latin America & info economía.

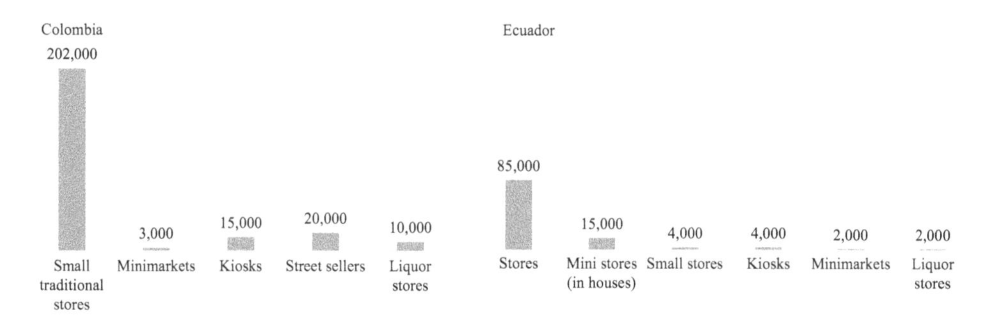

Figure 4.13 Type and importance of different sub-channels in the traditional sales channel

Number and type of sub-channels in the traditional sales channel in Colombia and Ecuador.

Source: Nielsen, 2011

The sales force has a key role in activating points of purchase. In the case of retail chains, the activities that can be performed on the point of purchase level depend on the guidelines of the retail chains. In the case of traditional and independent sales channels the activities that can be performed at the point of purchase depends on each individual point of purchase. Managing the point of purchase can be divided into activities to be performed and the frequency of their performance. The activities can either be performed by the sales force at the point of purchase, or be outsourced to distributors or other partners. The frequency and time of the activity needs to be optimized in terms of investment in material and resources vs. the expected increase in sales and margins. Point of purchase activation resources investment is economical as long as the marginal productivity is positive. As long as the increase in resources results in more output, the investment makes economic sense. The resource allocation by point of purchase needs to be optimized in terms of type of activities, by whom they should be performed, the total time invested by the point of purchase in terms of frequency of performing it and the length of the activity. It is applying the neoclassical concept

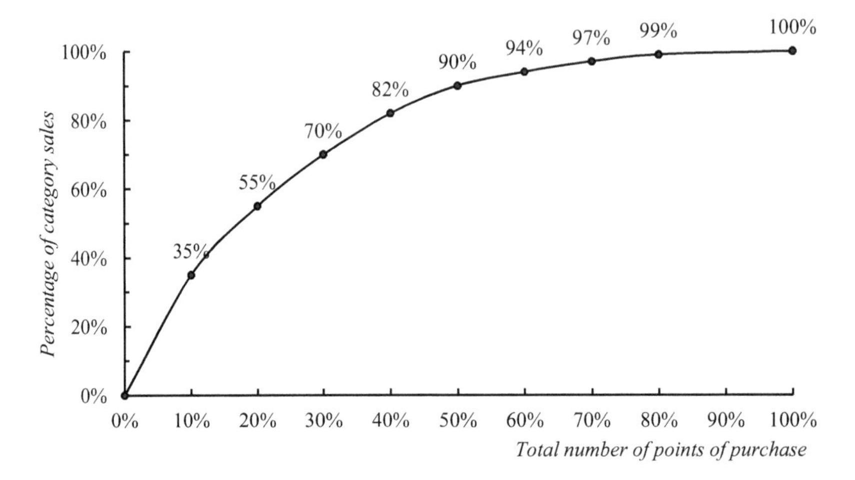

Figure 4.14 Concentration curve
Concentration curve of the points of purchase of the traditional sales channel in Latin America with the percentage of all points of purchase and the percentage of sales in a specific category.
Source: Author

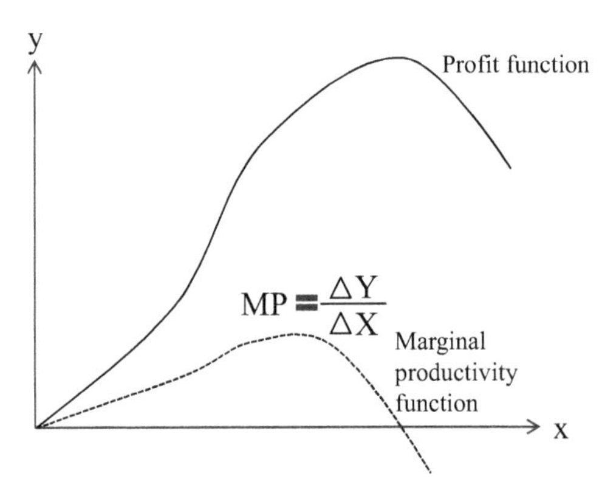

Figure 4.15 Marginal productivity function
Marginal productivity function that explains the additional profitability of additional resources. Investing more resources is only economical to the point where the function of marginal productivity reaches zero.
Source: Brewer, 2010

of marginal productivity to the optimization of shopper marketing resource investment by point of purchase.

Non-availability is a key driver of dissatisfaction among shoppers, and obviously of lost sales as well. Order taking, delivery and functioning supply chain operations are key dimensions for a successful shopper marketing.

The order-taking and supply-chain operations implications depend on the type of category. High value and low frequency purchase products often need a different order-taking

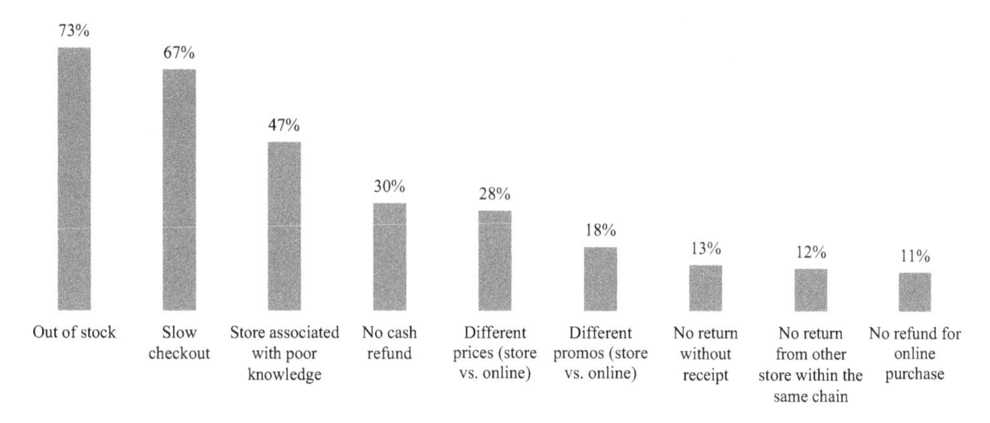

Figure 4.16 Factors having a negative influence on the shopping experience
Factors that most contribute to a negative shopping experience for shoppers in the UK.
Source: Cognizant, June 2011

and supply-chain system than categories of lower value and high frequency sales and turnover. In such categories the need for cost-efficient solutions are of higher concern as the margin per individual product and service sold is considerably lower. Often several order-taking and supply-chain solutions are used to ensure availability at the different points of purchase, reaching from direct service, joint ventures, distributors, wholesalers and third-party logistics solutions. The order taking can be done directly, over the phone, or digitally, either through the internet, or through specific applications. For large customers, such as retail chains, volumes and annual discounts are normally negotiated, including supply-chain solutions like customers' central warehouses. Orders can be automated through electronic data interchange (EDI) systems within the ECR framework to minimize out of stock, while optimizing the supply chain cost efficiency.

The optimum configuration of the route to market and management of the points of purchase touches the key question of in-sourcing vs. out-sourcing, as described in the Coase theory and the discussion of transaction costs, as first highlighted in the article "theory of the firm".[20] When to outsource route to market activities, such as the management of the point of purchase, depends on the effectiveness and efficiency in terms of expected results, investments, and costs of the activities to be performed, by whom they should be performed, and where they should be performed in relation to area and zone, as well as point of purchase. Solutions can be differentiated by segment of point of purchase, also depending on where more control out of strategic reasons is needed.

Order taking and supply chain operations are key to ensure availability of products and services. There is a step between out of stock and out of shelf, and there needs to be a system and incentives in place to ensure that this step is fulfilled. The order taking and supply chain needs are often scrutinized under the eye of cost efficiency, but they are at the same time the precondition for the effectiveness of point of purchase activation.[21] In traditional sales channels availability and minimizing both out of stock and out of shelf is often an important factor of competitive advantage.

Distributors often play a key role and provide service beyond just logistics to the point of purchase. They are normally more efficient due to a wider offering in terms of categories they carry and due to a more advantageous cost structure. For manufacturers with less sales, distributors often play a key role in distributing their products and services, as well as activating the point of purchase. The danger being that a distributor with a big variety of brands, products and services only gives limited attention to specific brands, products and services. Programs and agreements sometimes exist to incentivize the distributor to prioritize specific brands, products and services. Promotional programs can also be offered to the shopper to build a pull effect and increase the attractiveness of the point of purchase and the distributor to carry and deliver the brands, products and services. Other programs will target the distributor and his sales force, or the point of purchase and his salespeople to incentivize them to sell and prescribe specific brands, products and services. There exist agreements on exclusivity with distributors, either entirely, for specific categories, or specific products.

Designing the optimum route to market strategy is a tradeoff between potential sales and margins, and the cost efficiency, including strategic considerations. A route to market structure of many small points of purchase can be as efficient as one of only few large points of purchase. The driver of efficiency is the asset, resource and time investment to generate sales and margins. These can be the same in a route to market structure defined by a very high density of small points of purchase that can be managed with the same level of investment as few large points of purchase with a very low density. Different route to market alternatives have to be evaluated and compared over key criteria to design the optimum solution.

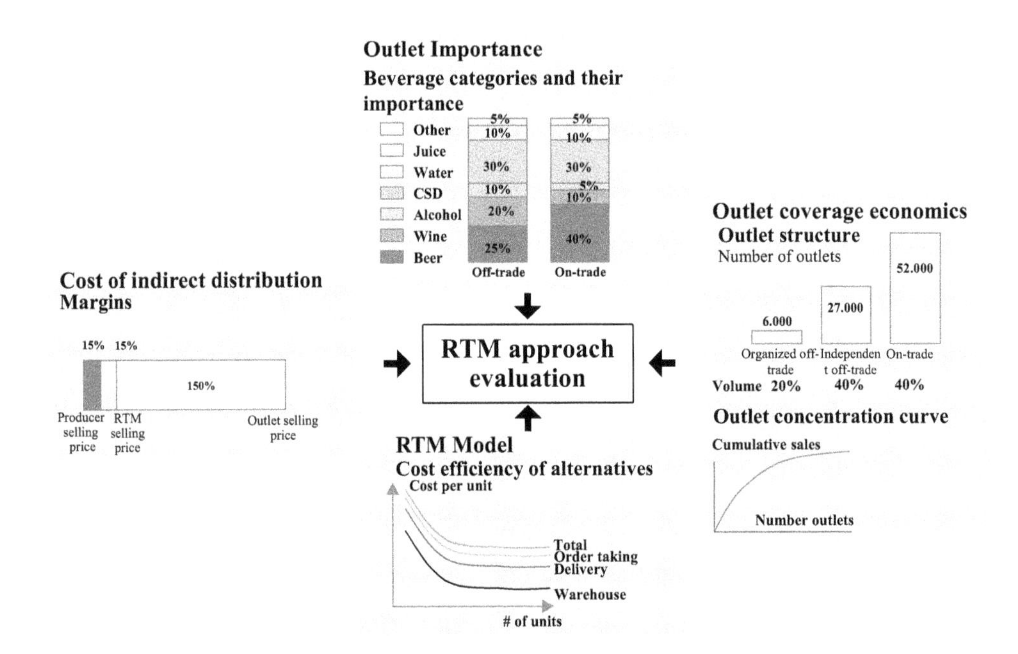

Figure 4.17 Model to evaluate the route to market strategy

Example of route to market strategy evaluation in beverages in Eastern Europe. Points to analyze are the importance of the different categories by main sales channel, the concentration curve and coverage economics of the point of purchase universe, the supply chain costs by point of purchase, and the margins of serving the point of purchase.

CSD: carbonated soft drinks.

Source: Author

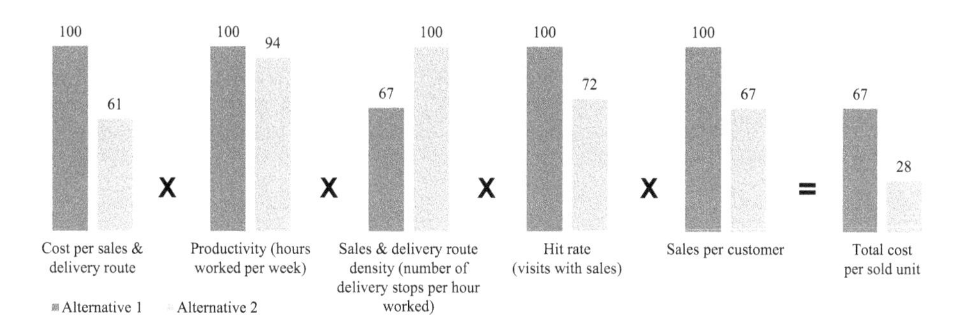

Figure 4.18 Framework to evaluate the cost efficiency of route to market alternatives
Example of the cost efficiency evaluation of two route to market alternatives, along the criteria of cost per sales and delivery route, productivity in working hours, point of purchase density in terms of number of visits per route, visits with sales, average sales per point of purchase. The result is the cost per sold unit. The illustration is indexed relative to both alternatives, with the index 100 as the more unfavorable result. The lower index indicates the advantage in percentage over the higher index. The cost per unit sold is the product of multiplying the other criteria and the result shows the relative advantage of one alternative over the other.
Source: Author

The interest of third parties to develop new brands, products and services is often limited as they do not generate much sales, at least at the beginning, and they prefer to focus on brands, products and services that are already successful with higher sales and margins. Therefore, a fundamental decision is the evaluation of the effectiveness of different route to market strategies. Is a more efficient route to market strategy conducive in the longer term to develop new brands, products and services. Different route to market strategies can be used in parallel, not only for different sales channels, countries, or regions, but also for different brands, products and services, and also during their different development stages.

There are different route to market strategy solutions, from direct management, over distributors, to different joint ventures with complementary categories. To combine the advantages of a higher activation focus and effectiveness of direct route to market strategies and the operational efficiencies of third-party route to market solutions third-party logistics models have been developed. Within third-party logistics (3PL), the sales development effort stays with the brand, product and service owner, and the operational logistics part is conducted by a third party specialized in efficiency.

The possibility of generating interest directly with consumers and shoppers through direct activation, for example, advertisements, digital touchpoints or promotions in channels to generate a pull instead of a push is an important consideration when evaluating route to market alternatives.

Each route to market model has its implications in terms of activation effectiveness, cost efficiency, investments, asset ownership and flexibility, and strategy realization. The configuration of the route to market system depends on the objectives and the reality of the market. Therefore, depending on the situation, different solutions may be needed for different markets, categories, and situations. Companies often use different route to market solutions in parallel. If the overarching route to market objective is cost efficiency the variety of route to market solutions is wider, while if the main objective is effectiveness, the variety is more limited.[22]

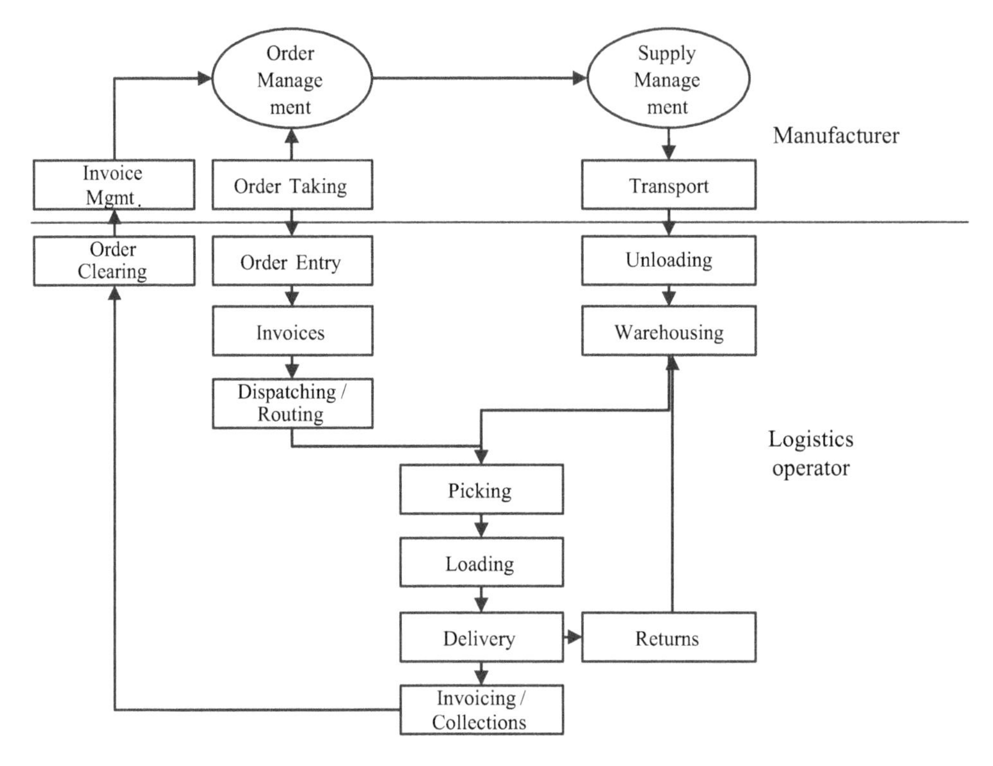

Figure 4.19 Third-party logistics (3PL) system
Example of a 3PL system in which the manufacturer takes care of order taking and the logistics operator is responsible for the distribution and invoicing of customers.
Source: Author

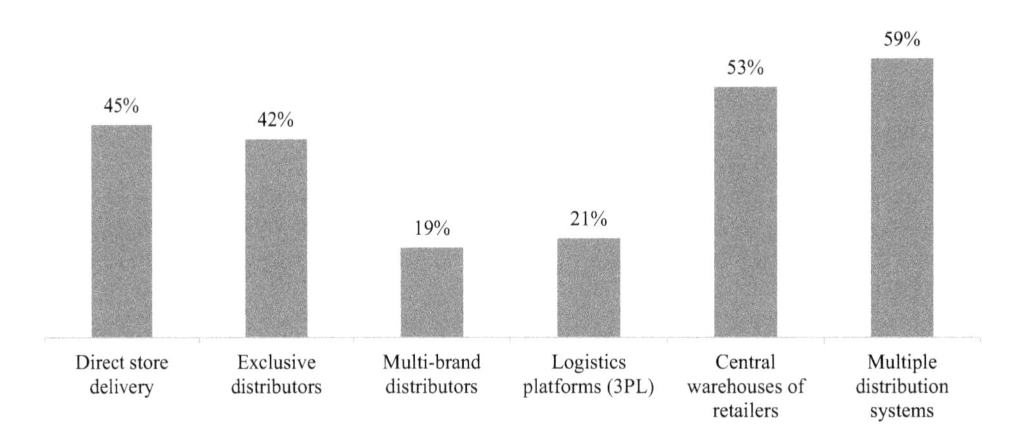

Figure 4.20 Type of route to market models used across 23 countries
Example and spread of different route to market models used by a leading beverage manufacturer across 23 countries in Europe, Africa, Asia and the Americas.
Source: Author

Modern and organized sales channels

With large clients key account management with a formalized negotiation process is usually established, often annually for the joint strategic objectives and during the year for tactical matters. That process varies depending on the status or importance of the products and services within the category and the retail chain. The retail chains often appoint category captains to develop the category using the classical category management process. More recently, with a deeper understanding of how the buying process works, a more shopper centric process is being used. Normally, the key account manager will be facing the purchasing managers of the key account to negotiate the brands, products and services within the category.

It is important to understand the role and functioning of retail chains, as having an agreement and a contract does not always ensure their implementation. This depends on the ability to ensure in-store activation. For this, it is key to understand the buying processes of the different retail chains. In some cases, the retail chains are fully centralized and manufacturers cannot influence implementation at any other level and the success of implementation depends on the trade terms, their monitoring and control. In other cases, the retail chains give higher levels of implementation responsibility to their regional teams or

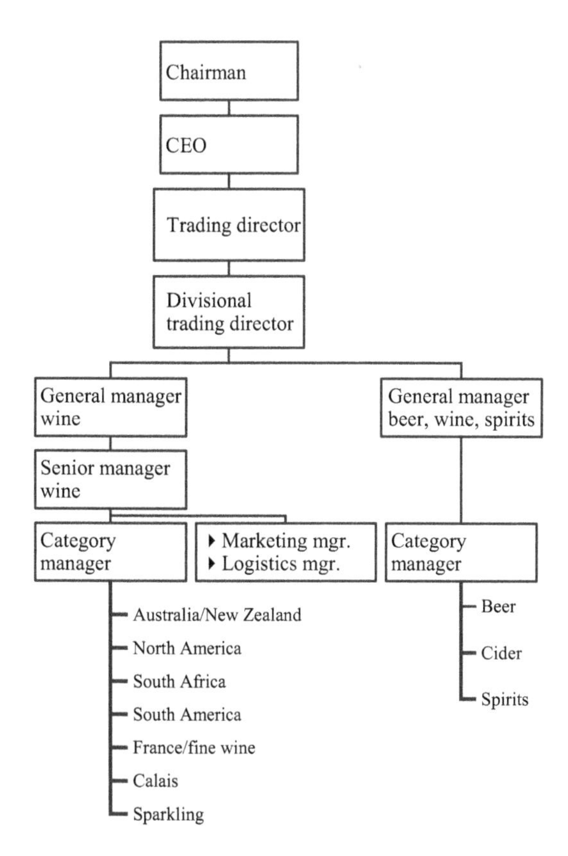

Figure 4.21 Retailer buying organization
Example of the buying organization of alcoholic beverages of a leading retailer in the UK.
Source: Author

individual stores, even letting the manufacturers handle the shelves and point of purchase activation, e.g. through merchandising agencies. For manufacturers this implies an opportunity to influence the activation better, but at the same time, it implies an increased complexity and a higher cost.

With the complexity of large customer management to ensure activation in line with the strategy and the negotiated agreements, the different contact points with the client need to be managed on all levels and across functions.

The retail industry has undergone big changes over the last decades and is continuing to do so. During this development the importance and role of retailers has changed, from pure distribution at its beginnings to shapers of how and what shoppers buy.

The first retail chain was founded in the early 1920s in the United States as a franchise business – the novelty being that shoppers themselves could select the goods on the shelves, put them in a shopping basket and pay at the cashier. Not only did this change the business model of retail to become more efficient and to start thinking in terms of sales by square meter (or foot), but it changed the way manufacturers had to market their products in terms of packaging, pricing and in-store activation.

In addition, it gradually changed the relationship between manufacturer and retailer. This relationship has become more and more complex, with power moving from being more in the hands of manufacturers to increasingly move to the hands of retailers. Not only has the power relationship changed but also the role of retailers, from just being efficient distribution

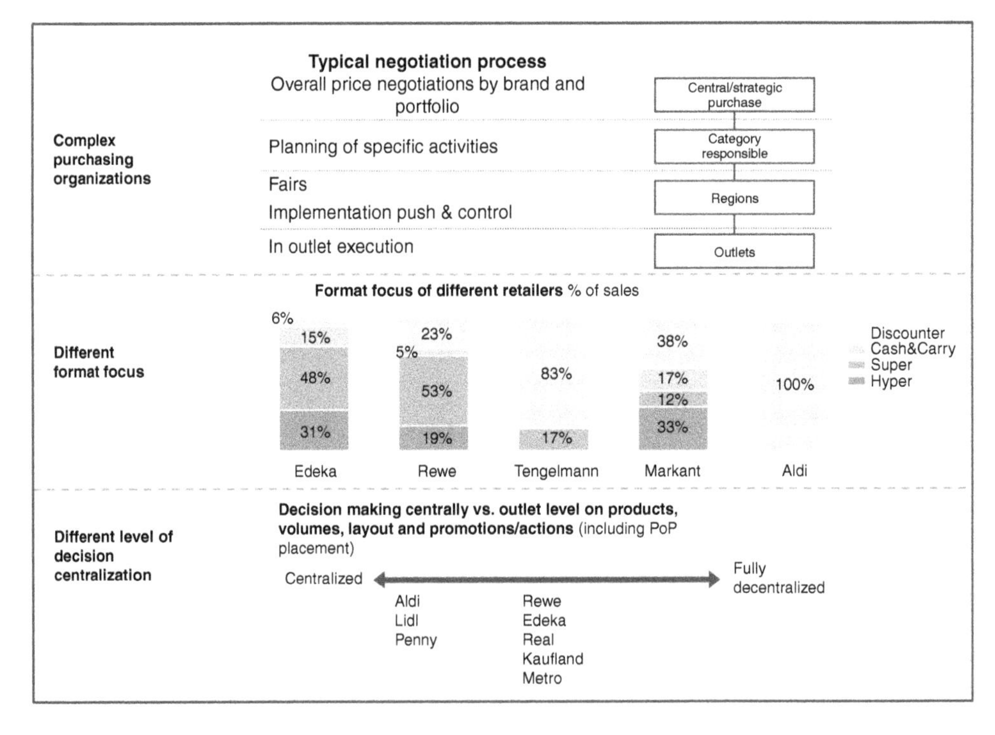

Figure 4.22 Structure of different retail chains in Germany
Example of the differences in the structure of retail chains in Germany in terms of the typical buying process, the format focus and the different levels of centralization of decisions.
Source: Author

channels to becoming marketing channels, and re-shaping the shopping landscape, with players like Amazon and Alibaba being at the helm.

As the negotiating power of retailers has increased and their role has changed, the relationship between manufacturer and retailer has had to change and become more professional in terms of the buying organizations of the retailers and the key account management approach of the manufacturers. The retailer is not the end point in the commercial value chain, but an intermediary to reach shoppers and ultimately consumers. Manufacturers and retailers therefore have, in some aspects, similar objectives. To focus on the joint objectives, rather than on the power struggle, the initiative of ECR started during the 1990s. Additionally, following the development in other industries in the 1980s, spearheaded by companies like Xerox or IBM, manufacturers started to develop their key account management capabilities to better manage the growing power and developing role of retailers.

Since the emergence of the first supermarket chain in the United States 100 years ago, modern retail has totally reshaped the distribution structure and re-defined the classical role between manufacturers and retailers. Traditionally, the role of manufacturers has been to develop products, brand these, communicate to, and activate consumers, normally through advertising and promotions using main media channels. The theory being that this would result in a pull effect, i.e. consumers demanding the products at stores. The role of retailers was to provide these products and brands as efficiently as possible. The metrics of this business model are relatively clear. It is about margins, and sales/margins per store square foot/ meter, per employee, and levels of inventory.

As retailers have grown in importance and consolidated, they have developed into a marketing channel themselves, introducing a new perspective on the market, and a new focus, the shopper. Retailers have understood that their customers were not the same as the consumers of the manufacturers and that their focus is on increasing sales per shopper by driving traffic to the store, focusing on the size of the shopping basket, not on specific products or brands, and on building loyalty of the shopper to ensure re-purchase in the same store and/or chain. In this reality, manufacturers have the task to develop a pull effect and to support the marketing effort of retailers to attain a push effect in the store. New shopper-oriented metrics have been added, such as traffic, basket size and loyalty.

The focus on the shopper vs. the consumer has led to disparate views between manufacturers and retailers. The consumer is the responsibility of the manufacturer, while the shopper is the responsibility of the retailer, giving the retailer important marketing clout. The business models of retailers have developed from focusing on margins and costs to including shopper data and loyalty initiatives. The classical example being Tesco, a British multinational grocery and general merchandise retailer, acquiring the shopper consultancy Dunnhumby.

The shopper focus and information advantage of retailers has made many of them take the step from only distributing and marketing products and brands to becoming brand owners themselves, competing directly with their suppliers. Today retailer brands not only exist in the price-fighter segment, but are also offered across different price and quality segments. In some instances, retailer brands have even opened up new categories, such as Ja! Natürlich in Austria in the 1990s, specialized in ecological products.

The retail industry has been successful in adapting to shopper trends and is continuing to do so, often being one step ahead of manufacturers.

The success of modern retail is shown through its domination of the distribution channel, especially in more developed markets where not only up to 70 percent of sales goes through this distribution channel but also where a few top players consolidate most of the sales.

Until the 1980s and 1990s, the focus was on big box retailing. Due to increasing income disparity, lower income shoppers are driving the growth of the discounter segment and retail brand offering. In parallel, the shopping experience, as well as shopping convenience, is becoming more important. Retailers are moving into the convenience store segment and developing new formats, like mixing discount and convenience stores, as done by the retailers Lidl and Aldi, or combining different formats, for example, retail and gas stations. In a stagnant market environment, moving into the convenience segment offers pockets of growth for retailers.

The biggest changes during the last decade have been the emergence of online and the mix of online and offline shopping. Amazon and Alibaba have developed into world leading retailers. The fastest growing chains are online retailers. The changes go beyond the division of offline and online to integrated solutions, like Amazon with Whole Foods, or Alibaba with Hema supermarkets, to align with the real shopping behavior of customers. Even further, companies like Alibaba, with their concept of New Retail that includes traditional channels, are targeting to meet the holistic service needs of shoppers.

Technology plays a vital role and is becoming more and more integrated into the service offerings of retailers through hyper connectivity solutions. Examples are Amazon and its cashless shopping solution, and Alibaba with the concept of the 11.11 shopping festival.

With the continuous change in the power relationship between retailers and manufacturers, the gatekeeper role of retailers has been accentuated. In the physical business model, space is a key scarce resource. One of the key metrics in retail has been and still is sales per square foot/meter. For retailers one of the key metrics is thus to maximize the sales per square foot/meter at the highest possible margin and optimum cost. While the manufacturer is focusing on brands, the retailer is focusing on attracting shoppers and making them fill their shopping baskets. Different brands or products can play different roles: as traffic builder, i.e. attracting shoppers to the store; as margin drivers; or as destination products, i.e. products for which the store or chain is a reference. The roles of different products for the retailer can be in stark contrast to the intended long-term brand positioning of manufacturers.

Shoppers make many final decisions on products in the store. This makes in-store marketing and activation a key success factor for both products and brands. It is not enough to be listed by a retailer; the products need to be on the shelf, on the right shelf, in the right position and with sufficient space to be encountered by the shopper and preferred over competing products and brands. To really have the attention of shoppers, additional placements and/or space can have a big impact. However, the manufacturer does not manage the space in the store. It is under the control of the retailer, who seeks to maximize its sales or margins by square foot/meter by offering the best combination of products and brands that will drive traffic and increase the value of the shopping basket.

The shift in the power relationship between manufacturers and retailers, plus the conflicting views of consumer vs. shopper and brand vs. shopping basket, has made it necessary to find a common language. In the 1980s, common ground was found in using categories. Category management was developed by the Partnering Group as a basis for the cooperation between retailers and manufacturers to better meet the needs of shoppers and ultimately consumers. Not the brand or specific products were to be the basis for discussions, but the category, and within the category, the different brands. Through the definition of categories, their role can be established, and within each category, the role of the different brands, of innovations and promotions can be defined. Categories are assigned space within the store, and within that space, each brand is allocated its rightful place, depending on its market position. To facilitate the cooperation, each category is assigned a category captain, normally the leading manufacturer, to cooperate with the retailer.

The category management approach addresses what is normally denominated the demand side of the relationship between manufacturers and retailers. The key advantage of big retailers is their ability to provide a wider and more attractive offer in a more efficient manner. Retailers have developed into very efficient supply chain operators. The supply chain is the second key part of the cooperation between manufacturers and retailers.

Optimizing the supply chain can result in some conflicts between manufacturer and supplier but in general, different from the demand side, it is driven by a common objective to improve cost efficiency. Conflicts occur from such things as minimizing inventory levels at retailers that can increase inventory levels of low rotation products at manufacturers, or specific needs from some retailers in terms of supply windows or type of pallets. Improvements such as electronic data interchange have been beneficial for both parties. Areas of discussion between manufacturers and retailers are often about which supply-chain solutions are most beneficial, and for whom, and how the potential benefits should be calculated, allocated and considered in trade terms.

The management of order taking and the supply chain is often part of ECR-type cooperation, which is positioning itself as a common standard. Modern retail is adapting its operational strategies to be able to optimize efficiencies.[23]

Managing the demand and supply side in a cooperative way has led to the development of ECR approaches. The idea is that the shared goal of both manufacturers and retailers is to develop consumer demand at the highest possible cost efficiency. The approach started in the United States with more focus on the supply chain, while in Europe there was a strong focus on the demand side. The JAG concept is one of the newer developments looking into cooperation to grow the market in the interest of both retailers and manufacturers.

As in any cooperation between buyer and supplier, the rules of the game need to come together in an agreement over financial mechanics, normally referred to as trade terms. The financial part of the agreement is the key source of many of the conflicts between retailers and manufacturers. In addition to shopper data and information, the price margin, listing fees and payment terms are the key determinants of financial success for retailers. Trade terms formalize the amount and type of activities that are to drive demand, such as promotions, launches, in-store and other activations. With price and logistics discounts and payment terms, these trade terms help to finance the inventory of retailers. They also include rules addressing shelf space, presentation, stock unavailability, sales material and in some cases the implications if one of the parties does not fulfill its responsibilities.

Due to the breadth of the relationship between manufacturer and retailer, ranging from marketing, trade marketing, supply chain and finance and spanning across the organizational complexity of the different retailers, the success of key account management has been mostly about the ability of key account managers to coordinate different departments. While the buying organization is the key department for retailers, as it is their main source of business success, this is often not the case with manufacturers, whose success is based more on product development, marketing, production and sales activation, rather than managing a specific retail account. At times, this leads to an imbalance between retailers and manufacturers in resources, expertise and preparation in the negotiation process.

One further key challenge for manufacturers is ensuring that the negotiated terms are in fact implemented by the retailer. Retailers have a multitude of individual stores, so the negotiated terms and shopper activations are not always correctly implemented. This can range from specific products being out of stock or not present on the shelves, to planograms,

Table 4.1 Examples of cooperation concepts between manufacturers and retailers

Area	*Concept*	*Content*
Demand-side driven approaches	Category Management (CatMan)	Shopping seen as an impulse to production and logistics processes.
Supply-chain driven approaches	Supply chain management (SCM)	Cooperation between companies to ensure optimum cost efficiency. Radio frequency identification (RFID) systems often being used to track products.
	Just in Time strategies (JIT)	An inventory management technique and type of lean methodology designed to increase efficiency, cut costs and decrease waste by receiving goods only as they are needed.
	Quick response (QR)	Delivery system harmonized with demand and all companies participating in a logistics approach based upon constant data interchange. First developed by the textile industry in the USA to fight the low-cost threat from abroad. It can be thought of as a specific JIT system.
	Continuous replenishment (CR)	Frequent replenishment that takes place from the supplier to the retailer in order to maintain a better flow in supply chain and minimize bullwhip effects, i.e. a shift in consumer demand creating increasing swings in inventory further up the supply chain. A type of vendor-managed inventory (VMI) system where the decision of quantity and time to replenish lies with the supplier and not the retailer.
	Vendor-managed inventory (VMI)	An arrangement in which both buyer (retailer) and supplier (manufacturer) share internal information to integrate their plans, forecasts and delivery schedules to ensure a smooth flow of goods and services. Manufacturers have access to inventory data and are responsible for generating purchase orders. VMI allows for the possibility of consignment inventory, where ownership only changes when the product is sold.
Integrated approaches	Efficient consumer response (ECR)	Could be thought of as a follow-up to the QR system: "successful reaction to consumer demand". Both concepts are from Kurt Salmon Associates; same concept as constraint-based supply-chain-management with the aim of increasing the speed of the product flow at the manufacturer to shorten lead times and improve throughputs. Integrates CatMan and SCM.
	Collaborative planning, forecasting and replenishment (CPFR)	Aims to enhance supply-chain integration by supporting and assisting joint practices. CPFR seeks cooperative management of inventory through joint visibility and replenishment of products throughout the supply chain.

Table 4.1 Cont.

Area	*Concept*	*Content*
	Supplier Relationship Management (SRM)/ Customer Relationship Management (CRM)	Handling interaction between buyers (retailers) & suppliers (manufacturers) using integration.
	Jointly agreed growth (JAG)	A five-step process for building a three-year rolling plan with annual milestones, where the buyer (retailer) and the seller (manufacturer) are accountable for functional liaison, planning, coordination, agreement, execution and follow-up. Cross-functional teams drive the analysis and planning. The approach gives trade partners a shared fact-based rationale on which to base decisions in the interests of both to drive growth.
Enablers	Electronic data interchange (EDI)	Protocol used for QR, billing data, etc.

Source: Author

Table 4.2 Ten steps of strategic account management of organized retail

Area	*Steps*	*Content*
Strategy	Retailer portfolio analysis	Assignment of roles to each retailer in terms of attainment of manufacturer's strategic objectives, e.g. profit cash cow, growth, brand building, reach, etc.
	Role alignment between manufacturer and retailer	Alignment of role with retailers in terms of shopper and shopping targets, e.g. convenience, discount, big box and operational implications.
Offering	Shopper-centric activation	Brand development and activation plans, based on category and shopper situations and needs by retailer.
	Micro offering	Detailing offering by formats/banners, regions, and even shopping areas.
	Category invigoration	Innovation and brand development to invigorate the category and drive traffic and sales at the retailer, and of the manufacturer.
Trade terms & contracting	Contracting for joint business development	Trade terms supporting joint value creation (JVC) initiatives based on a pay-for-performance (PfP) philosophy.
	Relevant metrics	Metrics connected with the trade terms linked to business development initiatives. Often proxies are used due to limitations in information sharing and data gathering.
Implementation	Activation implementation	In-store activation and sales force management.
	Operational efficiency	Supply chain cooperation and efficiency.
Organization	Premium customer management	Organization for customer relationship and implementation management.

Source: Author

additional placements, promotions or other activations not being correctly implemented. In other instances, central negotiations only cover certain aspects, so other aspects need to be negotiated on a regional, format or store level. In both cases, either sales may be lost or sales potential may not be fully captured.

The challenge that manufacturers face is how to cover the different aspects of managing a variety of categories, as well as functional-, format- and store-level aspects.

Successful key account management in the organized retail sphere is much about understanding how to align strategic objectives and success metrics. Due to the importance of individual retailers and the accelerating development of the industry, each retailer is in many cases an entire market in itself. In some cases, due to the international reach of both retailers and manufacturers, there is a need for global account management approaches.[24] Successful strategic account management needs a structured approach, ranging from a categorization of the accounts to the activation and control of the same. Below are ten steps of such a structured approach and key aspects to be considered in the management of strategic accounts.

1. Retailer portfolio analysis
   Retailers differ in terms of their importance to the manufacturer in developing its business. Understanding the role the retailer plays for the manufacturer defines the priorities not only in terms of resource allocation but also in terms of strategic challenges. Analyzing the profit situation and strategic challenges of each retailer and assigning a strategic role to each one helps to build a differentiated strategic approach to optimize the market development effort, resource allocation and profit situation.[25]
2. Role alignment between manufacturer and retailer
   Retailers are not only distributors per se. They differentiate themselves and target not only specific shopper segments but specific shopping missions as well. The offer needs to be aligned with the strategic profile of each retailer and its different formats as well as regional situation. Due to legal restrictions, manufacturers cannot decide on pricing levels or exclusively sell specific products to certain retailers. Therefore, the target shoppers of retailers need to be understood, and the offer (products, services, packaging, price, activation, promotions) attuned to fit with the need of the retailer to serve these shoppers.[26]
3. Shopper-centric activation
   Since the introduction of category management, the focus of activation has been on categories. The initial eight steps of category management were built around this concept. As shoppers have evolved and retailers have differentiated into various formats and become more elaborate in meeting shopper needs, category management has had to develop into shopper management. In shopper management, the focus is the shopper and how the strategies of retailers and manufacturers can be aligned to best activate the shopper.[27]
4. Micro offering
   The big promise of selling to big retailers, to be able to reach numerous shoppers through only one point of negotiation is only partly attainable. Retailers are continuously trying to expand and reach new shopper groups or serve new shopping missions. Expansion is about opening new stores in new territories, as well as entering into new formats. It is not sufficient simply to understand the strategy of the retailer and align, as far as possible, with it. Retailers optimize their offering by format and by outlet. Through increasing data density and data availability, retailers have access to more information on

how to better tune the offering toward specific shopper needs. Manufacturers need to fine tune the offering by type of store by studying shopping behavior across chains and store types, thereby optimizing sales and margins to the mutual benefit of manufacturer and retailer.[28]

5. Category invigoration
To stay a leader and relevant to retailers continuing to innovate and bringing new products to the market, based on an in-depth understanding of the shopper, are of the essence. For retailers, new products not only invigorate specific categories and build traffic, but also support the building of credibility around specific topics to connect shoppers with groups of adjacent categories to enlarge the shopping basket.[29]
6. Contracting for joint business development
At times, the conditions agreed in the trading terms are poorly executed. This can include availability of products, shelf space, position in the store, second placements, implementation of promotions, etc. This can lead to losses in sales and market share. To directly penalize retailers can be difficult, as well as detrimental to joint business development. Under these circumstances negotiations centered around problem solving, additional measures, and joint implementation plans to make up for the potential losses can be more fruitful.[30]
7. Relevant metrics
Detailed metrics from retailers can be difficult to obtain, as they normally do not share information on sales per format/banner or store, nor other detailed information. Nevertheless, it is crucial to have an understanding of retailer performance on a more detailed level as an input to product and service, as well as retail management strategies. Leading manufacturers develop sets of proxy information to substitute detailed data. These proxies are normally collected through the sales force, auditing companies and through connecting different information sources.

   With the support of the proxies a more detailed understanding is attained and cooperation with the retailers becomes more fact based.[31]
8. Activation implementation
Manufacturers and retailers normally agree on shopper activation plans. These shopper activations can include different aspects, such as advertisements, catalogs, flyers, gondolas, second placements, tastings, in-store promotions, etc. Planning and designing these are a big challenge in itself. The hidden, and often forgotten, challenge, though, is to ensure the implementation on all levels. The level of centralization in terms of decision making and in-store implementation differs by chain. As a result, many actions are not correctly implemented or even not implemented at all.

   Retail chains have different levels of freedom when it comes to store-level negotiations and activation. Dependent on the level of centralization and freedom in decision making at the store level, manufacturers need to adapt their organization to optimize the impact they have at the point of purchase and shopper activation..[32]
9. Operational efficiency
As pointed out previously, in the area of operations, especially supply chain, where there is a clear alignment of interests between retailer and manufacturer, cooperation is often quite advanced. It often includes cooperating to improve the efficiency of the supply chain end-to-end from transportation, to central warehousing, to the delivery and placement in the store. One key dispute can be the level of discounts expected by the retailer for different supply chain services, and if these discounts are higher than the potential cost for the manufacturer.[33]

10. Premium customer management
    The buying organizations of the leading retailers are often quite sophisticated. Category management, trade marketing and sales force resources need to be aligned to professionally meet the needs of retail customers and improve the position of the manufacturer. Challenges facing key account organizations are often unclear processes, struggles for resources and a lack of clarity over ownership of customer issues.[34]

The retail market is in the midst of important changes. E-commerce is already established and is continuing to develop. New shopping behaviors are emerging, like webrooming and showrooming, and shopper journeys are becoming longer and more complex. Retailers like Amazon and Alibaba are at the forefront of omnichannel strategies by integrating the physical and digital retail environments. Alibaba is launching its idea of the "new retail", integrating traditional channels into its system, developing a true shopper ecosystem transcending the classical idea of the dyadic customer–retailer relationship. Customer centricity becomes about the ecosystem and less about the sole interrelationship between shopper and retailer, and retailer and manufacturer. This development has and will have implications on how key account managers collaborate with and manage retailers, as the success metrics will evolve from focusing on margins and sales per square foot or meter to focusing more on shopper metrics. Metrics, like revenue growth, margins, return on capital employed (due to changes in store and technological investments) and basket size will grow in importance.[35] As key metrics change, the expectations of retailers will change, and there will be implications for how these expectations are managed..

Digital sales channels

Digital sales channels or e-commerce is often seen as something quite new. The reality is that digitalization has been around for a long time. Digitalization and e-commerce have been a constant process during the last 40 years that has been gathering speed exponentially. It has fundamentally changed the world of shopping, and is continuously doing so.

As early as 1980 electronic data interchange (EDI) was introduced, something that became one of the key enablers in making business between manufacturers and retailers more efficient. The starting point for online shopping could possibly be dated to 1979 when Michael Aldrich used Teletext to enable online transactions through a two-way message service. In 1981 the first B2B transaction with Thomson holidays from the UK was conducted; and in 1982 Mintel, an online service accessible by phone lines, was used for online purchases, to book train tickets, chat and check stock, prices etc. In 1984 the first online purchase at a Tesco store was performed. In 1990, Tim Berners-Lee created the first browser and web server, the future worldwide web.[36] What had been created for the academic world became commercialized through the birth of e-commerce, and in 1992 the first online bookstore, Book Stacks Unlimited, was introduced. In 1994, the first pizza was sold online, and in 1995 online banking through The Presidential Bank was introduced. In 1995, both Amazon and eBay were launched, and just three years later in 1998 PayPal was founded. In 1999, Jack Ma founded Alibaba in China. In 2003 Apple launched its iTunes store; in 2004 credit card companies created the payment card industry data security standards; in 2005 YouTube was launched; and in 2009 Bitcoin became the first decentralized cryptocurrency.[37]

E-commerce could be defined as sales generated by a connected activity, through either websites, mobile devices or applications. The moment of purchase is what at the end defines digital purchase channels and differentiates them from digital marketing channels. Digital

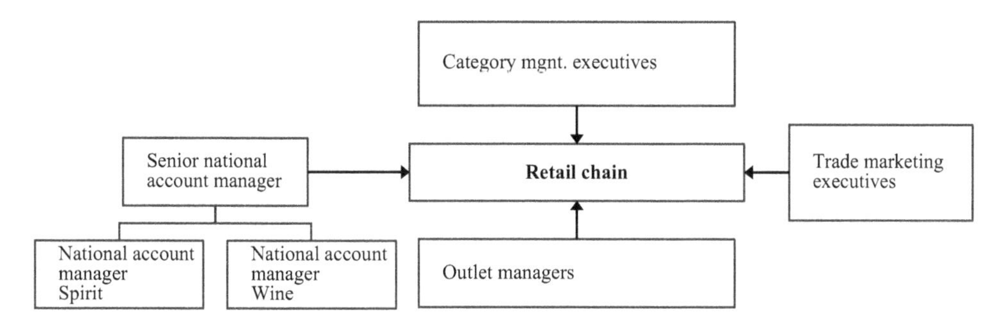

Figure 4.23 Organization of strategic account management
Example of the organization of strategic account management of a retailer by an alcoholic beverage manufacturer in the UK. One senior national account manager is responsible for the account with the support of specialized account managers for the two categories of spirits and wine. A category management executive is shared with another team and is responsible for category management projects with the retailer. The trade marketing executive is responsible for translating marketing strategies into channel and retail strategies and activation. Outlet managers visit and activate the different stores of the retailer in line with trade marketing initiatives and commercial strategies.
Source: Author

marketing includes all consumer and shopper engagement using digital channels to influence shoppers to purchase products, even if the shopper journey ends in a purchase in a brick-and-mortar point of purchase. E-commerce is buying online while digital marketing is moving shoppers down the purchase funnel. Digital marketing is to drive the shopper toward the checkout, e-commerce and brick and mortar alike. E-commerce purchase and its fulfillment, the moment beyond the point of purchase where the product, in the case of physical products, arrives into the hands of the shopper can be through click and collect or delivery, either from local stores or centralized shipment centers.

Fulfillment is an important challenge due to the costs associated with it. In brick-and-mortar retail, fulfillment costs have been streamlined. The last yard costs are normally carried by the shopper who comes to the store, fills his shopping basket, goes to the checkout, and brings the products back to the place of consumption. In brick-and-mortar retail, the big challenge has traditionally been the last mile, the cost to bring the goods from distribution centers to the individual brick-and-mortar stores. Within modern retail, the development of centralized warehouse solutions with optimized last mile delivery to the individual stores has improved efficiency, and the costs have been part of the trade terms between retailers and manufacturers. In e-commerce, distribution has developed into a key component. In brick-and-mortar environments, the shopper is usually in charge of the last yard distribution. While last mile distribution refers to delivering products and services to the point of purchase, last yard delivery refers to delivering the product and service to the ultimate point of consumption. Obviously, in immediate consumption channels, consumption and shopping coincide, as do the last mile and the last yard. In points of purchase where there is no immediate consumption, the shopper will buy a product and service to be consumed at a later moment and at another place. In the brick-and-mortar environment, the shopper has normally been responsible for the last yard. With e-commerce, last yard distribution, after the moment of purchase, has increasingly become part of the service to the shopper. Obviously, home delivery has been offered as a service by brick-and-mortar outlets as well, but not to the same extent. E-commerce offers several solutions, for cost reasons, such as click and collect in brick-and-mortar stores or at special lockers. In the e-commerce sphere, the costs of the last yard, bringing the goods to the place of consumption, have been transferred from the shopper to the supply side, retailers and manufacturers. In some instances, there will be a delivery fee, but this is often waived for purchases over a certain amount. This implies that the supplier side is faced with new aspects of the cost to serve to cover costs of individual shopping basket picking, more and smaller storage units closer to shoppers and consumers, and delivering to the point of consumption. To lower the barrier to online shopping many e-commerce platforms offer free returns. Free returns do not only increase the direct logistics costs, but the costs of products that cannot be resold, which either need to be destroyed, given away, or sold at a discount. Some companies talk of 30 percent return rates with significant implications on the cost to serve.[38] Packaging needs to be rethought. In the brick-and-mortar sphere, packaging is designed for upright visibility on retail shelves, but e-commerce requires packaging with minimal excess space and still strong enough to withstand the delivery journey. Managing the cost to serve and developing not only effective, but also efficient, supply chain solutions that are sustainable is one of the key challenges within e-commerce.

E-commerce is not one, but a diverse set of different sales channels. Direct channels are under the direct control of the manufacturer who can position and present products and services fully in line with the objectives and the brand marketing strategy. The disadvantages are obviously a lower reach. Through SEO, manufacturers can try to ensure high rankings for searches related to their products and direct these potential shoppers to their websites. When it comes to emailing, it is a tool to reach shoppers that have already provided their email address, e.g. previous buyers. Examples of tools to help develop email campaigns are MailChimp, HubSpot, ActiveCampaign, etc. There must normally be an address list for the emails not to be categorized as spams.

The majority of sales occur through retailers, and the biggest and leading retailers are historically brick-and-mortar stores. Amazon is the only fully e-commerce retailer that is among the world leading retailers. In China Alibaba is also a leading player. Brick-and-mortar retailers have added e-commerce to their program, entering the omnichannel sphere, and conversely Amazon has introduced brick-and-mortar solutions. Fulfillment through retailers often happens through click and collect, where shoppers order digitally and collect physically, at a given location and time window, or where the shopper is delivered to his

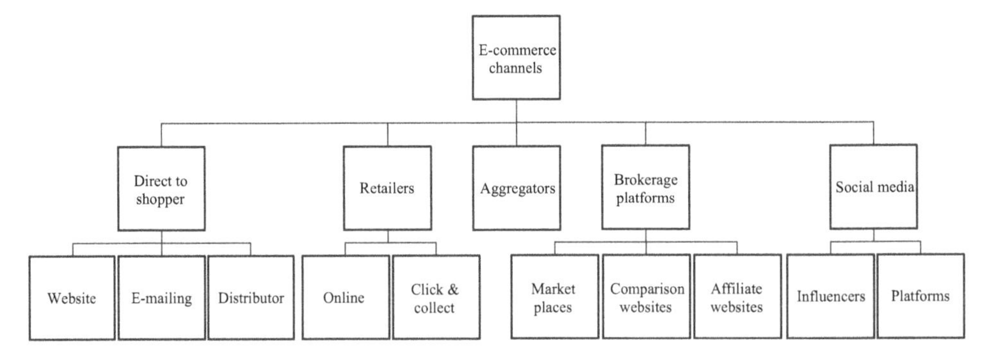

Figure 4.24 E-commerce channels
Categorization of e-commerce channels.
Source: Author

or her home. Sometimes, the delivery can be to pick-up lockers or stores nearby. Here the manufacturer is not in control of the presentation, but his products and services are part of the portfolio of the retailer and his objectives to attract and retain shoppers in line with his positioning, as well as to add to the shopping basket at each moment of purchase.

The aggregator business model is a network model, normally in specific industries, where the firm collects information about potential goods and service providers to make them its partners under the firm's brand. The goods and services are provided to shoppers under the same brand name. The providers can still act under their name under the umbrella brand of the aggregator platform. The idea is to establish a win-win situation for both parties where the partners focus on providing quality products and services to shoppers and the aggregator focuses on marketing and creating leads for the partners. The partner terms include rules on branding, quality standards and compensation, amongst others. Aggregator models are non-exclusive, and goods and service providers can partner with different aggregators. Aggregators have infiltrated many industries, such as travel, taxi services, restaurants, groceries, etc. Examples are Airbnb, Uber, Uber Eats, Munchery, Food Panda, Mjam, Gofers, etc.

Another important e-commerce channel is brokerage platforms. Here the platforms offer, as well as promote, different products and services. They are normally multi-brand with little preference for specific manufacturers and their brands. Marketplaces like Amazon, eBay, Zalando, or Taobao and Tmall in China are big and important platforms for shoppers that often already know which products they are looking for. Search engines help with presenting reviews, ratings and price comparisons. In addition, which products have been bought in combination are often shown, helping to build a shopping basket and present specific products and services. Marketplaces such as Amazon or Zalando are business to shopper marketplaces, while marketplaces like eBay are consumer to shopper marketplaces. Although some promotions and sponsoring are possible on marketplaces, the main comparison driver is price and reviews.

Comparison shopping engines are not directly e-commerce channels, but lead to platforms where products and services can be purchased. Still, they are an important tool for shoppers who look for specific products and services, and are relatively far down their shopping journey. Comparison shopping engines mainly help shoppers compare prices, and also reviews, to help them find the best deal. Examples are Idealo, PriceGrabber, Kelkoo, etc. Some activation can be done through product listings, but the presentation is more a result of the shopper marketing effort done in the channels to which the comparison shopping engines direct the shoppers, and the work done on product and service quality.

Affiliate networks like Rakuten, Affilinet, CJ Affiliate, etc., are brokers with which companies can agree to drive traffic to points of purchase, be it brick-and-mortar or digital, for purchasing specific products and services. The affiliate network will normally receive a certain sum of compensation based on specific outcomes like traffic or purchase. The affiliate network then needs to find ways to attract potential shoppers, normally through different deals. Normally the compensation is based on real sales, as metrics such as generating traffic to specific websites have shown to be challenging to measure correctly, with important implications on correct compensation levels. Affiliate marketing plays an important role as a tool in e-commerce and generates a significant share of e-commerce sales. In addition, although it is not always the final point of purchase, it plays a vital role as a final step in the shopper journey before the purchase.

Sales through social media give more opportunities to position products and services on dimensions other than price, and move toward content marketing. Social media marketing is normally considered reasonably effective when it comes to targeted campaigns. In the case of influencers the profile of the influencer needs to be aligned with the position of the product and service. Furthermore, the influencer needs to have a certain reach in targeting consumers and shoppers to make a marketing effort worthwhile. The most important platform is Instagram. When it comes to a platform like Facebook, it will help to target the right audience for the product and service. Other platforms are Snapchat, Reddit or Pinterest. Social media helps to inspire potential shoppers, remind past shoppers, and capture the attention of shoppers in the search phase. Products and services can be promoted through social posts, dynamic ads and videos. More than just being promoted, products and services can also be purchased directly on some social media platforms, e.g. Facebook.

The different search engines, with Google obviously the most important one, but also Bing, Yahoo, or DuckDuckGo, for example, are not directly e-commerce sales channels, but are important in directing sales traffic. Search engines help to attract potential shoppers who are actively searching for solutions and categories. Products and services can be promoted on the search engines through text ads, image ads, display ads, voice search, etc.

E-commerce channels, depending on the level of control and collaboration, have a huge opportunity to use data to deepen knowledge about shoppers and develop better targeted strategies and move from pure transactions to more retention and shopper development. The access to data for indirect sales is dependent on the level of collaboration with retailers, affiliates and influencers. The optimization of offerings and search results presented are driven by algorithms, with deductions normally based on fragmented data limited to online behavior. E-commerce is also limited when it comes to impulse purchases that can be important for specific categories.

In managing the e-commerce channels SEO is key to ensuring high rankings for searches related to products and brands, and directing searches to the most relevant websites, primarily brand and product websites. Beyond the brand and product websites content can be provided to engage shoppers, e.g. through banners, social marketing, bloggers, etc. Price comparisons and reviews build differentiation during search phases, and digital coupons and loyalty programs are effective in driving preference and purchase.

The classical manufacturer, retailer, shopper model is still in many ways the most important model in many categories, where the process is shared between manufacturer and retailer. E-commerce expands the possibilities for direct to shopper and consumer models, including subscription models, where the main part of the process stay with the manufacturer. In the brokerage and social media model the platforms gain commissions by bringing shoppers and sellers together, commissioned by either impressions or real purchases. Advertising, e.g. through banners, is an important source of income, especially for search engines. E-commerce makes it possible to collect much shopper behavior data. Sites and platforms, e.g. Google and Facebook, analyze and sell this data. Internet service providers are key players that generate revenues both from internet subscriptions and advertising.

The market-focused organization

To implement the route to market strategy and align it with the route to purchase strategy an adequate organization needs to be in place. Organization is based on the structure and people, processes to link the different functions and activities, the tools to support the work, and competencies and culture.

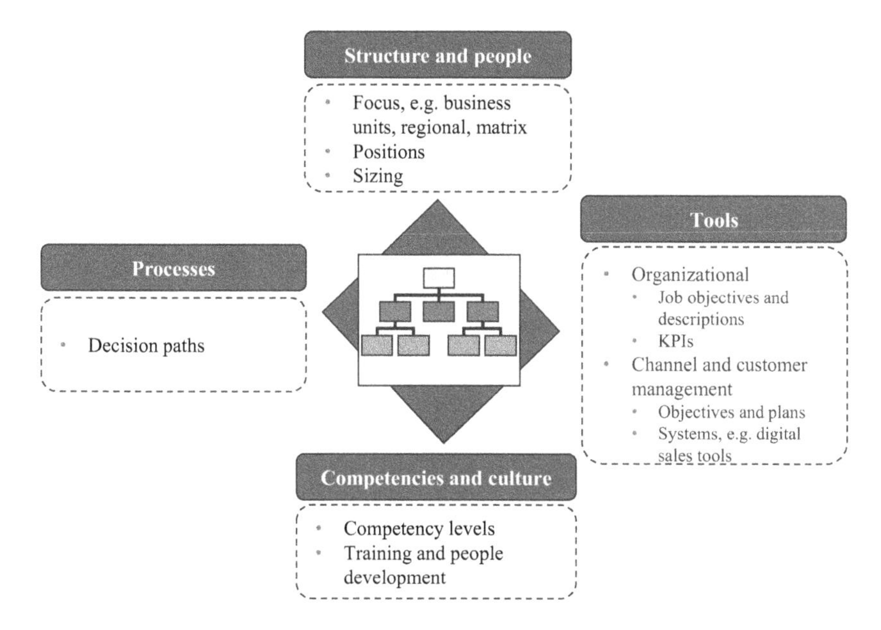

Figure 4.25 Designing organizations
Basic organizational design: structure and people, processes, tools, and competencies and culture.
Source: Author

There is no perfect organization. An organization is always a tradeoff between how to best link and divide activities in terms of their effectiveness and efficiency. Depending on strategic objectives and priorities, as well as specific market challenges, different solutions can be optimum. In a market-oriented organization, particularly one focused on profitable sales and shopper market drivers, the starting point in designing the organization is to understand the market and the challenges that need to be met to reach its objectives.

Designing an organization centers around the activities that need to be performed, by whom these activities will be performed, how they will be directed, monitored and supervised, and where responsibilities will lie. Sizing the organization, i.e. which positions and how many people per position are required, depends on the complexity and diversity of activities, i.e. how they can be grouped, and what supervision and span of control each position needs. The organization is thus designed from below, from the contact with the market, upward to the required groupings and supervision of activities, as well as the required support functions. The size of the organization is ultimately a function of marginal productivity. Activities that are closely interlinked to manage and serve customers often have to be divided due to efficiency and competency issues. In the route to market sales, order taking and the supply chain are strongly interrelated activities, but are usually divided into different departments. Good processes are needed to coordinate activities for a coherent customer experience across departments and functions. A coherent coordination across the functions involved in shopper management has a positive impact on results.[39]

Positions and the expected activities and responsibilities need to be clarified through job descriptions and key performance indicators, i.e. job expectations. The objectives

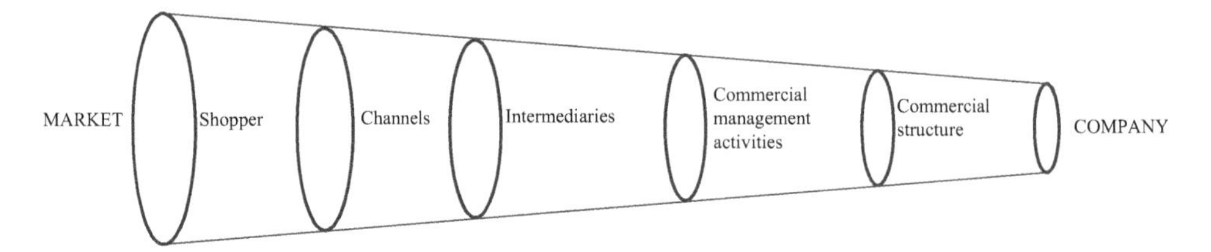

Figure 4.26 Outside-in perspective of organizational design
Design logic of commercial organizations with the market and challenges as the point of departure. Starting with understanding the market and the opportunities, the objectives and challenges, understanding how to best reach shoppers through sales channels, intermediaries, and analyzing which are the necessary commercial activities and the logical commercial structure to perform these activities.
Source: Author

and expectations by function and area are also formalized through objectives with dashboards as a means of management direction, supervision and control, as well as performance evaluation. Measurement is key to understanding the situation and in developing improvement actions.[40] Dashboards can be used across the key areas of the route to market, such as logistics, point of purchase management, collections and management control.

Further, tools to manage the points of purchase and the sales force are integrated sales force tools including activation, availability, and order-taking support. Through advanced data analysis, the performance can be monitored and improvement actions directed to identify and prioritize growth opportunities and competitive challenges.

Coca-Cola Femsa, one of the leading Coca-Cola bottlers, headquartered in Mexico, has launched a program of centers of commercial excellence supported and based on digital tools via their digital KOFmmercial platform. This advanced analytics platform allows the company to optimize prices and promotions, its customer portfolio and the facilitation of identification of additional market opportunities. In essence it is a platform for customer relationship management (CRM) that includes tools and back-office procedures for achieving granular segmentation, that allows the company to prioritize actions targeting specific clients to maximize the value of sales force visits and optimize the allocation of resources. The platform automates the sales force with a mobile handheld device including sales quota measurements, prioritizing portfolio coverage, a module for specific initiatives, 360° client data and faster order loading. The KOFmmercial platform allows the company to digitally connect commercial, marketing, manufacturing, sales and distribution for higher effectiveness and efficiency.

The support tools, like dashboards and shopper marketing sales management tools, are part of a development loop to identify opportunities to improve and define corresponding actions. This allows the organization the advantage of a learning curve to gain competitive advantage.[41] For this, an organization has to go beyond just reviewing results; it must also review and improve the reasons why it does things in a certain way, i.e., the assumptions on which the work is based.[42] In addition, organizations need to review the process of learning itself, the systems of analysis and the culture of reviewing and learning.[43]

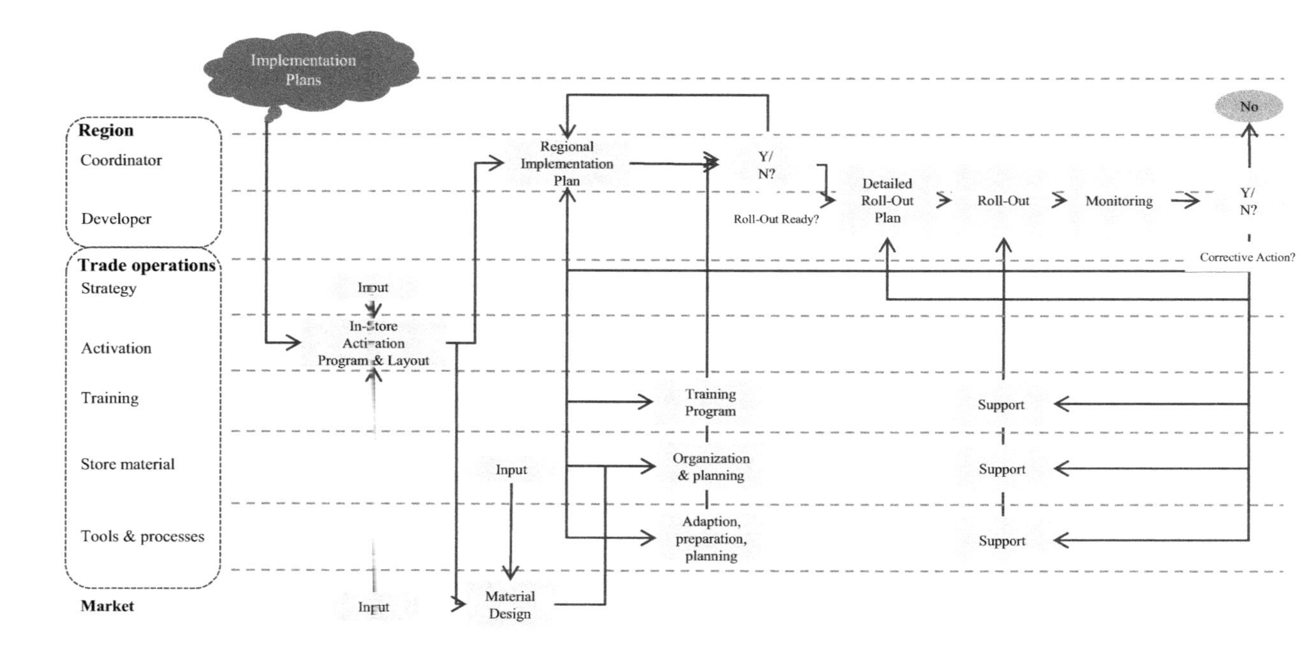

Figure 4.27 Process flow map of channel management in telecoms
Example of process flow for the implementation and control of channel marketing action plans in the telecom sector.
Source: Author

		LOGISTICS			STORE MANAGEMENT				COLLECTIONS		MANAGEMENT	
		Order & Payment	**Transport**	**Warehousing**	**Sales**	**Dispatching**	**Picking**	**Delivery**	**Invoicing**	**Collection**	**Information**	**Management**
EFFICIENCY	**KPIs**	• --	• Truck utilization • Drop size • Cost/unit	• Pallets/ manhour • Warehousing utilization • Cost/unit	• Orders/day • Size order (average drop) • Cost/unit	• Orders/utiliz ation/route	• Pallets/ manhour • Cost/unit	• Truck utilization • StopsXdrop size • Outlet density • Cost/unit	• Cost/unit	• Cost/unit	• --	• Debt level • Profit/margin levels • People rotation • Supervision level • People investment level
	KEY DRIVERS	• --	• People cost •Truck type/ size/cost • Maintenance needs/time • Drop frequency optimization	• People cost • Warehouse cost • Machines/ forklifts • Warehouse organization/ internal movements	• People cost • Hit rate • Routing	• Number of routes • People cost • Routing/ planning systems used	• % broken pallets • Picking area organization • Automization • People cost	• People cost/ people on truck • Truck size/type/ cost • Maintenance need • Route distance	• People cost • Systems	• People cost • Systems	• Systems	• People cost/ salaries • Efficiency levels • Training and development investment • Systems
EFFECTIVENESS	**ACCURACY**	• % correct orders	• % of goods brought back	• --	• % correct order	• % goods back • % goods missing	• % goods back • % goods missing	• --	• % correct invoice	• % correct money received	• Correct information	• --
	SERVICE LEVEL	• --	• Delivery on time • Picking up on time • Waiting time	• Stock levels (min. days by ABC products)	• --	• Time lag order-delivery	• --	• Delivery on time	• Time lag delivery-invoicing	• Time lag invoice–money received	• Time lag sending to manaufacturer	• --
	QUALITY	• --	• % of damaged goods	• % of damaged goods	• --	• --	• % of damaged goods	• % of damaged goods	• --	• --	• --	• --

Figure 4.28 Route to market dashboard
Example of the key dimensions of a route to market dashboard covering the areas of logistics, point of purchase management, collections and management control.
Source: Author

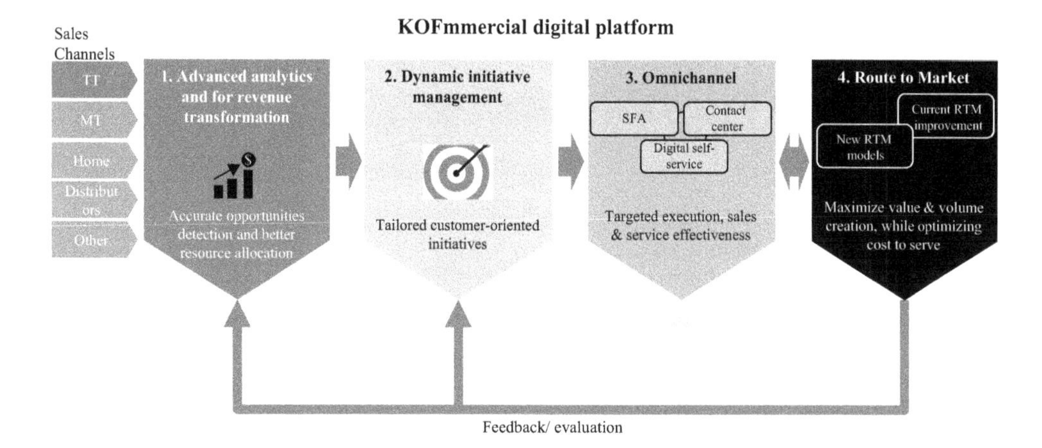

Figure 4.29 Femsa KOFmmercial digital platform

Overview of the digital commercial platform connecting key aspects of shopper marketing such as omnichannel and route to market to optimize and personalize initiatives and drive revenues.

SFA: sales force automation.

Source: Coca-Cola Femsa, October 2017

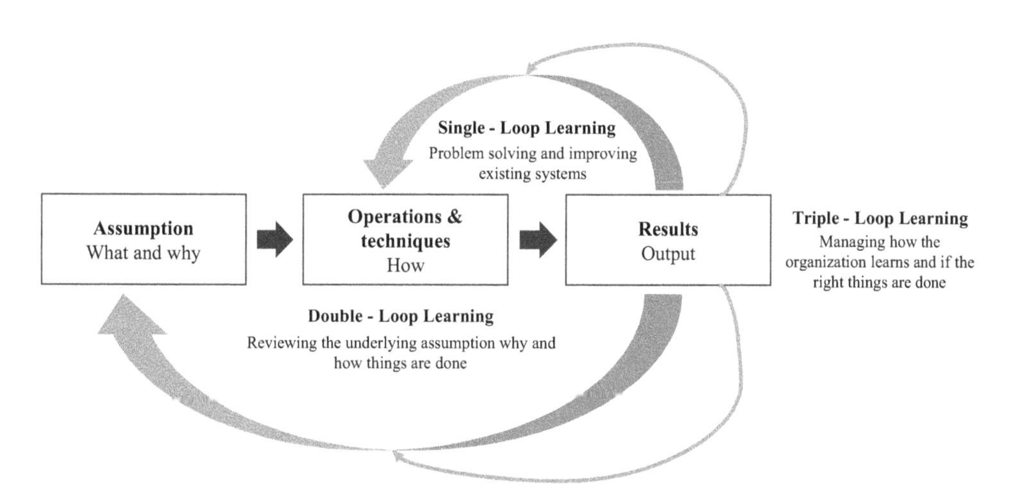

Figure 4.30 Organizational learning loops

The first loop focuses on solving problems and improving existing system. Double loop learning is the evaluation of why things are done and how they can be improved. Triple loop learning is a self-review of how the organization develops and learns.

Source: Adaptions by the author of Argyris & Schön, 1974; Argyris, 1977; (Argyris & Schön, 1978; Nielsen, 1993

Notes

1 (Stilley et al., 2010)
2 (Ayad, 2008)
3 (Grant & Fernie, 2008) and (Pramatari & Miliotis, 2008)
4 (Dadzie & Winston, 2007)
5 (Rani & Velayudhan, 2008)
6 (Miranda & Jegasothy, 2008)
7 (Zhuang et al., 2006) and (Nsairi, 2012)
8 (Turley & Milliman, 2000)
9 (Donovan et al., 1994) and (Ballantine et al., 2010)
10 (Yoon, 2013)
11 (Broekemier et al., 2008)
12 (Kaltcheva & Weitz, 2006), (Baker et al., 2002) and (Orth et al., 2012)
13 (Bigné-Alcaniz et al., 2008), (Wu et al., 2014) and (Harris & Goode, 2010)
14 (Yavas & Babakus, 2009), (Turley & Milliman, 2000) and (Ayad, 2008)
15 (Stüber, 2011)
16 (Park & Lennon, 2009) and (Kessler, 2004)
17 (Baker et al., 1994)
18 (El Comercio: Economia, 2017)
19 (Tang et al., 2014)
20 (Williamson et al., 1991)
21 (Ehrenthal & Stölze, 2013)
22 (Jindal et al., 2007)
23 (Kumar, 2008)
24 (Krentzel, 2008)
25 (McDonald, 2005)
26 (Krentzel, 2019b) and (Brown et al., 2017)
27 (Krentzel, 2018b)
28 (Krentzel, 2019b)
29 (Krentzel, 2019b)
30 (Krentzel, 2019b)
31 (Krentzel, 2019b)
32 (Krentzel, 2019b)
33 (Krentzel, 2019b)
34 (Cunningham, 2013) and (Noor & Ahmmed, 2013)
35 (Deloitte, 2017)
36 (Kenny, 2018)
37 (AltusHost, 2016)
38 (WAAM, 2019)
39 (Dewsnap & Jobber, 2009)
40 (Desforges & Anthony, 2013)
41 (Swieringa & Wierdsma, 1992)
42 (Argyris & Schön, 1974), (Argyris, 1977) and (Argyris & Schön, 1978)
43 (Nielsen, 1993)

5 Connecting the route to purchase with the route to market

The objective of activating shoppers at the point of purchase is to convert them into buyers. To activate the point of purchase, its role to the shopper in the shopping process needs to be understood. The role of the point of purchase is the result of the shopping missions and consumption need states it satisfies. Additionally, the different zones within the point of purchase fulfill different roles. Activation strategies need to be developed by clusters and zones of points of purchase.

Different activation strategies need to be developed for the different sales channels. In traditional channels activation programs are based on the picture of success by point of purchase cluster and zone, as well as point of purchase development and loyalty programs. In modern trade, category management programs are designed as part of the efficient consumer response (ECR) process. By incorporating consumption need states, shopper journeys, retailer strategies and a more accentuated commitment to the collaboration between manufacturer and retailer, these programs are gradually becoming more shopper marketing oriented. In digital channels and e-commerce, the activation is a more interactive dialogue of personalized and contextual messages, with the possibility of focusing more on consumption need states beyond the confines of physical in-store product presentation. There is a strong analytical and interactive component to the activation, which includes search engine optimization (SEO), content management, banners, shopper engagement and, increasingly, social platforms, like Facebook, Instagram and Twitter. Algorithm-based tools, like Google Ads, are used to match publishers and advertisers. In cooperation with online retailers, the category management approach needs to be adapted, like the e-commerce category leadership (ECL) framework.

A new competitive space centered around hyper-convenience is emerging. Manufacturers are entering into direct to consumer (D2C) solutions, retailers go online, and online retailers enter the brick-and-mortar world. Activation is becoming more recommendation driven, from search engines, ratings and reviews, to voice ordering, through, for example, Alexa. New technologies allow for checking in to stores instead of checking out, and the brick-and-mortar points of purchase become a seamless part of the shopper journey where the mobile device enables a continuous dialogue. The last yard moves from shopper to supplier responsibility and cost with a variety of new supply chain players, like CEPs (courier, express and parcel), and crowd supplier solutions facilitated by applications. With the tech giants (Google, Amazon, Facebook, Apple) and other new players an entirely new multi-stakeholder ecosystem, beyond the classical triangle of shoppers, manufacturers and retailers, is emerging. Companies will need to develop into ecosystem orchestrators in this new emerging shopper marketing reality.

Role of the point of purchase

Points of purchase have different roles for the shopper in their shopping trip. At the same time, they are one of the touchpoints during the shopper journey, as in the case of showrooming and webrooming. The starting point for any shopping trip is the consumption need state and the generated motivation to solve the need. The shopper embarks on his shopper journey, resulting in a purchase and point of purchase selection in line with his shopping mission. For the same category, but different consumption need states, both the shopper journey and the point of purchase can differ. Therefore, different activation approaches are needed for a similar product and service. The classic example is soft drinks to be consumed at home with the family compared to immediate consumption in a restaurant. The specific situation under which the purchase process is done will define the shopper needs and expectations, and thus the most fitting activation approach. Depending on the consumption occasion, the consumer and shopper will look for different solutions.[1] The importance of the occasion and the related attributes and motivations in selecting consumption solutions in terms of offer and place and their implications on the activation is the basis for occasion-based marketing.[2] Depending on the occasion, the shopper looks for specific attributes of the point of purchase that best satisfy that specific occasion.[3] Therefore, there is a clear association between type of point of purchase and different categories. Depending on the category, the consumption occasion, and the purchase situation, different channels and points of purchase are preferred by the shopper. As a result, the shopper is multichannel in his behavior.[4] Additionally, sociodemographic characteristics of the shopper are related to the choice of channel and point of purchase.[5] Points of purchase usually focus on specific audiences. Segmenting shoppers through the channels and points of purchase can be powerful, as it can explain shoppers' buying behavior and motivations related to the predominant occasion of the point of purchase.[6] Segmentations based on occasions give good insights into usage, motivations and purchase behavior, which are relevant dimensions to develop shopper marketing strategies.[7] The shopping mission, both offline and online, has a strong influence on the attributes or characteristics of the point of purchase preferred by the shopper.[8] This also explains the survival of traditional channels, e.g. in Latin America, as they meet the specific needs of the local shopper.[9]

Each type of point of purchase fulfills a role that helps the shopper to satisfy his or her needs depending on his or her purchase situation. The clarity of the role of the point of purchase is defined by its ability to satisfy the needs of the shopper in terms of offering solutions in line with the specific purchase situation. The purchase situation can be referred to as the shopping mission of the shopper, i.e. why the shopper embarks on the shopping trip. The type of shopping mission defines the type of point of purchase the shopper will prefer. The point of purchase is described by its attributes and characteristics, i.e. the service it can provide to the shopper. Type of channel already gives a first indication of the role of the point of purchase. Immediate consumption channels have a clear role to satisfy the consumption needs directly, while channels for later consumption are for later intended consumption. Bigger stores with a vast offering are more frequently used for stocking up, while small convenience stores are normally used for urgent and cravings shopping trips. The shopping missions the point of purchase serves defines its role, and depending on the role, the point of purchase will have specific attributes and characteristics that are related to the shopping missions. Due to the specific service it can provide to support the shopping missions of the shopper traditional channels still have an important role in many countries. More than just proximity, they can provide a more personalized services by knowing their customers and

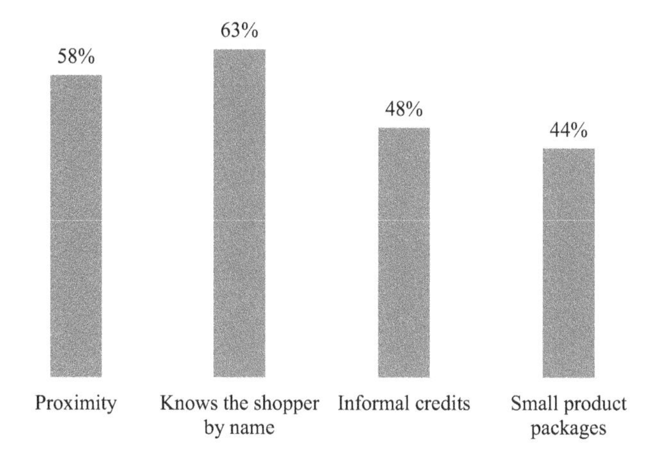

Figure 5.1 Service provided by the traditional channel
Service offering of the traditional channel in South America in comparison with modern retail.
Source: Booz Allen Hamilton, 2003; Author

provide informal credit, smaller packages and store-keeping units (SKUs) aligned with the economic reality of its clientele.

Modern, or organized retail, has developed different formats to meet the different purchasing needs, the shopping missions, of shoppers. Different formats range from convenience stores, mini-markets, supermarkets, hypermarkets, shopping clubs, wholesalers, department stores, etc. Additionally, there is internet retailing. The distinction between channel and sub-channel allows a finer differentiation to understand the roles of points of purchase. For example, for a manufacturer like Coca-Cola, the focus in hypermarkets could be on larger packages for family consumption occasions. In convenience channels it could be medium or smaller refrigerated packages for almost immediate consumption. In a restaurant a nice bottle or glasses to communicate the brand image would be more fitting. In a fitness center or in a waiting room there could be a vending machine. Depending on the role of the point of purchase, the manufacturer needs to design a shopper activation strategy in line with the role including type of product, services, material, equipment and communication. Additionally, specific activations need to be integrated into the strategy, e.g. promotions, products and service launches, events, tastings, etc.

Each sales channel and sub-channel meets a mix of different shopping missions.

Depending on the shopping mission the different zones in the store will have different roles to fulfill. A store therefore needs to be analyzed by zones of shopping, where they have different roles with different activation approaches.

The activation of the store needs to be adapted by zone in terms of products and services, materials, equipment, communication, promotions, events, etc.

The importance of different shopping missions differs by countries, emphasizing the point that relevant shopper marketing strategies are local.

Sales channels give an indication of the role of the point of purchase, but still there are differences within channels. As an example, the traditional channel includes many different sub-channels with different mixes of shopping missions and thereby roles to the shopper.

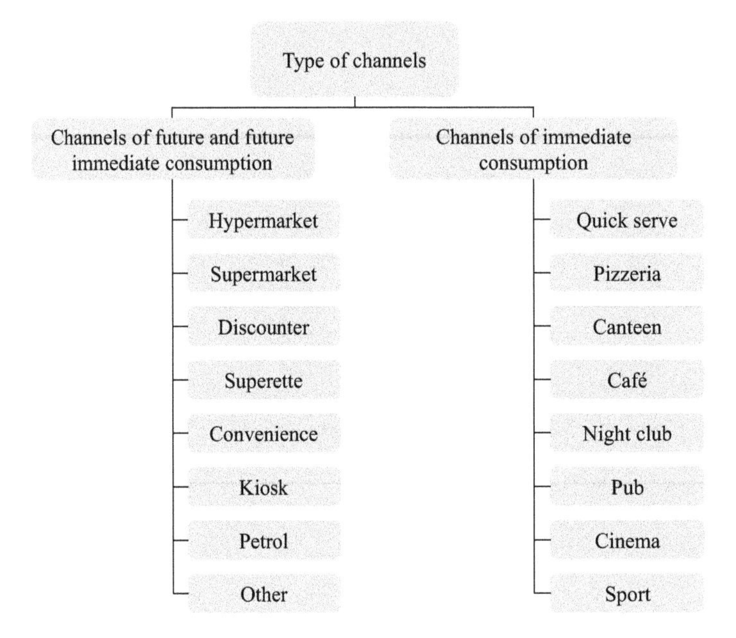

Figure 5.2 Sales channel segmentation
Example of sub-channels for immediate and future consumption in Scandinavia.
Source: Author

Allocating roles to points of purchase based on channels, and even sub-channels, can be too general for detailed shopper marketing strategies to optimize the potential for growth. Points of purchase across sales channels can have different roles within the same sub-channel. Activation strategies should be focused therefore more on the role, and the zones, than just on sales channels.

Shopping missions are not directly identifiable. They are deducted from the real or intended behavior of shoppers. To categorize the points of purchase of a market, shoppers' behavior needs to be analyzed to allocate the corresponding role. The characteristics of points of purchase need to match the types of shopping mission they serve. The shopping missions need to be operationalized through the attributes the shopper seeks to fulfill by specific shopping missions. By relating the point of purchase characteristics with the shopping missions, the role can be deducted and the adequate activation strategies designed. The categorization of points of purchase is then based on associating points of purchase characteristics with a specific mix of shopping missions.

Depending on the role of the point of purchase, the focus of product and service activation is different. For the points of purchase, the different categories and their brands play a specific role to attract shoppers. In addition, the way of activating the different stores according to their role differs. To fulfill its role, the point of purchase has to define its offering mix and the role of the different categories, brands, products and services. For retail, it is key to have coherency between the strategy, the objectives and the value proposition at the point of purchase. H&M, the Swedish clothing retailer, has defined specific formats and value propositions to meet different consumption need states and shopper expectations.

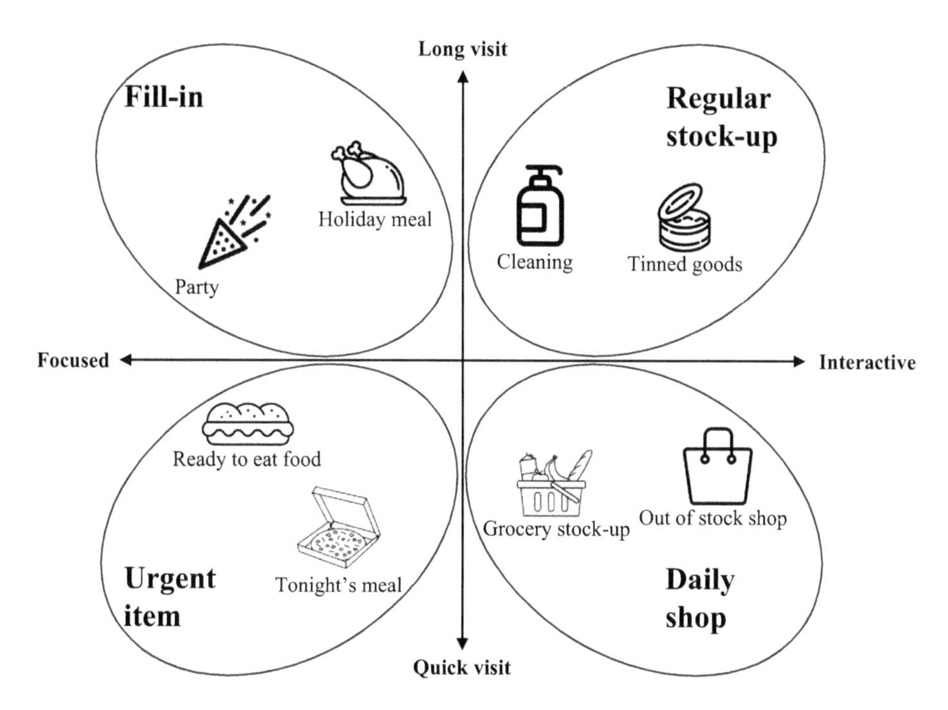

Figure 5.3 Shopping missions in hypermarkets and supermarkets
Example from Spain of key shopping missions categorized by length of visit and type of planning (focused on one category/product or interactive during shopping trip).
Source: Shoppermotion, 2019[10]

Buying behavior at the point of purchase is related to its role, but also to the attitudes, such as planning, and the shopping experience the shopper is seeking.[11] Together with the brand strategy the channel and the route to market strategies can be developed. This can be exemplified through the watch category and the two brands Rolex and Timex. Rolex has a high-status image. It is very expensive, of Swiss origin and usually the shoppers come from a high socioeconomic group or aspire to get there. Timex is a watch brand of American origin, of relatively high quality, and often with relatively advanced electronic functions at a more economical price. It is a watch more associated with functionality than with status. Although they belong to the same category, the target and the needs they fulfill are different and require different route to market strategies. Rolex watches are normally found in specialty stores with a high level of service, along with other high image categories, such as jewelry. Normally only stores selected by Rolex sell the brand. It is a strategy of selective distribution in line with the brand strategy. Timex watches can be bought in several channels. Classically, the most important channel used to be gas stations. To buy a Timex watch, the shopper does not have to look for a specialized or high-service-level point or purchase. Timex watches come packaged at a moderate price and do not need to be presented to the shopper by a salesperson.

To select the most suitable channels and points of purchase the implications of the brand, product and service strategy on channel and point of purchase attributes and characteristics

Pharmacy
Dairy
Fresh Meat & Seafood
Produce
Produce
Produce
Toiletries
Toiletries
22%
15%
28%
35%
Produce
Produce
Produce
10%
35%
30%
25%
Grocery Store
Floral
Baking Needs
Canned Foods
Snack Foods
Frozen Foods
Frozen Foods
Paper & Cleaning Supplies
Beverages
Wine & Spirits
32%
18%
21%
29%
Salad Bar
Magazines
Photo Kiosk
Bakery
Deli
Fill in
Regular stock-up
Urgent item
Daily shop

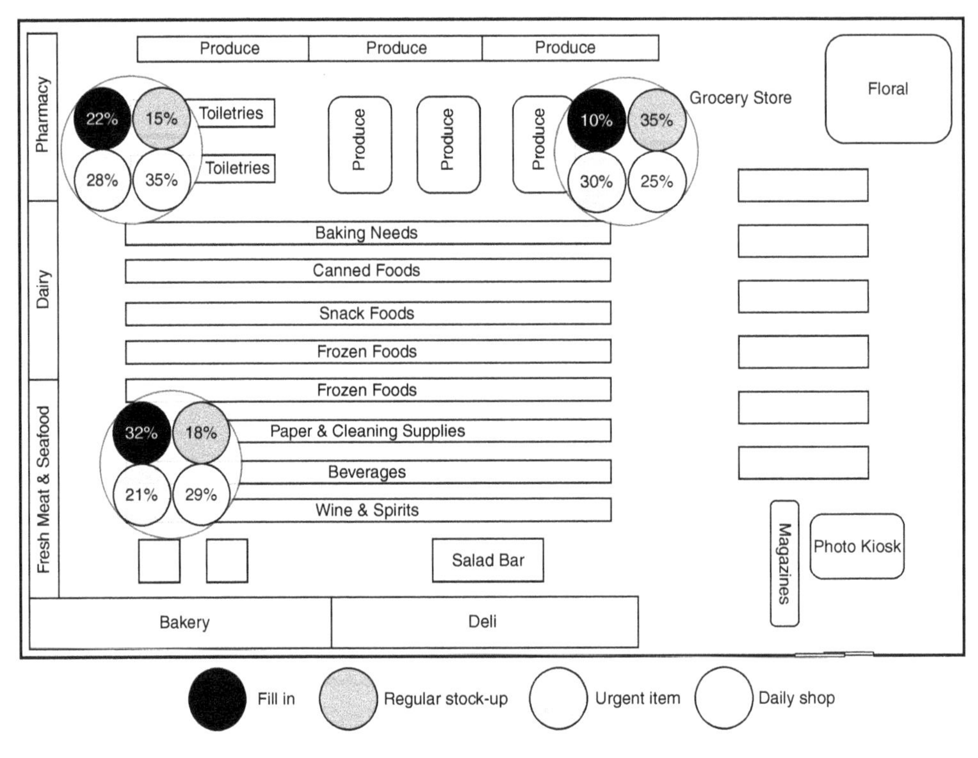

Figure 5.4 Importance of shopping missions by store zone
Example from Spain of key shopping missions and their importance by in-store zone.
Source: Shoppermotion, 2019

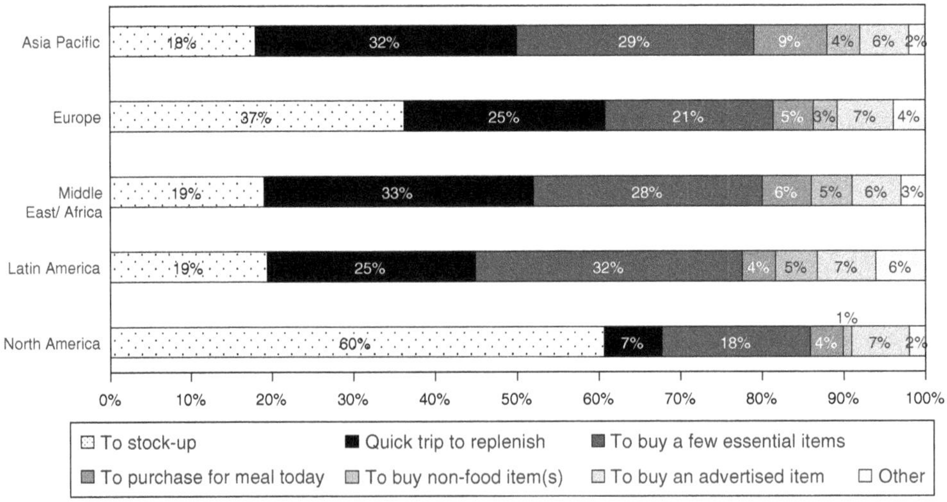

Asia Pacific
18%
32%
29%
9%
4%
6%
2%
Europe
37%
25%
21%
5%
3%
7%
4%
Middle East/ Africa
19%
33%
28%
6%
5%
6%
3%
Latin America
19%
25%
32%
4%
5%
7%
6%
North America
60%
7%
18%
4%
1%
7%
2%
0%
10%
20%
30%
40%
50%
60%
70%
80%
90%
100%
To stock-up
Quick trip to replenish
To buy a few essential items
To purchase for meal today
To buy non-food item(s)
To buy an advertised item
Other

Figure 5.5 Importance of shopping missions on different continents
Importance of key shopping missions across continents.
Source: Nielsen, Q1 2011

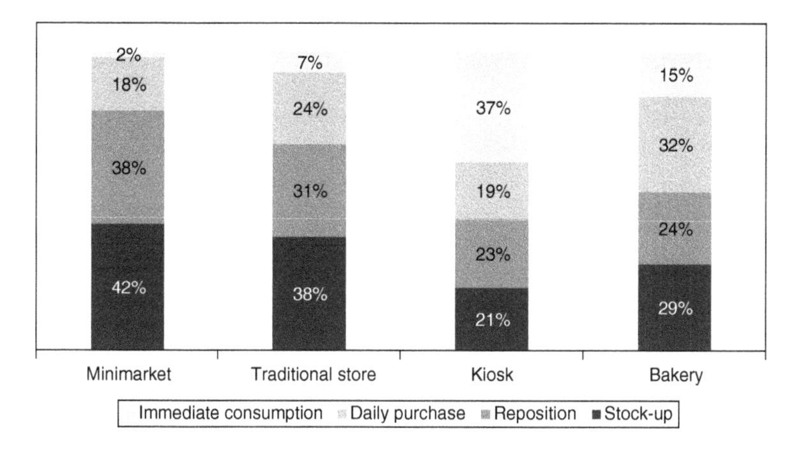

Figure 5.6 Importance of shopping missions in different sub-channels of the traditional channel
Example of mix of shopping missions for different sub-channels of the traditional channel in South America.
Source: Author

Figure 5.7 Mix of shopping missions by point of purchase cluster across channels
Example of points of purchase clustered by shopping mission mix across channels.
Source: Author

need to be analyzed. Eight criteria can be used to profile channels and points of purchase in relation to brand, product and service strategies.

The first criterion is the type of consumption. This is normally very important for categories, such as groceries and beverages. It describes the place of consumption, whether it will take place immediately at the point of purchase, or if the purchase is planned for later consumption and usage.

Secondly, the level of specialization and therefore the expertise and category focus is an important criteria, especially in more complex categories, or where the shopper is less knowledgeable.

		Cluster 1	Cluster 2	Cluster 3
Missions	Stock-up and reposition	95%	39%	31%
	Daily purchase	3%	46%	12%
	Immediate consumption	2%	15%	57%
Offer	Bulk sales	13%	62%	22%
	Fresh produce	28%	43%	--
	Bakery	2%	42%	26%
Characteristics	Aisles	2-3	1	Cashier
	Residential area	79%	58%	9%
	High traffic area	21%	42%	91%

Figure 5.8 Characteristics of clusters of points of purchase
Example of point of purchase clusters based on mix of shopping missions and their association with the offer and specific point of purchase characteristics.
Source: Author

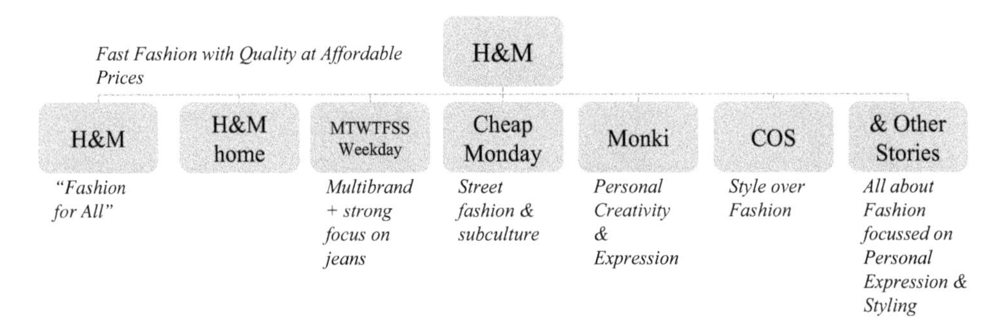

Figure 5.9 H&M retail formats
Retail formats of H&M (Hennes and Mauritz) with different value proposals. The different formats are also presented in different zones within the same shop.
Source: H&M, 2014

Thirdly, related to the previous point, is the level of service, which varies from self-service to high-service levels. For a dinner and romantic encounter, a self-service restaurant would perhaps not be the obvious choice. The fourth criterion, the price level, is normally associated with the level of service and level of product quality.

The fifth criterion, convenience, describes the urgency of the purchase, as well as the time and effort the shopper is ready to invest to purchase a product and service. For example, is the consumption need state a coffee on the go or preparing coffee at home for breakfast? Is

Figure 5.10 Route to market strategies for watches
Comparison of route to market strategies for Rolex, Swatch and Timex.
Source: Author

the shopper ready to go to a shop, even a specific shop, or is it important to have the goods immediately or even delivered?

The sixth criterion describes the possibility of experiencing the product and service live, and possibly test it. Is it a direct sales channel, like brick and mortar, indirect like digital, telephone sales, or a mail service sales channel, where the product and service cannot be experienced beforehand? Many products and services are not possible to experience, but can be sold through direct personal interaction, like travel, telephone and internet contracts, banking etc. These are also products and services where the internet as a sales channel has been quite successful. On the other hand, it would be difficult to enjoy a meal in a pub through the internet, although the shopper journey could have started digitally, through browsing possible locations and reviews, and making an online reservation.

The seventh criterion touches the important point of the level of exclusivity of the channel and point of purchase. Does it only sell products and services of a specific category, or even a specific supplier? Although H&M stores could be perfect for other clothing manufacturers, they are not allowed to sell through that channel. The choice is then either to open their own stores, or to use other multi-brand clothing stores.

The eighth and last criterion is the consolidation of the channel. Retail chains with their specific strategies have a stronger negotiating power and can influence how brands, products and services are presented and activated. With retail chains, a key account management approach is normally needed, and often collaborative models like ECR are applied.

The view of the shopper is crucial, and with omnichannel, different sales channels can be an appropriate point of purchase. The shoppers of today use multiple channels, both as complements and substitutes in an omnichannel way.[12] Shoppers re-evaluate the points of purchase, their role and the way they meet their needs and they are sometimes willing to switch between channels, points of purchase or formats if it suits their needs better.[13] With the evaluation of the channels from a brand and company strategy perspective the appropriate route to market strategy can be developed. Shopper and channel strategies have to be coherent across channels, based on their role and image.[14]

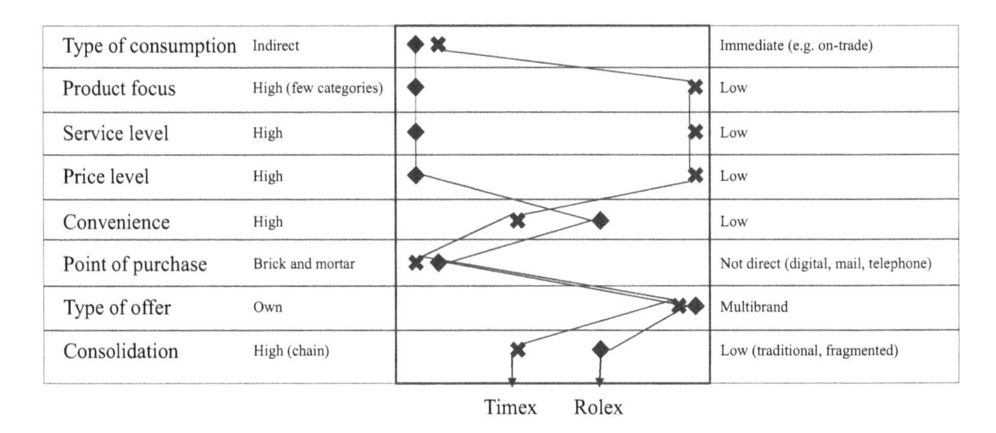

Figure 5.11 Channel categorization scheme
Categorization and comparison of channel selection criteria with Timex and Rolex as examples, using different dimensions to profile the preferred sales channels.
Source: Author

The objective of managing sales channels and the point of purchase is a shopper activation to convert shoppers into buyers. Simplified, consumption need states define what to activate and shopping missions define how to activate, all in coherency with the touchpoints along the shopper journey. Aligned with the strategic and commercial priorities of the manufacturer the route to purchase and route to market strategies can be designed. The point of purchase is the place, either brick and mortar, by distance, e.g. by telephone, or digitally, where the shopper encounters brands, products and services. Next to availability, activation is key to convert the shopper into a buyer and generate sales, by satisfying the purchase and consumption need states. The point of purchase is the point of linkage between the route to purchase and the route to market, and the activation ensures the final shopper conversion.

Activation of the shopper at the point of purchase

From picture of success to activation programs

In traditional and fragmented channels, including on-trade and immediate consumption channels that do not belong to chains, the point of purchase activation is normally done based on a picture of success. With the picture of success as a template the brand, product and service can be activated in line with shopper marketing guidelines. The picture of success template has to be developed by type of point of purchase.

Sales channels and points of purchase differ by market and activation guidelines need to be locally adapted.

The key difference between the picture of success and category management is the collaborative aspect. In category management the output is the result of a collaboration between retailer and manufacturer, normally with a third party to ensure the objectivity of the analysis. Traditional and fragmented sales channels do not have a centralized negotiation position, nor negotiating power. The development of the picture of success is the responsibility of the manufacturer, and the implementation is often done through a sales force, or through

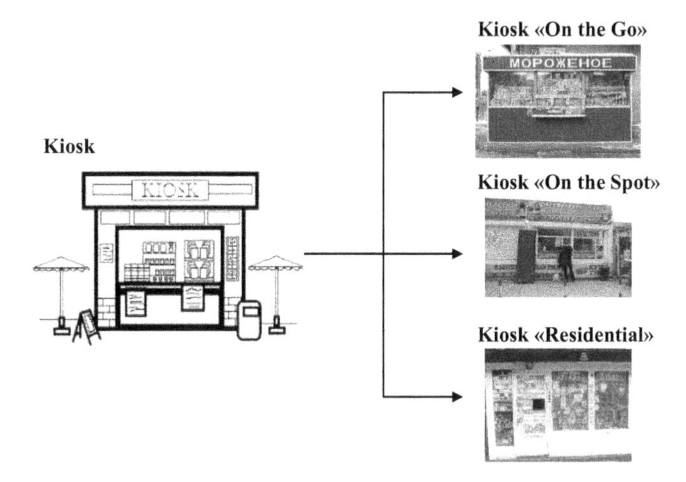

Figure 5.12 Types of kiosk
Example of an Eastern Europe kiosk sales channel with points of purchase with different roles.
Source: Author

instructing those at the point of purchase. The more important the manufacturer and his brands, products and services, the more possibilities there are to impose the picture of success over other suppliers. Many manufacturers also design pictures of success for the modern retail channel as a guidance for the sales force. Depending on the level of freedom of local points of purchase within the retail chain, more or less parts of the picture of success can be implemented by the manufacturer's sales force. The picture of success is normally adjusted to the category management and planogram guidelines for each retailer in these cases.

The building blocks of the picture of success are centered around the type of offer in terms of product, package, price and promotion, and the activation at the point of purchase in terms of equipment, place, presentation and the prescription (i.e. recommendation). As a basis, the target consumption need states and the mix of shopping missions have to be understood. The basic offer is more associated with the consumption need state, and the detailed offering, e.g. formats and packages, and activation of the point of purchase, with the shopping mission.

Regardless of the optimum activation of each segment of the point of purchase in line with the consumption need states and shopping missions, the level of investment needs to be considered. Some points of purchase are more attractive than others in terms of sales and sales increase potential. The investment in picture of success implementation in the chosen route to market strategy and resources needs to be gauged against the sales potential to optimize the investment.

Activating a point of purchase is more than just the picture of success. It includes programs to develop the point of purchase and its staff, as well as to build loyalty and preference toward the supplier. In addition, the salespeople at the point of purchase play an important role in building preference for brands, products and services through recommendation. The picture of success and activation program also need to be adapted over time, depending on changes in shopper behavior or due to specific seasonal events.

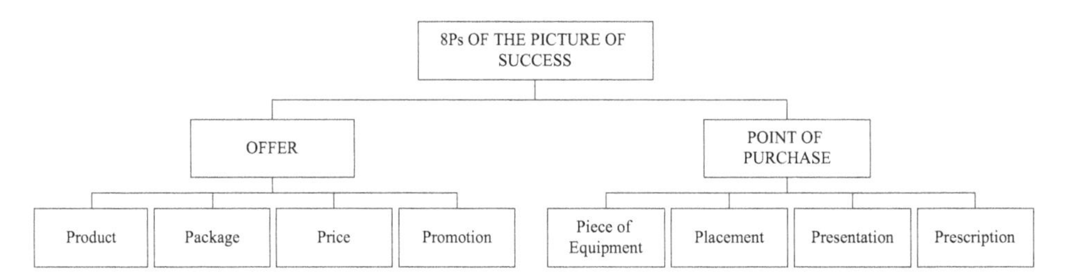

Figure 5.13 8Ps of the picture of success
Example of the main dimensions (8 Ps) when defining the picture of success in traditional channels.
Source: Author

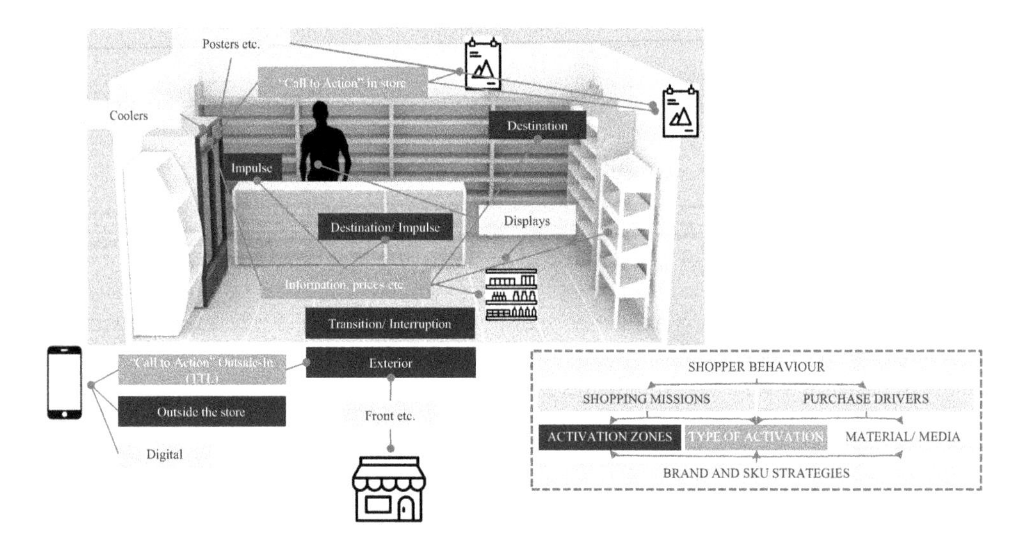

Figure 5.14 Structure of a picture of success
Structure of a picture of success for the traditional channel. Shopper behavior is driven by the shopping missions and the consumption need states, which influence the zones and the type of activation, as well as the material and media to be used, which again are driven by the strategy of the brand, product and service.
Source: Author[15]

The aim of the activation program is to optimize the profitability by point of purchase by optimizing the investment in relation to the potential value.

A big challenge in managing the picture of success is the implementation, not only the negotiation with the point of purchase, but the implementation itself to put the products and services and material in place, especially when other manufacturers are competing for the same space. Unlike the situation in modern retail, there is normally no manufacturer appointed as category captain to lead the development of the category at the point of purchase level. All manufacturers, depending on their importance to and relationship with the individual point of purchase owners, can influence the presentation and activation of their

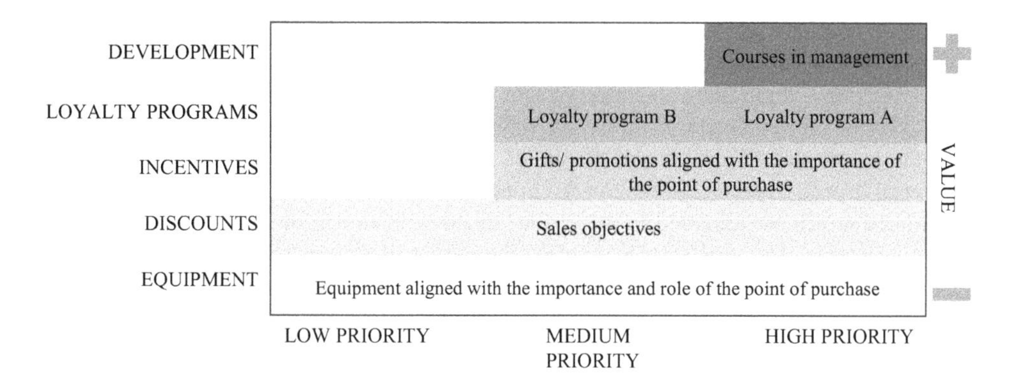

Figure 5.15 Investment in activation programs depending on point of purchase priority and value
Level and type of investment at the point of purchase depending on their priority and value.
Source: Author

brands. In addition, the focus of the owner of the point of purchase is not a specific brand, product and service, but the total performance and the optimum use of space. The different brands, products and services are merely there to support that objective. The challenge is thus to align with the interests of the point of purchase and gain the preferential position to implement the picture of success. An important decision is who will be responsible for the implementation and the management of the picture of success. It is associated with investment, either the manufacturer's as it has to invest in resources, its own or outsourced, or time and effort of the owner or the salesperson at the point of purchase. There are digital solutions, where the points of purchase can receive information on how to activate the store, including collaborative programs, where the point of purchase can send images of the implementation of the picture of success to control the implementation. Depending on the performance, there can be compensation from the manufacturer if the presentation is in line with certain standards.

Monitoring the implementation of the picture of success can be complicated due to two reasons. First, what to measure, i.e. which are the key parameters that would define a successful implementation of the picture of success? Secondly, how to measure it, as it is often difficult to have access to the relevant data at the right moment. A monitoring system needs to be simple, easy to execute and cost efficient. The objective of the picture of success is to enhance the conversion of the shopper into a buyer. The assumption is that a well-presented picture of success will facilitate this. The picture of success is thus a mediator between shopping and buying. Still, there are many other important factors involved that influence the decision of the shopper, e.g. price, promotions or competitor activities. Information is scarce in traditional and fragmented channels and normally not shared. A manufacturer might know his own sales at the point of purchase, but if the sales are through third parties or through several suppliers, the sellout of the point of purchase is not equal to the sell-in by the manufacturer. There are often unreported, unofficial sales in the traditional sales channels that makes it even more difficult to receive the correct information. One possible way to evaluate the implementation of the picture of success is through indirect monitoring systems, where the basic assumption is that a well-presented picture of success will have a positive impact on shopper conversion and sales. Such systems are sometimes referred to as merchandising scores. Merchandising is the name of the management of products and services, and associated material and equipment at the point of purchase. Merchandising scores convert the picture of success into key rules for the presentation at the point of purchase and specific scores are associated with these rules depending on the level of implementation. Rules can refer to the right portfolio of products and services, the number of SKUs presented, the location and position on shelves, the presence of material and equipment, as well as the presentation in comparison to the competition. Compliance scores are assigned to these rules to assess the level of implementation of the picture of success. The challenge is not only the design of a merchandising score, but also its implementation and cost. The coverage, i.e. number of points of purchase served out of the relevant universe, and the frequency of monitoring need to be defined in the most cost-efficient manner. Finally, it needs to be defined how to use such scores to be able to improve the implementation of the picture of success, e.g. should it be linked to the compensation system of the sales force or of the point of purchase, or should it be used for specific actions to improve activation?

From category management to shopper management

The classic category management approach starts with the definition of the category. Categories are products that meet similar needs, and that are interrelated or substitutable. They should also be able to be placed and activated together at the point of purchase.[16]

Within modern and organized retail, category management approaches are used to collaborate to optimize the activation from the perspective of the shopper and in line with retailer and manufacturer strategies. The challenge of brand owners in modern sales channels is that they do not control the activation, and so this needs to be based on the agreement with the retailer. Retailers engaging in category management approaches normally appoint a category captain, often one of the leading manufacturers, to optimize the presentation of the category at the retailer. The category captain needs to be objective in terms of brands, with the assumption that growing the category in volume and/or value will benefit all brands, as well as the retailer. There are inherently several conflicts to the approach. The retailer's focus is the shopper and the value of the shopping basket, whereas the manufacturer's focus is the consumer and the brand. There is also a risk that category management with one of the brand leaders as category captain will cement the status quo and complicate the situation for smaller brands.

Category management was introduced in the 1980s as a collaboration between retailers and manufacturers. Organizations within the ECR framework were founded to help in the methodological development to enhance the collaboration between retailers and manufacturers.[17]

The concept of category management emerged out of the total quality movement, first developed in Japan and then adopted by companies such as Hewlett Packard and P&G in the 1980s. As the output of companies is compiled of multiple processes, and even if every process is optimized, the final total output can be sub-optimum.[18]

In the early 1990s, the consumer-packed goods (CPG) industry formed the Efficient Consumer Response Committee to address the many collaborative problems and conflicts between retailers and manufacturers. The committee, composed of major stakeholders in manufacturing, retailing and distribution, agreed on a common denominator for industry

RED	Parameter	Grocery			E & D			Conv.		
		D	G	S	D	G	S	D	G	S
Visicooler	1. Is a coca cola cooler present									
	2. Is the cooler as per standard	4	4	4	4	4	4	4	4	4
	3. Is the cooler in prime location	10	10	10	10	10	10	10	10	10
	4. Is the visicooler in a working condition	3	3	3	3	3	3	3	3	3
	5. Is the visicooler light working	2	2	2	2	2	2	2	2	2
	6. Is the cooler 100% pure	10	10	10	10	10	10	10	10	10
	7. Is the cooler brand order compliant	6	6	6	6	6	6	6	6	6
	Total	**35**	**35**	**35**	**35**	**35**	**35**	**35**	**35**	**35**
Availability	1. Can				4			4		
	2. RGB - CSD			12	22	25	25	14	18	18
	3. RGB - Maaza			4	8	10	10	4	4	4
	4. Mobile - CSD	16	16	10	6	5	5	13	13	14
	5. Mobile - Maaza	4	4	4				3	3	4
	6. Large PET - CSD	16	16	10						
	7. Large PET - Maaza	4	4							
	8. TP - Maaza							2	2	
	Total	**40**	**40**	**40**	**40**	**40**	**40**	**40**	**40**	**40**
Activation	1. Warm display rack	10	10	8				10	10	10
	2. Is the rack pure and changed	10	10	7						
	3. Shelf display	5	5	5						
	4. Crate display with wrap			5			5			5
	5. Flange/ Standee/ GSB/ DPS board/ Flex board				5	5	5	10	10	10
	6. Aerial mobile hanger							5	5	
	7. Menu board/ Menu card						15			
	8. Combo communication				15	15				
	9. Branded table mat/ table vinyl				5	5				
	Total	**25**	**25**	**25**	**25**	**25**	**25**	**25**	**25**	**25**

Figure 5.16 Coca-Cola merchandising score system
Example of Coca Cola RED (right execution daily) scoring sheet in India. Dimensions considered are coolers, the availability of the right portfolio and the activation of the store. A sample of stores are normally evaluated with a maximum of 100 points to be distributed. In this case, 40 for coolers, 25 for availability, and 35 for activation, distributed differently by different channels.

Note: E&D: Eating and Drinking channel; Conv: Convenience channel; D: Diamond outlets; G: Gold outlets; S: Silver outlets; RGB: Return Glass Bottle; CSD: Carbonated Soft Drinks; TP: Tetra Pack; GSB: Glow Sign Board; DPS board: Dealer Printed Sign board.

Source: Author

collaboration: the category. Both shoppers and retailers focused on categories rather than brands when planning their purchase or offering. As a result, the category became the dimension around which the CPG ecosystem would operate.[19]

Category management was implemented with a rigorous eight-step process with specific inputs, outputs and metrics at each step. Although the information and data used in category management have increased dramatically and the software tools used to manipulate the data have improved in the last two decades, the basic steps have mainly stayed the same. The category management approach enjoys a high level of adoption by the industry and the success is due to five fundamental changes in the way companies collaborate and analyze the market:

1. Changes in the culture of collaboration between retailers and manufacturers: A process does not simply change years of adversarial relationships between business partners that have been rewarded for taking advantage of the person at the other side of the table. Both retailers and manufacturers have had to start relying on each other and agree on objective data to be used in analyzing the situation. Category management has succeeded by moving the conversation between retailer and manufacturer from arguing about who receives the lion's share of a fixed amount to how to enlarge the amount to share. Category management suggests that both business partners can benefit by meeting the needs of shoppers. The most important achievement of category management has been to exchange relevant data and to build trust between partners.
2. Focus on the shopper: Focusing the collaboration on the common shopper and how to satisfy his or her needs has directed the discussion toward a common goal, away from the focus on conflicting objectives of the retailer and the manufacturer.
3. Development of new skills: Category management is data rich and analysis focused. With category management the sales and buying process has moved from focusing on pure negotiation skills to include analytical skills.
4. Creation of a fact-based environment: The availability of new data and analytical tools has changed the discussion. With objective data, negotiations can center around facts rather than being based on anecdotal assumptions. The credibility of category management lies in its fact-based approach, which has led to its acceptance within the CPG ecosystem.
5. Increased profitability through a reduction in choice-related costs: Category management has increased margins, especially, but not exclusively, the retailers' margins by reducing the proliferation of choice within categories. The benefits of reducing choice has been described in an ECR paper on Efficient Item Assortment that introduced the concept of "transferable demand" of SKUs with similar attributes. The report showed the relatively low risk of eliminating SKUs with similar attributes to other SKUs.[20] Early studies conducted by ECR organizations showed that 20 percent of SKUs could be eliminated, while still increasing sales of the category, primarily by eliminating low-performing brands and giving space to better-performing brands. Reducing the range increases the cost efficiency at every step along the supply chain of manufacturers and retailers.[21] In addition, a reduced range reduces the shelf space for many categories, allowing retailers to introduce new categories and new products and services within the restrictions of the store's selling space.

The adoption of ECR practices has been especially successful in the area of the supply chain, where there have been fewer conflicts of interest compared to the commercial area of category management.[22]

The optimal presentation of the optimal category portfolio includes aspects such as location, presentation and layout of shelves and different activations, e.g. promotions. In the presentation and layout, the portfolio in terms of brands, products and services is defined, as well as their location, their space allocation and price levels by SKU. The basis is the decision tree, which is the schematic representation of the shopper's decision process. The idea is that the presentation of brands, products and services should represent the decision process of the shopper to facilitate choice and decision making. The decision tree is then

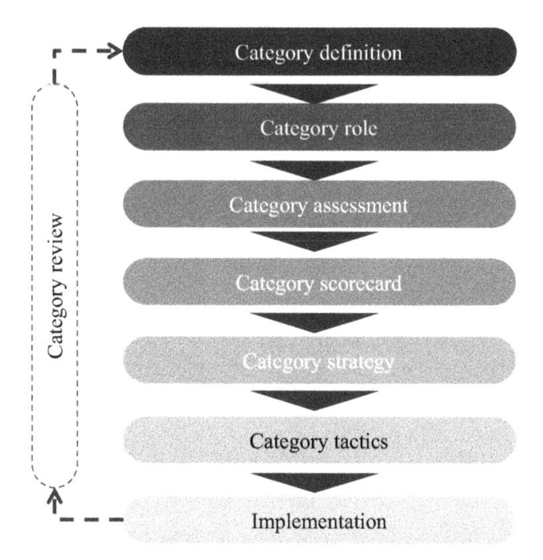

Figure 5.17 The eight steps of category management
The classic category management steps.
Source: ECR Europe & The Partnering Group, 1998

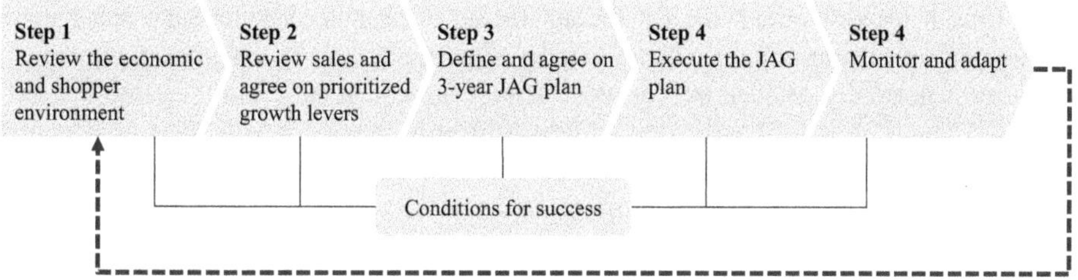

Figure 5.18 The JAG process
Framework of the JAG process.
Source: ECR, 2009

detailed into a planogram that is the detailed map of the presentation of the category on the shelf.

There are initiatives to make the category management process more strategic through an even better alignment between retailer and manufacturer to increase sales and profitability levels. In one such initiative, jointly agreed growth (JAG), the manufacturer and the retailer agree on common goals with clear action programs supported by the necessary resources to ensure implementation in line with the commitment.

In contrast to category management the starting point in shopper marketing is the consumption need state. The consumption need state not only defines direct interchangeability between products, but focuses on the needs being satisfied. It can therefore include different categories, dependent on the consumption needs, motivations and occasions. Understanding the consumption need states gives valuable insights into the motivations, as well as the

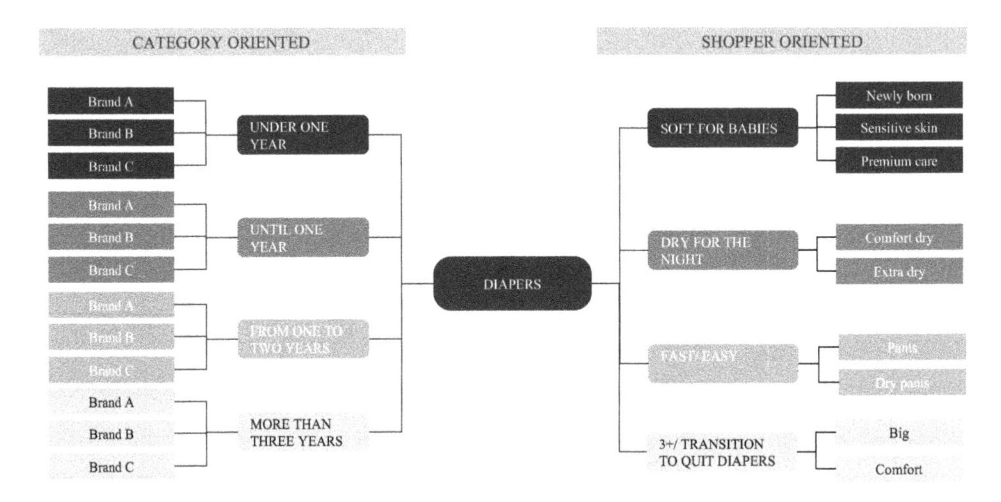

Figure 5.19 Decision tree based on categories vs. based on consumption need states
Example of decision tree for diaper purchase in Scandinavia based on category management and based on shopper management.
Source: Author

complementary categories and services defining the same consumption need states. At the same time it provides the basis for the activation of brands, products and services within each specific consumption need state. In a decision tree driven by category management, the category is normally divided into product-driven sub-categories, and then into the different brands. From a shopper-based view, this would only make sense if the brand perception equals the solution. In a shopper-based decision tree, the decision points are the usage, the occasion, and then which brands, products and services are part of the optimum solution to the shopper.

For a correct representation of the needs and purchase process of shoppers the classical category management approach has some disadvantages, and a shopper-oriented approach better represents the real shopper behavior.[23]

The classic category management does not explicitly take into consideration the strategy of the retailer or even the different strategies by format. The role of a category and the role of the retailer differ by type of retailer, format and even type of point of purchase. In addition, the shopper journey and the coherency of activation from before to the point of purchase is not considered. The success of category management approaches is dependent on the agreement and commitment between retailers and manufacturers, as proposed in the JAG approach.[24] To build a successful approach focused on the shopper the classical category management model should be complemented to incorporate the shopper, the retailer and a clear commitment between retailer and manufacturer.

An example is the presentation of consumption need states of H&M in their stores, as well as in their online presence. The advantage for manufacturers with their own retail outlets is obviously full control of the presentation and activation.

The activation of the point of purchase, especially in the brick-and-mortar environment, includes more dimensions than just the presentation in terms of location, shelf layout, equipment, prices and promotions. Other dimensions include music, olfactory factors and

		Retail	Manufacturer
Missing shopper perspective	**Shopper insights not used**	14%	16%
	Missing shopper perspective	23%	16%
Missing focus on solutions (consumption need states)	**Focus only in categories**	17%	18%
	Barriers between categories	14%	30%
Missing creation experience in line with the retailer strategy	**Missing alignment with retailer strategy**	20%	17%
	Missing creativity of merchandising solutions	13%	4%

Figure 5.20 Need for shopper-oriented category management
Percentage of retailers and manufacturers that see a need for more shopper-centric category management.
Source: Author, based on Deloitte & Winston Weber and Associates, 2015

the way in which the categories are arranged, all of which influence the size and structure of the shopping basket.[25] Poorly presented brands, products and services do not only have a negative impact on shopper conversion, but on the brand image as well.[26]

Digital activation

Digitalization has important implications for shopper marketing. The introduction of RFID (radio frequency identification) technology in the 1980s made it possible to track products and to make the supply chain more efficient, an important ingredient in the evolving ECR collaborations between retailers and suppliers. With the expansion of the internet, online searches and presentation of products and services became possible in the 1990s and 2000s, as well as e-commerce, direct to consumer sales, omnichannel, and brokerage platforms. The next phase is hyper-connectivity through the internet of things (IoT) and artificial intelligence (AI), which will change the mechanics of shopping. Changes will include entire connected shopping ecosystems and moving from checking out to checking in through cashierless technologies, inter-connection between mobile devices and shopping, as presented by Alibaba at its 11.11 shopping events. This development is a clear step from channel focus to consumer and shopper centricity. Instead of marketers determining the when and where through one-way communication with broad messages for all, the consumer and shopper will determine the when and where through a more interactive dialogue of personalized, relevant and contextual messages.

Digital activation increases the opportunities for activating consumption need states beyond just categories, products and services. If it is not a fully planned search or purchase for specific products, shoppers are increasingly looking for solutions and adjacent

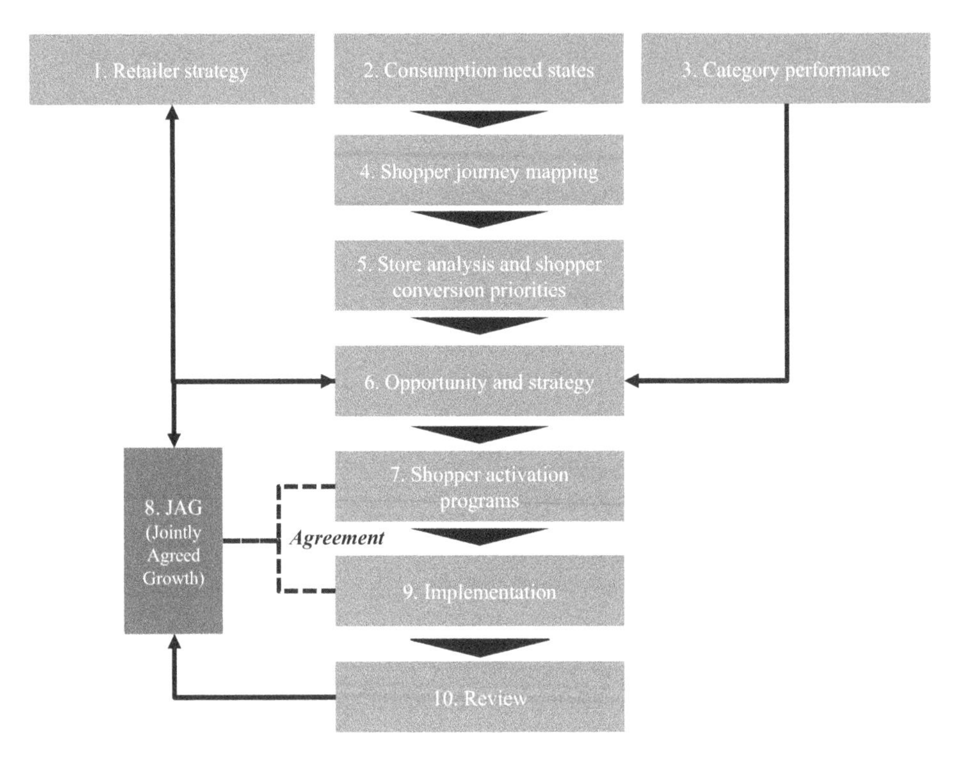

Figure 5.21 Strategic shopper-centric category management model
Steps of a strategic shopper-centric category management model.
Source: Author based on Deloitte & Winston Weber and Associates, 2015; ECR, 2009

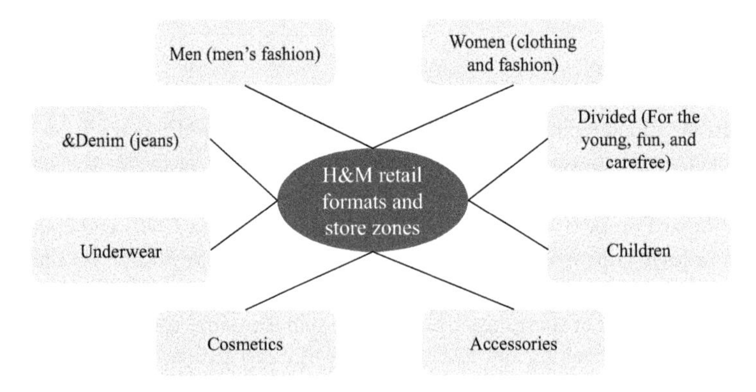

Figure 5.22 Consumption need states activation by H&M
Example of how H&M (Hennes and Mauritz) defines and activates its consumption need states.
Source: H&M, 2014; Author

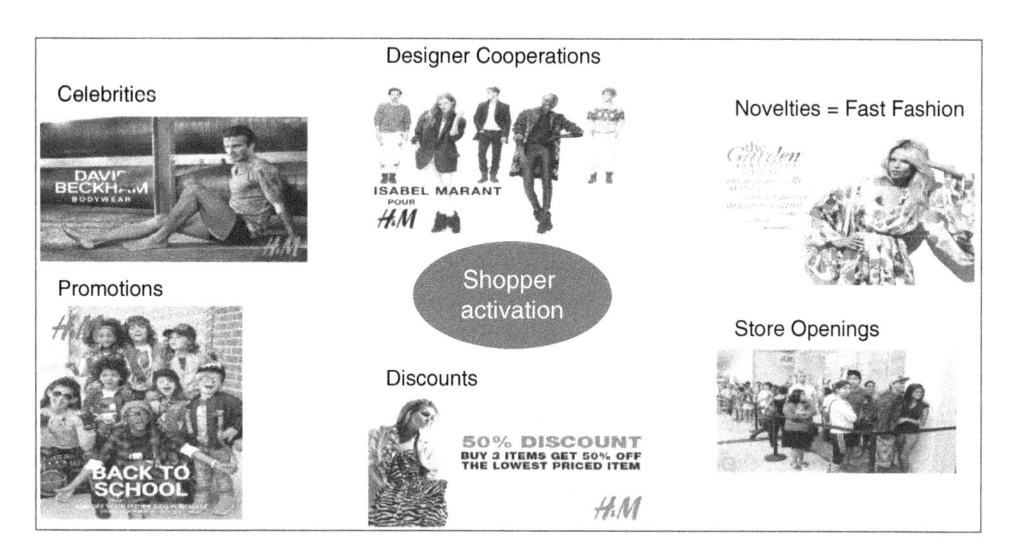

Figure 5.23 Shopper activation by H&M
Example of how H&M (Hennes and Mauritz) activates shoppers in a brand-coherent manner.
Source: H&M, 2014; Author

services. One example is the rise of meal kits for home delivery; full food solutions rather than individual products. Digital gives the freedom to break the shackles of physical category shelving, the limitations of brick-and-mortar stores, and offers the opportunity of a shopper- and consumer-centric organization of products and services. Categories can be organized within broader consumption need states in a digital presentation that allows for multiple searches and combinations, e.g. breakfast, back to school, and not solely one specific, which is often the case in the physical environment of brick and mortar. These consumption need states can span multiple product types, storage requirements and even services. One example is the collaboration with aggregators that can be activated on two levels. Firstly, through partners, e.g. by promoting combined solutions. One example could be beverages with the partners of food aggregators. The other level is a shopper activation directly with the aggregator. One example is the joint promotion of Uber Eats and Coca-Cola of free delivery during Christmas 2018 in France.[27]

The approaches toward digital and e-commerce activation depend on the objectives and the stage of the shopper in the shopper journey, whether it is to attract new shoppers; whether the shoppers are browsing or already in the choosing mode; or whether it is to develop and engage existing shoppers. When it comes to attracting shoppers to e-commerce, the strategy is to build traffic, normally with a wider scope of potential shoppers targeted. Attracting potential shoppers or light users normally means a broad approach across digital media channels, using SEO, paid searches, banners, presence on retailer, brokerage and social media platforms.

For shoppers in browsing mode the objective is to facilitate the purchase, increase the desire to purchase, by helping in the search and purchase process. This is especially important for categories and solutions with lower e-commerce penetration and percentage of sales. On retailer and brokerage platforms, next to SEO in general content management is key to building higher engagement and providing information to shoppers in active browsing mode and comparing different solutions. Supporting activation includes paid searches and product promotion with banners and digital ads on websites in line with the shopper targeting.

When shoppers are already engaged in the category or in a specific solution mode, the challenge is to ensure the purchase and focus on the benefits of products and services. Content management is a key dimension, as are reviews and videos explaining the product and service. The classical approaches of SEO and paid search product promotions and digital ads are still helpful activation tools.

For shoppers who have already added products and services, or entire solutions to their cart, the challenge is to expand the basket, normally by adding adjacent or complementary products and services. Activation includes paid search recommendations, content management, reviews, digital coupons, digital ads, email marketing, etc.

Shopper engagement approaches are used for shoppers who have already purchased. The objective is to drive a return to sites for future purchases by increasing satisfaction and building an ongoing relationship. Social marketing, loyalty programs, and email marketing all play a vital role, next to the more general approaches of digital ads, videos and directing shoppers and consumers to the brand website.

Banner advertising is a general tool that creates brand awareness, generates leads, and supports retargeting, something that has expanded into Facebook and Instagram sponsored ads. Facebook and Twitter now account for a large amount of spending on online display advertising.

Targeting is key to understanding which activation approach to prioritize depending on the stage in the shopper journey. Digital marketing has the advantage of the availability of vast amounts of data and the possibility of advanced analytics approaches. Still, large amounts of data and advanced analytics do not ensure relevance and effective targeting. It just increases the possibility of robust targeting. Types of targeting can include:

- Audience targeting that is based on demographic characteristics and sometimes broad interests. This is broad targeting and often available at a lower cost when buying media.
- Behavioral targeting, based on e.g. websites visited, products searched. Sometimes even offline behavior can be researched, such as stores shopped, products purchased, and media viewed.
- Daypart targeting, which targets people who are active at certain times of the day.
- Retargeting is targeting people that have engaged previously with the content of certain websites, from visiting to purchasing products and services.
- Geotargeting focuses on the location of shoppers. It can be at the zip code level, or more granular, including store locations, and in some cases the in-store location.
- Device targeting is targeting and retargeting based on specific devices used, e.g. smartphones.

One approach to understanding and predicting shopper behavior is look-alike modeling. It is an understanding of precise shopper characteristics based on specific shoppers' past behavior. These insights can then be applied to a much wider group of shoppers that have similar characteristics.

Important sources for targeting include first-party, second-party and third-party data. First-party data is a company's own information from websites and programs, including customer relationship marketing. Second-party data is information from another organization's first-party data. It is less commonly used due to privacy and data-sharing concerns, but it is sometimes used in supplier and retailer collaborations. Third-party data is information collected,

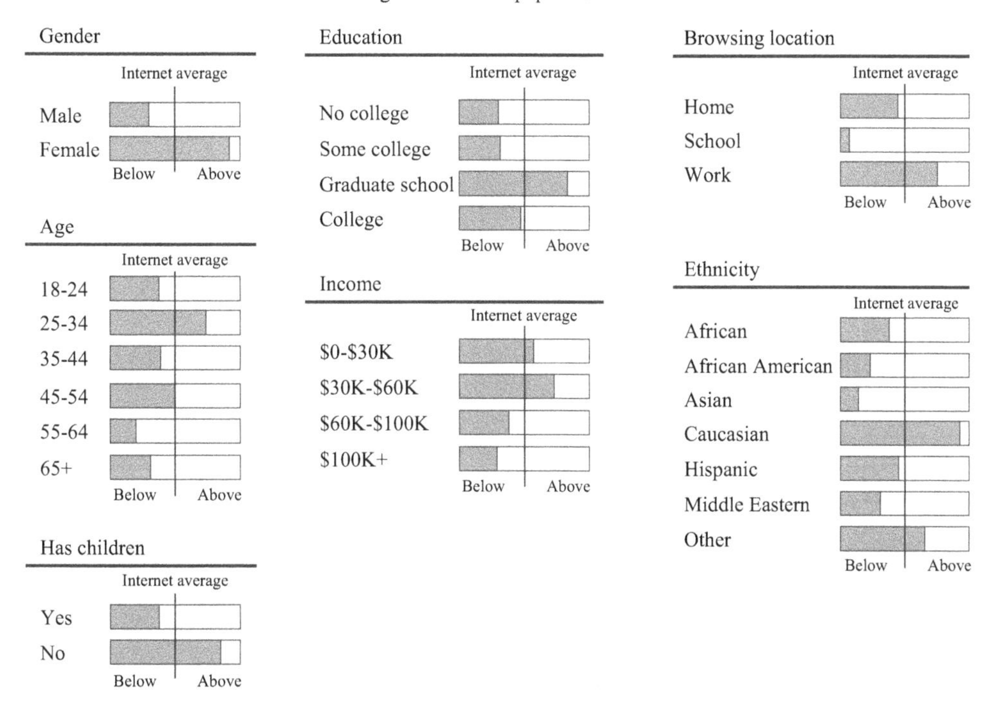

Figure 5.24 Website visitor demographics
Visitor demographics of health retailer site in the UK compared to the general internet population.
Source: Author

aggregated and sold by another organization. In e-commerce, targeting and analysis of web-scraping data is an important tool. It is generally done with software that simulates human web surfing to collect specified bits of information from different websites. Web data extraction is also referred to as web harvesting and in essence is a form of data mining. Data displayed by most websites can only be viewed using a web browser. Web-scraping software automates the process of analyzing data, which otherwise would need to be copied and pasted in a manual manner. Web-scraping software automatically loads and extracts data from multiple pages of websites based on defined requirements. With search engine optimization (SEO) and keyword research using tools like Google Ads and social listening approaches, traffic flows, drivers and content reactions can be surveyed. SEO reviews of the most critical keywords within a category can help to drive up products and services in the rankings on search engines and other e-commerce channels. With social listening, commentaries from consumers and shoppers can be distilled regarding their attitude to and relationship with products, services and brands.

Google Ads is the world's largest entity matching publishers with advertisers. Website publishers contract with Google to place advertisements on their sites, e.g. text, images, videos. Google then suggests the type of ads to run on a given site based on traffic, content and number of advertisers interested. Publishers are paid by cost per click (CPC) and

Figure 5.25 Key online search sources
Top search sources for health retailer site in the UK.
Source: Author

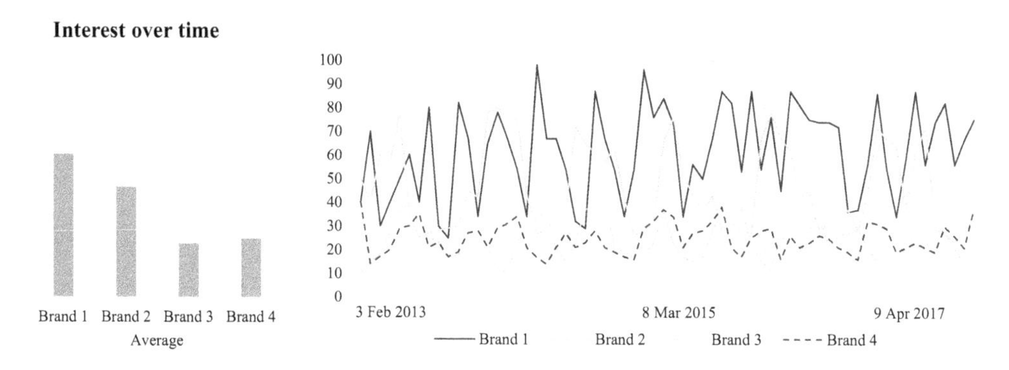

Figure 5.26 Brand interest online search
Searches of the top four brands of vitamins & supplements in the UK in 2018.
Source: Author

advertisers bid how much they are willing to pay. Google uses algorithms to match publishers and advertisers. The sites with the highest number of unique visitors and that incorporates the most valuable keywords receive the highest CPC. The auction for ads is dynamic and continuous, so the CPC is changing continuously. For smaller publishers it can be difficult to join the program and meet the minimum payout. Peer-to-peer networks and block chains have developed, such as Bit Teaser, which started in January 2015 and charges and pays in bitcoins.

Retailers that are fully e-commerce oriented or omnichannel players are a vital part of e-commerce sales. Category management and ECR approaches have been fundamental in the development of collaboration between retailers and suppliers. With e-commerce, collaboration needs to be adapted to the new digital reality. The Partnering Group together with the Category Management Association have developed an overview of how to organize such collaboration. They call it e-commerce category leadership (ECL), which denotes a collaborative supplier and retailer approach for shopper engagement to drive accelerated business results through e-commerce channels.[28] Through a collaborative approach of joint planning, development and testing shopper needs can be better met, and shopper baskets developed, e.g. through better cross selling. One key difference to classical category management is that beyond the category as an organizing principle, solutions that create distinct, manageable groupings of products and services, that consumers and shoppers perceive as interrelated to meet their needs, can be used in ECL projects. The Partnering Group sketches five steps that should be agile, and therefore, although normally sequential, could be changed due to the situation and the specific needs. The five steps are define, discover, design, develop and deliver, referred to as the ECL 5D process.[29]

For a successful ECL process, suppliers and retailers need first to agree on the process with clear steps, inputs, outputs and metrics. Secondly, they need to re-imagine categories, as the online shopping process is not bound by physical presentation constraints as in the brick-and-mortar sphere. This means rethinking the categories into wider solutions and how shoppers understand and search for these. Websites are more versatile, as different types of search and decision trees can be accommodated. Some shoppers will have a high level of planning, while others may just be browsing for solutions to their consumption need states.

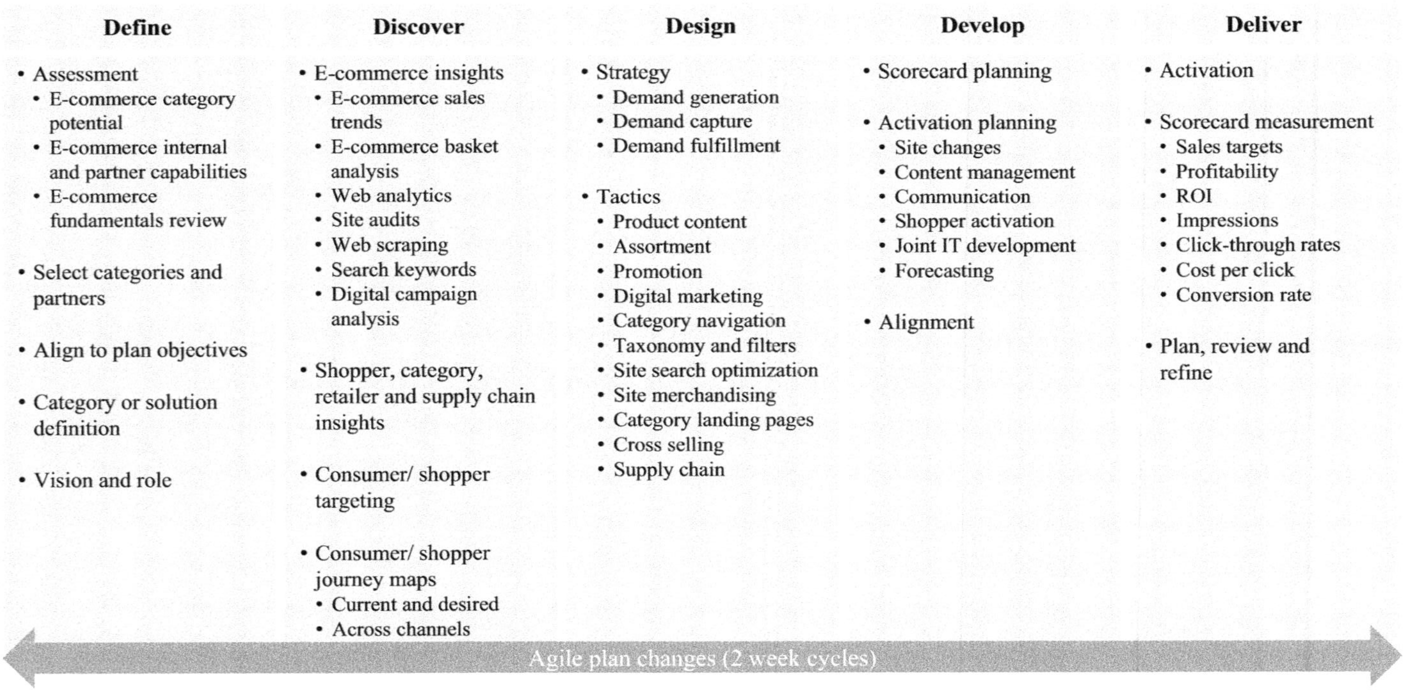

Define

- Assessment
  - E-commerce category potential
  - E-commerce internal and partner capabilities
  - E-commerce fundamentals review
- Select categories and partners
- Align to plan objectives
- Category or solution definition
- Vision and role

Discover

- E-commerce insights
  - E-commerce sales trends
  - E-commerce basket analysis
  - Web analytics
  - Site audits
  - Web scraping
  - Search keywords
  - Digital campaign analysis
- Shopper, category, retailer and supply chain insights
- Consumer/ shopper targeting
- Consumer/ shopper journey maps
  - Current and desired
  - Across channels

Design

- Strategy
  - Demand generation
  - Demand capture
  - Demand fulfillment
- Tactics
  - Product content
  - Assortment
  - Promotion
  - Digital marketing
  - Category navigation
  - Taxonomy and filters
  - Site search optimization
  - Site merchandising
  - Category landing pages
  - Cross selling
  - Supply chain

Develop

- Scorecard planning
- Activation planning
  - Site changes
  - Content management
  - Communication
  - Shopper activation
  - Joint IT development
  - Forecasting
- Alignment

Deliver

- Activation
- Scorecard measurement
  - Sales targets
  - Profitability
  - ROI
  - Impressions
  - Click-through rates
  - Cost per click
  - Conversion rate
- Plan, review and refine

Agile plan changes (2 week cycles)

Figure 5.27 E-commerce category leadership (ECL) process
Overview of the five agile steps of the ECL process.
Source: The Partnering Group, 2018

Webshop based on level of planning (Pharmacy)

Low level of planning
New shoppers and/ or looking for information

Consumption need states
- Topical information
- Categories and products fitting with the needs

Solutions - Offering
Categories and product groups

Differentiated solutions dependent on the type of shopper
- Top brands
- Own and exclusive brands
- Other brands

High level of planning
Knowledgeable shoppers

Efficient navigation
- Quickly encounter searched products
- Efficient search machine

Specific categories, products and brands

Presentation of alternatives
- Offers and promotions
- Popular cross purchases
- Propose alternatives, e.g. own and exclusive brands

Figure 5.28 Digital decision tree
Example of decision tree structure for OTC pharmaceuticals in Europe.
Source: Author

Thirdly, e-tailers and manufacturers need to agree on data sharing and the development of quality insights. E-commerce provides massive amounts of data, including web analytics and shopper databases. Converting data into action requires targeted data sharing, objectivity and specific analytical skills combining retailers' knowledge of cross-category and shopper trends with suppliers' expertise of their product categories and consumers. Fourth, the concept of category captain needs to be reassessed. In a more consumption need state-oriented approach, solution partners are needed rather than category captains. This is a more project-oriented approach involving more partners to tackle cross-category topics.

Digital and e-commerce change the metrics due to the different drivers to the brick-and-mortar sphere, as well as the availability of different type of data. Metrics such as sales, margin, or profit per square meter (or foot), footfall (number of visits), or number of stores lose importance, while revenues and margins across channels in an omnichannel reality, basket size as a metric of cross-category solutions and return on capital employed, due to technological investments, gain in importance. In addition, the cost to serve due to the new delivery reality with last yard delivery has become an important metric to fully understand the profitability across channels and shopper segments. Marketing metrics such as return on investment (ROI), awareness, sales and loyalty are equally important in the digital world.[30]

When analyzing online and e-commerce behavior, it is important to understand the flow from consumer and shopper awareness to action. Impressions are a metric used to quantify the display of an advertisement on a webpage. Impressions are also referred to as ad views. Counting impressions is essential to how web advertising is accounted and paid for in search engine marketing. Impressions do not measure clicks, only that an ad has been displayed; it measures the occurrence of a web page being found and loaded. Charging for impressions is normally on a cost per thousand impressions basis (CPM, with M for mille). The advertisement is then removed when a daily budget, set by the supplier, is achieved. The click-through rate (CTR) measures the percentage of people that saw an advertisement and clicked on it. As internet users are becoming immune to advertisements, click-through rates are normally quite low, often under the 1-percent level. Click-through rates are normally charged as CPC. The CPC method is based on the number of times visitors click on an advertisement. Another measurement is the bounce rate, the percentage of site visits that are single-page sessions with the visitor leaving without viewing a second page. It is usually used as a measurement of a website's overall engagement.

The final objective of e-commerce is to drive sales and convert shoppers into buyers. The conversion rate is the percentage of click-throughs that lead to actual sales. The conversion is normally charged on a cost per action basis, e.g. a payment for every website visitor who completes a task, e.g. filling out a form, or making a purchase. This is often referred to as cost per acquisition (CPA).

As social platforms are increasing in importance social shares, e.g. sending photos, videos, product recommendations and website links to friends are becoming an important metric for understanding consumer and shopper engagement.

When it comes to email campaigns metrics like open rates, e.g. emails opened compared to those sent, and unique open rates are often used, e.g. emails opened by recipient (if one recipient opens the same email several times it is still counted as one) compared to emails delivered.

Understanding the activation effectiveness and costs of different digital marketing tools is the basis for defining the optimum traffic mix for the e-commerce effort.

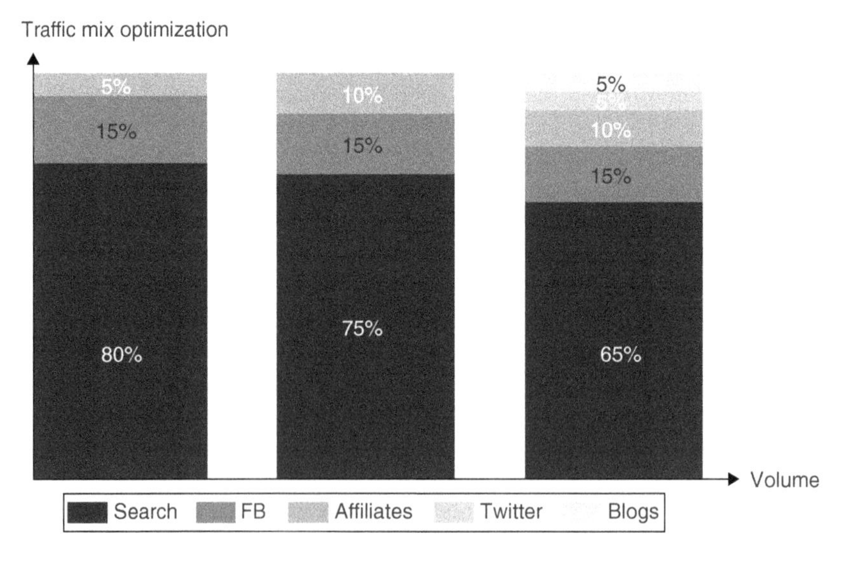

Figure 5.29 Traffic mix optimization by targeted volume

Optimization of traffic drivers for e-commerce for vitamins & supplements in the UK in 2018.

Source: Author

Ecosystem shopper marketing

The need for recommendation-driven activation strategies

In the new shopping ecosystem manufacturer brands are and will be increasingly pressured from two sides, especially those in more commoditized categories, and those not able to make the step into becoming mega-brands with a pervasive presence and activation. Contrary to the strong trend of an emerging middle class in developing countries, the economic divide in the developed markets is broadening. At one end of the spectrum, shoppers are looking for value to stretch their spending. At the other, the Amazon Prime type of shopper, mainly households with an income over 100,000 USD a year, are looking for more and new expressions of convenience.

Traditional shopper marketing strategies for brand hegemony is becoming outdated. Since the introduction of retail brands, manufacturer brands have been under pressure. The introduction of retail brands fundamentally changed the role between manufacturers and retailers. Retailers moved from being an efficient distribution channel to also become direct competitors. With the emergence of big box retailers and discounters manufacturer brands have been squeezed by price, as well as by the retailer's prerogative to shopper insights. The growing economic divide in developed markets is a key force in the continuous growth of the discounter and retailer brand segment. Discounters are also adapting to newer shopper needs of convenience by introducing convenience discounter formats, like Aldi in the UK. According to Nielsen discounter sales increased from 14.9 percent in 2001 to 22.2 percent in 2016. The global value share of private labels was 16.7 percent in 2016, and within the developed markets of the European Union 31.4 percent, with Spain and the UK at the helm with 42 percent and 41 percent, respectively.[31] At first, retail brands were focused on price and the economy segment. In a second step, retailer brands entered the premium space of value-added brands, formerly seen as the privilege of manufacturer brands. Rebranding Tesco's Finest, the premium range of the UK retailer with over 1,600 SKUs led to an uplift of £420 million of sales in 2018.[32] Retailer brands also meet new consumer trends, not or only insufficiently met by manufacturer brands. In 1994 the Austrian retailer Billa, today part of the German Rewe-Group, launched the ecology-friendly retail brand Ja! Natürlich. By 2010, the brand had reached sales of 290 million Euros with 1,100 SKUs in Austria. Retail brands are even reaching outside their own chains, like the German online pharmacy Doc Morris, formerly part of the Celesio group, and now acquired by the Swiss Zur Rose group, that has started to sell its branded band-aids in the Austrian drugstore BIPA. With more premium retail brands, shopper segments somewhat up the scale are being targeted and new discounter formats are capturing some of the convenience shopping occasions. All this is supported by improved market knowledge and refinement of shopper and channel strategies in terms of segmentation, price optimization and brand and product development to cover different consumption need states and consumer and shopper segments.

The model of retail brands has been developed over decades, and manufacturers have developed an arsenal of defense strategies to fend off these attacks, mainly along two dimensions, brand and cooperation. On the cooperation axes, the ECR approach has been refined, and many manufacturers have produced some of the retailer brands. The advantage of manufacturers has been their focus in terms of target consumers, as well as in investments to build brands, thereby, in the best case, building awareness and trust with consumers and shoppers. Through innovation, manufacturers are increasing the value and relevance of the category, helping to keep ahead of retailer brands, and simultaneously helping retailers to attract shoppers and increase the value of the shopping basket.

Manufacturer strategies built on brand building, collaboration and execution have been developed for the classical retail landscape, constituted mainly by producer, retailer and shopper. With the introduction of the modern retailer in the 1920s in the USA, the brand and how it was presented superseded the importance of the store clerk's recommendations to the shopper. The role of advertising through some key media during prime time, the presentation in store, through placement, point of purchase material, packaging, as well as retail flyers, coupons, etc. became the prime brand builders. This was a one-way conversation directed from the manufacturer toward the consumer and shopper during his relatively simple and short shopper journey. The brand strategies to counter economy products, as well as premium retail brands have been, as far as possible, perfected. To fend off the threat from retailer brands, manufacturers have refined their approach to segmentation, pricing, activation and execution, thereby understanding in detail the price premium they can charge, and how to best reach different customer segments, also with value, or fighter brands, if needed. Through investment in brand trust and innovation, manufacturers have been leading the development of categories, also in the interest of retailers in terms of drawing traffic and shopping basket size. Manufacturers have relied on the traditional way of one-directional and visual brand activation, through advertising, presence, location, space, packaging and point of purchase material, including flyers and coupons from retailers. Needless to say, the more commoditized the category, the more difficult is the branding strategy of manufacturers.

Shopper journeys have undergone radical changes, leading to the need for new activation strategies in the emerging shopping ecosystem. Today 90 percent of shoppers use three or more touchpoints on their journey compared to just a few years ago, when 70 percent used two or fewer touchpoints.[33] Research from Nielsen shows that 66 percent of respondents see electronic interaction as replacing face-to-face interaction in the future.[34] In this new environment one-directional, awareness building is being replaced by information seeking, conversations and peer-to-peer recommendations across the internet, applications, and social media platforms. Additionally, how to activate consumers and shoppers is changing, and thereby reducing the traditional arsenal of manufacturer brands to build preference. In particular the big four technology companies are changing the rules and moving the triangle of manufacturers, retailers and consumers/shoppers into a multi-stakeholder ecosystem. Technology and digitalization expand the connection with products from mainly visual to more recommendation-driven activation. Recommendation-driven activation started with search engines, then incorporated ratings, and is now moving to voice ordering. Through smartphones, it is not limited to the online world, as omnichannel concepts evolve, and shopping becomes about checking in, rather than checking out, shoppers are connected also in the brick-and-mortar world, and recommendations can supersede classical visual activation in the store.[35]

Technology and digitalization have redefined convenience and introduced new players into the shopping ecosystem. The former triangular biotope of consumer/shopper, manufacturer and retailer is continuously changing into a full ecosystem, including the tech giants GAFA (Google, Amazon, Facebook, Apple), aggregators, apps, influencers, a new delivery biotope, and in fact the shoppers themselves in a new role as reviewers.

Digitalization and technology are putting manufacturers under pressure on how to activate their brands, and who will lead the ecosystem surrounding consumers and shoppers. The new pressure on manufacturer brands is about the hegemony of recommendation and activation along the shopper journey, about more personalized offers better meeting consumer and shopper needs, and it entails more protagonists striving for ecosystem dominance, including the big four technology companies.[36]

The tech giants are planning to spend more than 1 trillion USD on voice-based shopping solutions. Already today, shoppers asking Amazon's Alexa to buy batteries only get one option, Amazon Basics.[37] Around 70 percent of word searches done on Amazon's browsers are for generic goods and not for specific brands. Among tests done for unbranded searches, 55 percent of first recommendations were Amazon choice products. It is predicted that by 2020 128 million Echo devices will be installed in households. Amazon's top ten private labels get the lion's share of the exposure that the e-tailer's private brands receive from customers, accounting for a resounding 81 percent of all the customer reviews left for Amazon private labels.[38] In addition, Google has entered the race and has incorporated food-ordering features into its mobile apps.[39]

The growth of the importance of retailers, and especially discounters, changed the way manufacturers had to work in terms of refining their methods of segmentation, pricing, branding and activation, and they had to introduce key account approaches and new ways of collaboration, most notably ECR. In the new reality, manufacturers need to develop tools and structures of advanced marketing analytics, ecosystem management, and more recommendation-driven activation.[40]

The new competitive space of hyper-convenience and last yard service

Digitalization has fundamentally disrupted the competitive landscape and, more than a technological revolution, it is a marketing revolution in how customer needs can be fulfilled through new business models. Hyper-connectivity enables hyper-convenience. The much discussed omnichannel is just a reaction to the search for hyper-convenience, which is now the competitive space for retailers as well as manufacturers. When brick-and-mortar retailers introduce same-day delivery and online retailers struggle with instant delivery options, they are trying to occupy the same competitive space of hyper-convenience. Adding personalization explains how manufacturers are entering into this competitive space, e.g. through subscription models.[41] Winning in the competitive space of hyper-convenience means fully connecting the route to purchase with the route to market.[42]

The number of new players to deliver hyper-convenience, applications, equipment through IoT solutions or voice ordering solutions such as Alexa shows that this is an entire new ecosystem interacting to serve customers. This convenience ecosystem is no longer fully represented by the traditional and linear value chain perspective divided between upstream and downstream activities, a view that classically puts the route to market and supply chain in the back seat to support marketing and sales. In the new marketing reality of the convenience ecosystem, route to market and supply chain become marketing, upstream becomes downstream, and the route to market and supply chain need to move from the back seat to the front seat, from planning and operations to a real-time customer management function.

Amazon Go has already shown that the future of brick-and-mortar is about checking in, not about checking out. In Stockholm, Sweden, Nordic Tech House received permission in 2018 to install facial recognition equipment in stores to facilitate shopper check-in.[43] Knowing the shopper means that personalized information and promotions can be sent to his or her smartphone, changing the activation game in store as well.[44] The shopping ecosystem is expanding not only through the tech giants and providers of check-in, and other store technology, but also by apps for digital shopping, and food aggregators, meal kits and delivery service providers and their apps.[45] As eating out increasingly becomes eating in, manufacturers selling products for these channels, e.g. beverages, are not only selling into the channel, but in fact need to activate their brands through these providers and their apps as well. By 2022, digital food delivery may comprise 11 percent of the total market, compared to 6 percent in 2017.[46]

The emerging competitive space for consumer goods companies and retailers is not about online vs. offline, but about hyper-convenience. A new ecosystem of new players and solutions driven by digitalization and technological innovations is enabling companies to deliver and present products where they create value to customers.

Between 2010 and 2016, the market share of Gillette dropped from 70 percent to 54 percent amid the market entry of new players like Harry's and Dollar Shave Club. Both brands work through direct-to-consumer and subscription models. Additionally, the average price of razors decreased by 12 percent in 2017. Walmart online sales grew by 44 percent in 2017. In 2018, Walmart introduced pick-up groceries in 1,200 stores, and introduced grocery delivery using their stores as fulfillment centers in more than 100 metropolitan areas, covering 40 percent of US households.[47] In a report from 2016, McKinsey identified 308 start-up companies focused on prepared food.[48] A recent article in *Boss Magazine* mentioned several start-ups, like Deliv, Doorman, Dropoff, Pickup and Postmates.[49] In February 2019 CNCB reported that Amazon will become a logistics company, and is building its own air fleet. Amazon has also invested in systems like Amazon Dash, allowing customers to more automatically re-order products, or Amazon Key, for delivery into homes through smart lock systems. Walmart introduced a similar system through Deliv, and acquired Parcel in 2017.[50]

Traditionally, route to market and supply chains have been focused on efficiency and outsourcing opportunities, as they have been viewed as more operational upstream activities of the value chain. In the emerging ecosystem and competitive landscape of hyper-convenience, the route to market and the supply chain become a vital part of the marketing offer to the customer to create value and gain competitive advantage.

The route to market and supply chain constitutes a major part of companies' total sales costs. Some sources position the cost of the supply chain between 50 percent and 70 percent of total sales costs and over 50 percent of those costs are attributable to the last mile.[51] In the competitive space of hyper-convenience, last mile service is not enough. The last mile is about bringing a product or service to a customer, normally a channel outlet, but in the reality of hyper-convenience the challenge is to bring the product or service where the end-user will use it, where it creates the value it is meant to create. It is beyond the last mile, it is the last yard.[52] In the traditional route to market and supply chain model the last yard has been the responsibility of the shopper.[53] The model has normally been the manufacturer selling to retail, and retail selling to shoppers, who need to come to brick-and-mortar stores to assemble their purchases by looking for products, checking out and bringing the goods home for their final use.

Managing the last yard, i.e. delivering products and services and presenting them the way they were meant to create value, has become a key concern for companies and it is where the last mile and last yard connect to become integrated route to purchase and route to market solutions. Companies like Diageo and Pernod Ricard even talk about route to consumption to clearly indicate that last mile distribution, channel activation, as well as final customer activation, be it in a channel or at home, are indivisible. Still, the logic follows the logic of the value chain, with logistics serving marketing. In addition, in that logic, upstream activities are more about efficiency, while downstream activities develop the real value. Often, this means the outsourcing of the last mile, and the deployment of a sales force to activate channels.[54] Route to market and supply chain are often viewed as support functions to marketing, mainly about planning and managing efficiencies within clearly pre-defined service levels. Within these levels, third parties are managed, measured and compensated. Retailers and manufacturers have developed a joint system to work together that clearly mirrors the value chain approach, and the division between upstream and downstream activities. With the introduction of the ECR concept in the 1980s the division between supply and demand-side management was firmly established. Supply side is about efficiency at a certain pre-determined service level, and is often fully or partly outsourced. Demand side is about developing shopper needs and fulfilling these. The last yard is mainly in the hands of the shopper, and the challenge is to influence in-store performance through presence and presentation, expanding the last mile challenge from managing out of stock to managing out of shelf. In this system, operations until the last mile are firmly under the control of manufacturers and retailers, and in some cases involving distributors, especially in more fragmented sales channels. Manufacturers have bridged their supply chain and demand activation through building more sophisticated route to market systems to perform better in store and reach more, especially smaller, outlets by optimizing outsourcing vs. insourcing of different functions. This includes improving efficiencies in more commoditized sales activities, e.g. merchandising and shelf filling. The prevalent paradigm is that the route to market and supply chain need to gain more and more efficiency to liberate resources to be reinvested downstream, to develop customers. To better serve the specific needs of shoppers more refined sales channel segmentations have been continuously introduced. But, with an increasing diffusion of needs, offerings and channels, the classical model based on strict last mile supply chain criteria, such as very specific ordering and delivery dates, and minimum order quantities, is reaching its limits. This is even more so as shoppers and consumers expect manufacturers and retailers to provide personalized last yard service. Shoppers look for hyper-convenience better adapted to their needs, the last yard becoming an inevitable part of the product or service sold, and a much higher level of personalization in terms of SKUs, amounts, destination, and timing will be a differential part in the emerging competitive space of hyper-convenience. It is also contrary to the classical goal setting of efficiency-based routes to market and supply chains with strict service parameters.

The new emerging ecosystem is connecting new players with customers outside the direct control of retailers and manufacturers. New players and solutions give sales channels and points of purchase the opportunity to break out of the chains of rigorous order and delivery systems, and frees shoppers from lengthy pre-planned shopping trips with pre-defined offer ranges. Manufacturers are starting to integrate omni-ordering systems, e.g. any system (salesperson, tele-sales, e-order, apps, etc.), anytime (not rigorous, fixed order taking and delivery windows), not only to improve the service, but also to drastically reduce the lost order ratio. Coca-Cola has invested in the start-up Bringg that has developed the MyCoke Express app to take full advantage of the gig economy and thereby reducing delivery lead times from three to five days to same or next day deliveries.[55] Hereby, points of purchase can order quickly, view possible suppliers, their prices and ratings, and have a quick delivery using crowd service solutions. Through such apps, manufacturers can also have a direct relationship with points of purchase further down the long tail, that they normally would not visit, that individually may not be that valuable, but aggregated are crucial to the business. With merchandising apps, like Traxx, Snapshop, Yoobic, Fieldagent etc., outlets can become part of the activation system for manufacturers. In addition, as third parties consolidate and become more professional adding data exchange and analysis to their services, the classical last mile under the managed lead of manufacturers is developing into collaborative route to market systems, with new players and the redefinition of roles.

A key challenge to manufacturers and retailers is how to solve consumers' and shoppers' expectations for solutions to their hyper-convenience needs, and to fulfill the promise of the last yard. The conundrum is that consumers and shoppers expect last yard service, but are not ready to pay for it. A 2016 McKinsey study revealed that 70 percent of shoppers want to pay the cheapest price possible, 28 percent would pay extra for same day delivery, 5 percent would pay extra for more reliable and timed delivery, and 2 percent would be ready to pay more for instant delivery. However, if they had to pay more than three Euros, they would prefer to pick up the products, e.g. at lockers. As a logical consequence the McKinsey study from 2016 sees big changes in how last yard service will be attained by 2025. If same day/instant delivery is 20–25 percent by then to meet customer convenience expectations, manufacturers and retailers will have to solve the service–cost conundrum. This would imply a new and already emerging service model dominated by X2C (anything to consumer) solutions, like autonomous ground vehicles with lockers, drones, droids, but also semi-autonomous ground vehicles, crowd-service and traditional solutions.[56]

As the competitive space moves into hyper-convenience, reinventing the last mile and winning the last yard through a more personalized service becomes a key challenge. This moves the route to market and supply chain into downstream territory. Companies, especially in the tech business, have developed cross-functional supply chain control towers. Dell is an example that manages more than 600 parts depots across the globe, and dispatches technicians to customers, if needed, through real-time supply chain systems to ensure quick responses to customer needs. With supply chain control towers, companies hope to gain agility and introduce dynamic decision-making through cross-functional supply chain management with different suppliers and players. Supply chain control towers could be a step toward fourth-party logistics management, also involving and managing different third-party logistics. Many of these concepts are centered on efficiencies and relatively well-defined roles of suppliers and players. Last yard domination and leadership in the emerging ecosystems are becoming key competitive differentiators as downstream and customer management activities in the competitive space of hyper-convenience and personalization. In this context, key questions are what should be insourced and what could be outsourced, and how to better integrate route to market, supply chain, route to purchase and marketing to develop real-time solutions. As shown by Amazon, Walmart and Coca-Cola, who are insourcing and shaping their ecosystem, the route to market and supply chain are increasingly becoming a source of competitive advantage and a key dimension of the definition of the service offer to customers and shoppers.

The need for ecosystem-oriented shopper marketing

Technology and digitalization are changing the name of the game. A new shopping ecosystem is emerging with new players like tech giants, food aggregators and apps that are changing the classical triangle of shoppers, manufacturers and retailers, as well as the traditional way of brand activation. The new emerging shopping ecosystem puts into question the traditional strategies of manufacturers to fend off attacks on their brands, especially from retail brands. Manufacturers need to flank their traditional strategies to fight off retail brand attacks with approaches to ecosystem management and new activation strategies, more centered on recommendation.

In a report on collaboration in the connected economy 74 percent of managers stated that the future success of companies depends on their abilities in ecosystem management, and that a clear internal cross-functional collaboration approach is needed.[57] The idea of value networks, instead of value chains, as generators of value through complex dynamic exchanges between enterprises, customers, suppliers, strategic partners and the community was introduced as early as 2000.[58] Competition is not between companies in specific industries, but between ecosystems.[59] In this reality, companies need to function like orchestrators to deliver new experiences. The need to organize and manage the ecosystem, define the strategy and identify potential participants is an emerging art.[60] However, as such, an ecosystem is innovative by nature. It is not possible to plan and foresee it entirely. Ecosystems could be regarded as micro-economies where the value of the entire micro-system is the overarching goal, meaning companies need to be open to innovation and new players, as well as understand when to cooperate, invest or acquire players for the best of the ecosystem.[61] It ultimately means a redefinition of the industry, new forms of cross-functional collaboration, with new functions emerging.[62]

Notes

1 (Dubow, 1992)
2 (Hall et al., 2001)
3 (Carpenter & Moore, 2006), (Carpenter & Balija, 2010) and (Carpenter & Brosdahl, 2011)
4 (Inman et al., 2004)
5 (Prasad & Aryasri, 2011)
6 (Kushwaha & Venkatesh, 2007)
7 (Kushwaha & Shankar, 2011)
8 (Kahn & Schmittlein, 1989) and (Prud'homme et al., 2007)
9 (D'Andrea, Lopez-Aleman & Stengel, 2006)
10 The icons in Figure 5.3 were retrieved from the following: party (www.flaticon.es/icono-gratis/aguafiestas_104542), holiday meal (www.svgrepo.com/svg/209842/turkey-chicken), cleaning (https://vectorstate.com/imagedetails/102834480/IST_15344_69461-Isignstock-Contributors-Bottle%2Dwith%2Dliquid%2Dsoap%2Dicon%2DSimple%2Dillustration%2Do.html), tinned goods (www.vectorstock.com/royalty-free-vector/canned-food-icon-simple-style-vector-23916564), ready to eat food (www.vectorstock.com/royalty-free-vector/sandwich-icon-vector-22623126), tonight's meal (https://thenounproject.com/term/pizza-box/906701/), grocery stock-up (https://thenounproject.com/term/grocery-basket/1471124/), out of stock shop (www.vectorstock.com/royalty-free-vector/shopping-bag-icon-vector-21156727)
11 (Park et al., 1989), (Bucklin & Lattin, 1991) and (Atkins & Kim, 2012)
12 (Shankar & Kushwaha, 2010)
13 (Findlay & Sparks, 2008)
14 (Berkhout, 2015) and (Carlson & O'Cass, 2011)
15 The icons in Figure 5.14 were retrieved from www.iconninja.com/phone-smartphone-apple-iphone-device-mobile-icon-7622; https://thenounproject.com/search/?q=poster&i=2651064; https://thenounproject.com/search/?q=grocery%20shelf&i=628038;https://thenounproject.com/search/?q=store&i=1369767
16 (Wang, 2014)
17 (ECR Europe, 2003)
18 (Deming, 1992)
19 (ECR Europe, 2005), (ECR Europe & Roland Berger Strategy Consultants, 2003), (ECR Europe & Deloitte Consulting, 2003), (ECR Europe & Roland Berger & Partners, 1999), (ECR Europe & PriceWaterhouseCoopers, 1999), (ECR Europe & Roland Berger & Partner GmbH, 1998), (ECR Europe and Earnst & Young, 1999), (ECR Europe and Roland Berger & Partners, 1998), (ECR Europe & The Partnering Group, 1998), (ECR Europe & Accenture, 1998), and (ECR Europe & Accenture, 2007)
20 (Wade, 2013)

21 (ECR Europe & AT Kearney, 1998)
22 (Kumar, 2008)
23 (Krentzel, 2018b)
24 (ECR Europe, emnos & The Partnering Group, 2011)
25 (Oakes et al., 2013), (Parsons, 2009), (Bezawada et al., 2009) and (Turley & Chebat, 2002)
26 (Castro et al., 2013)
27 (O'Brien, 2018)
28 (The Partnering Group, 2018)
29 (The Partnering Group, 2018)
30 (Deloitte, 2017)
31 (Nielsen, 2018)
32 (Honey, 2019)
33 (Clarke, 2018)
34 (Nielsen, 2015)
35 (Adhi et al., 2019)
36 (Reily & White, 2018)
37 (Creswell, 2018) and (Danziger, 2018)
38 (Kaziukėnas, 2019)
39 (Locker, 2019)
40 (Krentzel, 2019c)
41 (Luna, 2018)
42 (Krentzel, 2018a)
43 (Lindblad, 2019)
44 (Adhi et al., 2019)
45 (Brown, 2019)
46 (Morgan Stanley, 2017)
47 (Faelli et al., 2019)
48 (Joerss et al., September 2016)
49 (Boss editorial team, n.d.)
50 (Schoolov, 2019)
51 (Joerss et al., September 2016)
52 (Kaplan, 2019)
53 (Myerson, 2017)
54 (Dawar, 2013)
55 (Bringg, 2019)
56 (Joerss et al., September 2016)
57 (IBM, June 2016)
58 (Allee, 2000)
59 (Moore, 1999)
60 (Lang et al., 2019)
61 (Parker & van Alstyne, 2018)
62 (Porter & Heppelmann, 2015)

Bibliography

Adams, J.S., 1963. Toward an understanding of inequity. *Journal of Abnormal and Social Psychology*, 67, pp. 422–36.

Adhi, P., Burns, T., Davis, A., Lal, S. & Mutell, B., 2019. A transformation in store. [Online] Available at: www.mckinsey.com/business-functions/operations/our-insights/a-transformation-in-store [Accessed 1 November 2019].

Ahrens, G. & Dressler, M., 2011. *Online-Meinungsführer im Modemarkt: Der Einfluss von Web 2.0 auf Kaufentscheidungen*. Wiesbaden: Gabler Verlag Research.

Ajzen, I., 1991. The theory of planned behavior. *Organizational Behavior & Human Decision Processes*, 50(2), pp. 179–211.

Ajzen, I., 2005. *Attitudes, personality and behavior*. 2nd ed. Maidenhead: Open University Press.

Albarracín, D. & Wyer, R., 2000. The cognitive impact of past behavior: Influences on beliefs, attitudes, and future behavioral decisions. *Journal of Personality and Social Psychology*, 79(1), pp. 5–22.

Alderfer, C., 1972. *Existence, relatedness, and growth: Human Needs in Organizational Settings*. New York: Free Press.

Allee, V., 2000. Reconfiguring the value network. *Journal of Business Strategy*, 21(4), pp. 36–9.

Alpert, J. & Alpert, M., 1990. Music influences on mood and purchase intentions. *Psychology & Marketing*, 7(2), pp. 109–34.

AltusHost, 2016. The history of e-commerce, online shopping evolution, and buyers' behavior. [Online] Available at: www.altushost.com/the-history-of-e-commerce-online-shopping-evolution-and-buyers-behaviour/ [Accessed 13 November 2019].

Anderson, R., 1973. Consumer dissatisfaction: the effect of disconfirmed expectancy on perceived product performance. *Journal of Marketing Research*, 10(2), pp. 38–44.

Andrews, J., Srinivas, D. & Akhter, S., 1990. A framework for conceptualizing and measuring the involvement construct in advertising research. *Journal of Advertising*, 19(4), pp. 27–40.

Argyris, C., 1977. Double loop learning in organizations. *Harvard Business Review*, Issue September–October, pp. 115–25.

Argyris, C. & Schön, D., 1974. *Theory in practice: increasing professional effectiveness*. San Francisco, CA: Jossey-Bass.

Argyris, C. & Schön, D., 1978. *Organizational learning: a theory of action perspective*. Reading, MA: Addison-Wesley Publishers.

Atkins, K. & Kim, Y.-K., 2012. Smart shopping: conceptualization and measurement. *International Journal of Retail & Distribution Management*, 40(5), pp. 360–75.

Ayad, A., 2008. Optimizing inventory and store results in big box retail environment. *International Journal of Retail & Distribution Management*, 36(3), pp. 180–91.

Babin, B. & Babin, L., 2001. Seeking something different? A model of schema typicality, consumer affect, purchase intentions and perceived shopping value. *Journal of Business Research*, 54(2), pp. 89–96.

Baker, J., Grewal, D. & Parasuraman, A., 1994. The influence of store environment on quality inferences and store image. *Journal of the Academy of Marketing Science*, 22(4), pp. 328–39.

Baker, J., Parasuraman, A., Grewal, D. & Voss, G., 2002. The influence of multiple store environment cues on perceived merchandise value and store patronage intentions. Journal of Marketing, 66(2), pp. 120–41.

Ballantine, P., Jack, R. & Parsons, A., 2010. Atmospheric cues and their effect on the hedonic retail experience. *International Journal of Retail & Distribution Management*, 38(8), pp. 641–53.

Bamberg, S., Ajzen, I. & Schmidt, P., 2003. Choice of travel mode in the theory of planned behavior: the roles of past behavior, habit, and reasoned action. *Basic & Applied Social Psychology*, 25(3), p. 175.

Bandura, A., 1977. *Social learning theory*. Englewood Cliffs, NJ: Prentice-Hall.

Bansal, H. & Voyer, P., 2000. Word of mouth processes within a service purchase decision context. *Journal of Services Research*, 3(2), pp. 166–77.

Bastistich, J., 2013. A new customer journey. [Online] Available at: www.slideshare.com [Accessed 29 April 2013].

Basuroy, S., Mantrala, M. & Walters, R., 2001. The impact of category management on retail prices and performance: theory and evidence. *Journal of Marketing*, 65(4), pp. 16–32.

Beardon, W., Netemeyer, R. & Teel, J., 1989. Measurement of consumer susceptibility to interpersonal influence. *Journal of Consumer Research*, 15(4), pp. 473–81.

Becker, G. & Posner, R., 2009. *Uncommon sense: economic insights, from marriage to terrorism*. Chicago, IL and London: University of Chicago Press.

Belk, R., 1974. Application and analysis of the behavioral differential inventory for assessing situational effects in buyer behavior. In: S. Ward & P. Wright, eds., *Advances in Consumer Research*. Ann Arbor, MI: Association for Consumer Research, pp. 370–80.

Belk, R., 1974. An explanatory assessment of situational effects in buyer situations. *Journal of Marketing Research*, 11(2), pp. 156–63.

Belk, R., 1975. Situational variables and consumer behavior. *Journal of Consumer Behavior*, 2(3), pp. 157–64.

Bell, D., Corsten, D. & Knox, D., 2011. From point of purchase to path to purchase: how preshopping factors drive unplanned buying. *Journal of Marketing*, 75(1), pp. 31–45.

Bellizi, J. & Hite, R., 1992. Environmental color, consumer feelings, and purchase likelihood. *Psychology & Marketing*, 9(5), pp. 347–63.

Berekoven, L., Eckert, W. & Ellenrieder, P., 2006. Marktforschung: *Methodische Grundlagen und praktische Anwendung*. 11th ed. Wiesbaden: Gabler.

Berkhout, C., 2015. Retail marketing strategy: *Delivering shopper delight*. Philadelphia: Kogan Page.

Berry, L., Seiders, K. & Grewal, D., 2002. Understanding service convenience. *Journal of Marketing*, 66(3), pp. 1–17.

Bezawada, R., Balachander, S., Kannan, P. & Shankar, V., 2009. Cross-category effects of aisle and display placements: a spatial modelling approach and insights. *Journal of Marketing*, 73(3), pp. 99–117.

Bigné-Alcaniz, Ruiz-Mafé, C., Aldás-Manzano, J. & Saviz-Blas, S., 2008. Influence of online shopping information dependency and innovativeness on internet shopping adoption. *Online Information Review*, 32(5), pp. 648–67.

Bloch, P., 1981. An exploration into the scaling of consumers' involvement with a product class. In: K. Monroe, ed., *Advances in Consumer Research 8*. Ann Arbor, MI: Association for Consumer Research, pp. 61–5.

Bolsalea, 2019. ¿Qué es el webrooming?. [Online] Available at: www.bolsalea.com/blog/2016/04/que-es-el-webrooming/ [Accessed 13 November 2019].

Bone, P. & Ellen, P., 1999. Scents in the marketplace: explaining a fraction of olfaction. *Journal of Retailing*, 75(2), pp. 243–62.

Booz Allen Hamilton, 2003. Creando valor en canales minoristas para consumidores emergentes: rompiendo mitos sobre los consumidores emergentes aprendiendo de los minoristas pequeños. Un estudio exploratorio conducido para el Coca-Cola Retailing Research Council – América Latina, *s.l.*: Coca-Cola Retailing Research Council – América Latina.

Boss editorial team, n.d. The agony of X2C: last mile delivery. [Online] Available at: https://thebossmagazine.com/last-mile-delivery-customer-experience/ [Accessed 4 June 2019].
Braunstein, C., Huber, F. & Herrmann, A., 2005. Ein Ansatz zur Erklärung der Kundenbindung auf Basis der Theorie des geplanten Verhaltens. *zfbf*, 57(3), pp. 187–213.
Brewer, A., 2010. *The making of the classical theory of economic growth*. London and New York: Routledge.
Brightpearl and Multichannel Merchant, 2017. The State of Omnichannel Retail. [Online] Available at: https://info.brightpearl.com/the-state-of-omnichannel [Accessed 31 March 2019].
Bringg, 2019. My Coke Express: Restocking Merchants On-Demand. [Online] Available at: www.bringg.com/resources/case-studies/coke-express-restocking-merchants-demand/ [Accessed 4 June 2019].
Broekemier, G., Marquardt, R. & Gentry, J., 2008. An exploration of happy/sad and liked/disliked music effects on shopping intentions in a women's clothing store service setting. *Journal of Services Marketing*, 22(1), pp. 59–67.
Brown, B., Iftahy, A., Magni, M. & Saway, A., 2017. *The future of key-account management in the Middle East*, *s.l.*: McKinsey.
Brown, S., 2019. Best shared shopping list apps to save you from going back to the store. [Online] Available at: www.cnet.com/news/best-shared-shopping-list-apps-to-save-you-from-going-back-to-the-store/ [Accessed 3 October 2019].
Bruhn, M., Schoenmueller, V. & Schäfer, D., 2012. Are social media replacing traditional media in terms of brand equity creation. *Management Research Review*, 35(9), pp. 770–90.
Bruner, G., 1990. Music, mood, and marketing. *Journal of Marketing*, 54(4), pp. 94–104.
Bucklin, R. & Lattin, J., 1991. A two state model of purchase incidence and brand choice. *Marketing Science*, 10(1), pp. 24–39.
Bureau of Labor Statistics, 2017. United States Department of Labor. [Online] Available at: www.bls.gov/ [Accessed 12 November 2019].
Bylykbashi, K., 2015. Brands are struggling to join up multichannel customer journeys. [Online] Available at: www.marketingweek.com/brands-are-struggling-to-join-up-multichannel-customer-journeys/ [Accessed 13 November 2019].
Cadent Consulting Group, 2020. Marketing spending industry study. [Online] Available at: https://cadentcg.com/publication/2020-marketing-spending-industry-study/ [Accessed 31 March 2020].
Carlson, J. & O'Cass, A., 2011. Managing website performance taking account of the contingency role of branding in multi-channel retailing. *Journal of Consumer Marketing*, 28(7), pp. 524–31.
Carpenter, J. & Balija, V., 2010. Retail format choice in the US consumer electronics market. *International Journal of Retail Distribution Management*, 38(4), pp. 258–74.
Carpenter, J. & Brosdahl, D., 2011. Exploring retail format choice among US males. *International Journal of Retail & Distribution Management*, 39(12), pp. 886–98.
Carpenter, J. & Moore, M., 2006. Consumer demographics, store attributes, and retail format choice in the US grocery market. *International Journal of Retail & Distribution Management*, 34(6), pp. 434–52.
Castro, I., Morales, A. & Nowlis, S., 2013. The influence of disorganized shelf displays and limited product quantity on consumer purchase. *Journal of Marketing*, 77(4), pp. 118–33.
Celsi, L. & Olson, J., 1988. The role of involvement in attention and comprehension processes. *Journal of Consumer Research*, 15(2), pp. 210–24.
Central Intelligence Agency, n.d. The world factbook. [Online] Available at: www.cia.gov/library/publications/the-world-factbook/ [Accessed 21 June 2017].
Chao, E. & Utgoff, K., 2006. 100 years of U.S. consumer spending data for the nation. New York and Boston, MA: U.S. Department of Labor.
Chatterjee, P., 2010. Multiple-channel and cross-channel shopping behavior: role of consumer shopping orientations. *Marketing Intelligence and Planning*, 28(1), pp. 9–24.

Clarke, M., 2018. 78 Customer Engagement Statistics for Generating More Engaged Customers. [Online] Available at: https://blog.zoominfo.com/78-customer-engagement-statistics/ [Accessed 15 November 2019].

Coca-Cola, 2008. 360 degree plan to win in Thailand. Shopper Marketing Silver Winner: Coca-Cola MOTORing to win. David Ogilvy Awards presented by the Advertising Research Foundation.

Coca-Cola Femsa, October 2017. KOFmmercial digital platform. SAP Hybris Global Summit.

Cognizant, June 2011. Second annual 2011 shopper experience study: taking the store to the shopper. [Online] Available at: https://risnews.com/2nd-annual-2011-shopper-experience-study-taking-store-shopper [Accessed 31 March 2020]..

Cognizant, 2014. Delivering compelling customer journeys. The Cognizant UK shopper experience study 2014. [Online] Available at: www.cognizant.com/whitepapers/Cognizant-UK-shopper-study-2014.pdf [Accessed 31 March 2020]..

Cohen, J. & Reed II, A., 2006. A multiple pathway anchoring and adjustment (MPAA) model of attitude generation and recruitment. *Journal of Consumer Research*, 33(1), p. 1.

Consumergoods.com, 2019. Path to Purchase IQ. [Online] Available at: https://consumergoods.com/shopper-marketing-definition [Accessed 1 December 2019].

Crawford, L., 2012. *The shopper economy: the new way to achieve marketplace success by turning behavior into currency*. New York: McGraw-Hill.

Creswell, J., 2018. How Amazon Steers Shoppers to Its Own Products. [Online] Available at: www.nytimes.com/2018/06/23/business/amazon-the-brand-buster.html [Accessed 21 July 2019].

Cunningham, K., 2013. Reducing channel conflict. *Journal of Marketing Development and Competitiveness*, 7(1), pp. 78–83.

Dadzie, K. & Winston, E., 2007. Customer response to stock-out in the online supply chain. *International Journal of Physical Distribution and Logistics Management*, 37(1), pp. 19–42.

D'Andrea, G., Lopez-Aleman, B. & Stengel, A., 2006. Why small retailers endure in Latin America. *International Journal of Retail & Distribution Management*, 34(9), pp. 661–73.

D'Andrea, G., Ring, L., Lopez-Aleman, B. & Stengel, A., 2006. Breaking the myths on emerging consumers in retailing. *International Journal of Retail & Distribution Management*, 34(9), pp. 674–87.

Danielson, S., 2017. Trade and the International Division of Labor. [Online] Available at: http://debitage.net/humangeography/economic.html#Division [Accessed 10 November 2019].

Danziger, P., 2018. How Amazon plans to dominate the private label market. [Online] Available at: www.forbes.com/sites/pamdanziger/2018/05/06/how-amazon-plans-to-dominate-the-private-label-market/#3c1b515372d9 [Accessed 22 May 2019].

Dawar, N., 2013. When marketing is strategy: why you must shift your strategy downstream from products to customers. [Online] Available at: https://hbr.org/2013/12/when-marketing-is-strategy [Accessed 4 June 2019].

Dellaert, B., Arentze, B. & Timmermans, H., 2008. Shopping context and consumers' mental representation of complex shopping trip decision problems. *Journal of Retailing*, 84(2), pp. 219–32.

Deloitte, 2017. *A brave new world: the retail profitability challenge. s.l.*: Deloitte.

Deloitte & Winston Weber and Associates, 2015. *From category management to shopper-centric retailing: It can be done — here's how. s.l.*: Deloitte.

Deming, W., 1992. *Quality, productivity and competitive position*. Los Angeles, CA, Quality Enhancement Seminars.

Desforges, T. & Anthony, M., 2013. *The shopper marketing revolution: consumer – shopper – retailer: how marketing must reinvent itself in the age of the shopper*. Highland Park, IL: RTC Publishing.

Dewsnap, B. & Jobber, D., 2009. An exploratory study of sales-marketing integrative devices. *European Journal of Marketing*, 43(7/8), pp. 985–1007.

Dezalay, Y. & Garth, B., 2002. *The internationalization of palace wars: lawyers, economists, and the contest to transform Latin American States*. Chicago, IL: University of Chicago Press.

Dholakia, U., 1997. An investigation of the relationship between perceived risk and product involvement. In: M. Brucks & D.J. MacInnis, eds., *Advances in Consumer Research*, vol. XXIV. Provo, UT: Association for Consumer Research, pp. 159–67.

Dholakia, U., 2001. A motivational process model of product involvement and consumer risk perception. *European Journal of Marketing*, 35(11/12), pp. 1340–62.

Dickson, P., 1982. Person-situation: segmentation's missing link. *Journal of Marketing*, 46(4), pp. 56–64.

Diehlmann, L., 2011. *Shop social live total. s.l.*: The Hub, Research Report.

Dodd, J., 2011. *Follow the path to purchase. s.l.*: Admap.

Donovan, R., Rossiter, J., Marcoolyn, G. & Nesdale, A., 1994. Store atmosphere and purchasing behavior. *Journal of Retailing*, 70(3), pp. 283–94.

Dubow, J., 1992. Occasion-based vs. user-based benefit segmentation: a case study. *Journal of Advertising Research*, 32(2), pp. 11–18.

Ebling, C., 2008. Dynamische Aspekte im Kaufverhalten: Die Determinanten von Kaufzeitpunkt, Marken- und Mengenwahl. (Diss.). Wiesbaden: Gabler Wissenschaft.

ECR, 2009. *Jointly agreed growth (JAG) – The next frontier in retailer/supplier collaboration.* Barcelona: ECR Conference.

ECR, 2015. *ECR category management/shopper marketing benchmark study in 14 European countries. s.l.*: ECR.

ECR Europe, 2003. *ECR Europe's guide to collaborative consumer relationship management. s.l.*: ECR Europe.

ECR Europe, 2005. *The case for ECR: a review and outlook of continuous ECR adoption in Western Europe. s.l.*: ECR Europe.

ECR Europe & Accenture, 1998. *Shelf ready packaging (retail ready packaging) – Addressing the challenge: A comprehensive guide for a collaborative report. s.l.*: ECR Europe.

ECR Europe & Accenture, 2007. *ECR Europe blue book on shelf ready packaging: Summary presentation. s.l.: s.n.*

ECR Europe & AT Kearney, 1998. *Assessing the profit impact of ECR. s.l.*: ECR.

ECR Europe & Deloitte Consulting, 2003. *Collaborative PoS data management. s.l.*: ECR Europe.

ECR Europe, emnos & The Partnering Group, 2011. *The consumer and shopper journey framework. s.l.*: ECR Europe.

ECR Europe and Ernst & Young, 1999. *Efficient product introductions: the development of value-creating relationships. s.l.*: ECR Europe.

ECR Europe & The Partnering Group, 1998. *Efficient assortment: best practice report. s.l.*: ECR Europe.

ECR Europe & PriceWaterhouseCoopers, 1999. *Promotion tactics: adding focus, adding value. s.l.*: ECR Europe.

ECR Europe & Roland Berger & Partner GmbH, 1998. *Efficient replenishment project: "Working three-gether" – transport consolidation with the involvement of logistic provider (phase II). s.l.*: ECR Europe.

ECR Europe and Roland Berger & Partners, 1998. *How to create consumer enthusiasm: roadmap to growth. s.l.*: ECR Europe.

ECR Europe & Roland Berger & Partners, 1999. *How to implement consumer enthusiasm: strategic consumer value management. s.l.*: ECR Europe.

ECR Europe & Roland Berger Strategy Consultants, 2003. *ECR – Optimal shelf availability: increasing shopper satisfaction at the moment of truth. s.l.*: ECR Europe.

Editorial Board, 2016. Mexico's soda tax success. [Online] Available at: www.bloombergview.com/articles/2016-01-08/mexico-s-soda-tax-success [Accessed 22 July 2017].

Egol, M., Raju, S. & Sayani, N., 2013. *Reimaging shopper marketing: building brands through omnichannel experiences. s.l.*: booz&Co Perspective.

Ehrenthal, J. & Stölze, W., 2013. An examination of the causes for retail stockouts. *International Journal of Physical Distribution*, 43(1), pp. 54–69.

El Comercio: Economia, 2017. Consumo masivo: Bodegas vendieron más que los supermercados. [Online] Available at: http://elcommercio.pe/economia/mercados/consumo-masivobodegas-vendieron-mas-que-supermercados-noticia-1970794 [Accessed 12 January 2018].

Elkin, T., 2001. *Shopper marketing insight: embracing digital touchpoints. s.l.*: eMarketer.

Engel, J., Blackwell, R. & Miniard, P., 1995. *Consumer behavior*. 8th ed. New York: The Dryden Press.

Eurostat, 2017. Eurostat statistics explained. [Online] Available at: http://ec.europa.eu/eurostat/statistics-explained/index.php/Household_composition_statistics [Accessed 2 March 2017].

Faelli, F., Webster, R., Pratt, E. & Johns, L., 2019. *How brands can navigate turbulence with a disruption radar. s.l.*: Bain & Company.

Fam, K., B. Merrilees, J.E. Richards & L. Jozsa, 2011. In-store marketing: a strategic perspective. *Asia Pacific Journal of Marketing and Logistics*, 23(2), pp. 165–76.

Fayol, H., 1962. *Administration industrielle et générale: Prévoyance, organisation, commandement, coordination, control*. Paris: Dunod.

Federal Reserve Bank of St. Louis: Economic Research, 2017. FRED Economic Data. [Online] Available at: https://fred.stlouisfed.org/series/DPCERE1Q156NBEA [Accessed 21 June 2017].

Festinger, L., 1957. *A theory of cognitive dissonance*. Stanford, CA: Stanford University Press.

Findlay, A. & Sparks, L., 2008. "Switches": store.switching behaviours. *International Journal of Retail & Distribution Management*, 36(5), pp. 375–86.

Flint, D.J., Hoyt, C. & Swift, N., 2014. *Shopper marketing: profiting from the place where suppliers, brand manufacturers, and retailers connect*. Upper Saddle River, NJ: Pearson Education.

Flynn, L. & Goldsmith, R., 1993. A causal model of consumer involvement: replication and critique. *Journal of Social Behavior and Personality*, 8(6), pp. 129–42.

Freedman, J., 1964. Involvement, discrepancy and change. *Journal of Abnormal and Social Psychology*, 69(3), pp. 290–95.

Friedman, M., 1962. *Capitalism and freedom*. Chicago, IL: University of Chicago Press.

Fukuyama, F., 1989. The End of History? *The National Interest*, Issue 16, pp. 3–18.

Future exploration network, 2008. 7 driving forces shaping media. Silicon Valley: Future of Media Summit.

Ganesh, J., Arnold, M. & Reynolds, K., 2000. Understanding the customer base of service providers: an examination of the difference between switchers and stayers. *Journal of Marketing*, 64(3), pp. 65–87.

Gehrt, K. & Shim, S., 2003. Situational segmentation in the international marketplace, the Japanese snack market. *International Marketing Review*, 20(2), pp. 180–94.

Gilbride, T., Inman, J. & Stilley, K., 2013. What determines unplanned purchase? A model including shopper purchase history and within-trip dynamics. Paper presented at the Wharton Marketing Camp, Wharton School – University of Pennsylvania.

GMA, 2011. *Shopper marketing 5.0: creating value with shopper solutions. s.l.*: GMA.

GMA/Deloitte, 2007. *Shopper marketing: capturing a shopper's heart, mind and wallet. s.l.*: The Grocery Manufacturers Association.

Goldsmith, R. & Emmert, J., 1991. Measuring product-category involvement: a multitrait multimethod study. *Journal of Business Research*, 23(4), pp. 363–71.

Grant, D. & Fernie, J., 2008. Exploring out-of-stock and on-shelf availability in non-grocery high street retailing. *International Journal of Retail & Distribution Management*, 36(8), pp. 661–72.

Green, P. & Rao, V., 1972. Configuration synthesis in multidimensional scaling. *Journal of Marketing Research*, 9(1), pp. 65–8.

Greenwald, A. & Leavitt, C., 1984. Audience involvement in advertising: four levels. *Journal of Consumer Research*, 11(1), pp. 581–92.

Grewal, D., Roggeveen, A. & Nordfält, J., 2014. *Shopper marketing and the role of in-store marketing*. Bingley: Emerald Group Publishing Limited.

Grönros, C., 2000. *Service management and marketing: a customer relationship management approach*. 2nd ed. Chichester: John Wiley & Sons.

GS1, 2008. *Mobile commerce: opportunities and challenges*. Brussels: *s.n.*

GSMA, 2015. *The mobile economy. s.l.*: GSM Association.

GSMA, 2019. Intelligence Consumer Insights Survey. [Online] Available at: www.gsma.com/ [Accessed 31 March 2020].

H&M, 2014. H&M. [Online] Available at: www.hm.se [Accessed 19 February 2014].

Haley, R., 1968. Benefit segmentation: a decision-oriented research tool. *Journal of Marketing*, 32(3), pp. 30–5.

Hall, J., Lockskin, L. & O'Mahoney, G., 2001. Exploring the links between wine choice and dining occasions: factors of influence. *International Journal of Wine*, 13(1), pp. 36–53.

Hall, J., Oppenheim, P. & Lockshin, L., 2001. Deriving wine marketing strategies by combining means-end chains with an occasion based chain segmentation analysis. In: A. Groeppel-Klien & F. Esch, eds., *European Advances in Consumer Research* vol. 5. *s.l.*:Association for Consumer Research, pp. 82–9.

Hammann, P. & Erichson, B., 2006. *Marktforschung*. 2nd ed. Stuttgart: Lucius & Lucius Verlagsgesellschaft mbH..

Harris, B., 2010. Bringing shopper into category management. In: M. Stahlberg & V. Maila, eds., *Shopper marketing: how to increase purchase decisions at the point of sales*. London: Kogan Page, pp. 28–32.

Harris, L. & Goode, M., 2010. Online servicescapes, trust, and purchase intentions. *Journal of Service Marketing*, 24(3), pp. 230–43.

Harris-Walker, L., 2001. The measurement of word-of-mouth communication and an investigation of service quality and customer commitment as potential antecedents. *Journal of Service Research*, 4(1), pp. 60–75.

Harry's, 2019. www.harrys.com. [Online] Available at: www.harrys.com/en/gb?sticky=true [Accessed 13 November 2019].

Herzberg, F., 1974. *Work and nature of man*. London: Crosby Lockwood Staples.

Hillesland, J., 2013. *Fundamentals of retailing and shopper marketing*. Harlow, England; New York: Pearson.

Hitt, J., 1996. The theory of supermarkets. *New York Times Magazine*, 10 March, pp. 56–61.

Holbrook, M. & Hirschman, E., 1982. The experiential aspects of consumer behavior: consumer fantasies, feelings and fun. *Journal of Consumer Research*, 9(2), pp. 132–40.

Ho, L. & Chung, M., 2007. The effects of single-message single-source mixed word-of-mouth on product attitude and purchase intention. *Asia Pacific Journal of Marketing and Logistics*, 19(1), pp. 75–86.

Honey, 2019. Tesco Finest. [Online] Available at: https://honey.co.uk/work/tesco-finest/ [Accessed 21 November 2019].

Hook, M., 2015. Study: 87% of Retailers Agree Omnichannel is Critical to their Business, Yet Only 8% Have "Mastered" it. [Online] Available at: www.brightpearl.com/company/press-and-media-1/2017/12/15/study-87-of-retailers-agree-omnichannel-is-critical-to-their-business-yet-only-8-have-mastered-it [Accessed 13 November 2019].

Houston, M. & Rothschild, M., 1978. Conceptual and methodological perspectives on involvement. In: S.C. Jain, ed., *Advances in consumer research*, vol. 5. Ann Arbor, MI: Association for Consumer Research, pp. 184–7.

Hovland, C., Harvey, O. & Sherif, M., 1957. Assimilation and contrast effects in reaction to communication and attitude change. *Journal of Abnormal and Social Psychology*, 55(7), pp. 244–52.

Huang, Y., Hui, S., Inman, J. & Suher, J., 2013. The effect of in-store travel distance on unplanned purchase with applications to store layout and mobile shopping apps. Working paper, University of Pittsburg, PA.

Hupfer, N. & Gardner, D., 1971. Differential involvement with products and issues: an exploratory study. In: D. Gardner, ed., *Proceedings of the 2nd annual conference of the Association for Consumer Research*. *s.l.*: *s.n.*, pp. 262–70.

Huskins, P. & Goldring, N., 2009. Turning shopper insights into results. *Retail World*, 62, p. 24.

IBM, June 2016. The ecosystem equation: collaboration in the connected economy. A Harvard Business Review Analytic Services Report.

Inman, J., Shankar, V. & Ferraro, R., 2004. The roles of channel-category associations and geodemographics in channel patronage. *Journal of Marketing*, 68(2), pp. 51–7.

In-Store Marketing Institute, 2009. *Shopper marketing glossary. s.l.*: In-Store Marketing Institute.

Interbrand, 2016. Best global brands. [Online] Available at: www.interbrand.com/best-brands/best-global-brands [Accessed 2 April 2016].

Iyer, E., 1989. Unplanned purchasing: knowledge of shopping environment and time pressure. *Journal of Retailing*, 65(1), pp. 40–57.

Jilani, Z., 2017. Think Progress. [Online] Available at: https://thinkprogress.org/chart-top-u-s-corporations-outsourced-more-than-2-4-million-american-jobsover-the-last-decade-2ea66dfc0e35 [Accessed 6 June 2017].

Jindal, R., Reinartz, W., Krafft, M. & Hoyer, W., 2007. Determinants of the variety of routes to market. *International Journal of Research in Marketing*, 24(1), pp. 17–29.

Joerss, M., J. Schröder, F. Neuhaus, C. Klink & F. Mann, September 2016. *Parcel delivery: the future of last mile. s.l.*: McKinsey & Company.

Jonas, K. & Doll, J., 1996. Eine kritische Bewertung der Theorie überlegten Handelns der Theorie geplanten Verhaltens. *Zeitschrift für Sozialpsychologie*, 27(1), pp. 18–32.

Judt, T., 2010. *Ill fares the land*. New York: Penguin Press.

Kaas, K. & Fischer, M., 1992. Der Transaktionskostenansatz. *Das Wirtschaftsstudium*, 22(8–9), pp. 686–93.

Kahn, B. & Schmittlein, D., 1989. Shopping trip behavior: an empirical investigation. *Marketing Letters*, 1(1), pp. 261–4.

Kaltcheva, V. & Weitz, B., 2006. When should a retailer create an exciting store environment? *Journal of Marketing*, 70(1), pp. 107–18.

Kapferer, J.-N. & Laurent, G., 1985. Consumers' involvement profiles: a new practical approach to consumer involvement. *Journal of Advertising Research*, 25(6), pp. 48–56.

Kapferer, J.-N. & Laurent, G., 1993. Further evidence on the consumer involvement profile: five antecedents of involvement. *Psychology and Marketing*, 10(4), pp. 347–55.

Kaplan, D., 2019. The last yard: the final logistics frontier. [Online] Available at: www.supplychaindive.com/news/last-yard-mile-final-logistics-frontier/555770/ [Accessed 4 June 2019].

Kassarjian, H., 1981. Low involvement: a second look. In: K.B. Munroe, ed., *Advances in consumer research*, vol. VIII. Ann Arbor, MI: Association for Consumer Research, pp. 31–34.

Kaufman, C., 2015. The Concept of Convenience in Marketing: A Definition and Suggested Approach in the Study of Household Time-Savings. In: *Developments in Marketing Science: Proceedings of the Academy of Marketing Science*. Cham: Springer, pp. 11–15.

Kaziukėnas, J., 2019. Amazon Private Label Brands. [Online] Available at: www.marketplacepulse.com/amazon-private-label-brands [Accessed 11 November 2019].

Keaveney, S. & Parthasarathy, M., 2001. Customer switching behavior in online services: an exploratory study of the role of selected attitudinal, behavioral and demographic factors. *Journal of the Academy of Marketing Sciences*, 29(4), pp. 374–90.

Kendzierski, D., 1990. Decision making versus decision implementation: an action control approach to exercise adoption and adherence. *Journal of Applied Social Psychology*, 20(1), pp. 27–45.

Kenny, J., 2018. The History of Online Shopping. [Online] Available at: https://medium.com/@johndkenny/the-history-of-online-shopping-d6ef35ab80d9 [Accessed 13 November 2019].

Kessler, C., 2004. Editorial: Branding in store – marketing in the 21st century. *Journal of Brand Management*, 11(4), pp. 261–4.

Keynes, J., 1936. The general theory of employment, interest and money. New York: Harcourt, Brace.

Kidwell, B. & Jewell, R., 2003. The moderated influence of internal control: an examination across health-related behaviors. *Journal of Consumer Psychology*, 13(4), pp. 377–86.

Kidwell, B. & Jewell, R., 2008. The influence of past behavior on behavioral intent: an information-processing explanation. *Psychology & Marketing*, 25(12), pp. 1151–66.

Kinley, T., Conrad, C. & Brown, G., 1999. Internal and external promotional references: an examination of gender and product involvement effects in the retail apparel setting. *Journal of Retailing and Consumer Services*, 6(1), pp. 39–44.

Kirmani, A., Sood, S. & Bridges, S., 1999. The ownership effect in consumer response to brand line stretches. *Journal of Marketing*, 63(1), pp. 88–101.
Klein, N., 2007. *The shock doctrine: the rise of disaster capitalism*. New York: Metropolitan Books, Henry Holt.
Klingenberg, B., 2000. *Kundennutzen und Kundentreue. Eine Untersuchung zum Treue-Nutzen aus Konsumentensicht*. Munich: FGM-Verlag.
Knight, F. & Emmet, R., 1999. *Selected essays by Frank H. Knight*. Chicago, IL: University of Chicago Press.
Koelemeijer, K. & Oppewal, H., 1999. Assessing the effects of assortment and ambience: a choice experimental approach. *Journal of Retailing*, 75(3), pp. 319–45.
Kollat, D. & Willet, R., 1967. Customer impulse purchasing behavior. *Journal of Marketing Research*, 4(1), pp. 21–31.
Kotler, P. & Armstrong, G., 2006. *Principles of marketing*. 11th ed. Upper Saddle River, NJ: Pearson Prentice Hall.
Kotler, P. & Armstrong, G., 2014. *Principles of marketing*. 16th ed. Boston, MA: Pearson.
Kotler, P., Keller, K. & Koshy, A., 2007. *Marketing management: analysis, planning, implementation and control*. 12th ed. New Delhi: Prentice Hall of India.
Krämer, M., 2010. Preiskomplexität: Gestaltungsmerkmale, Kundenwahrnehmung und Auswirkungen (Diss.). Wiesbaden: Gabler Verlag.
Kreller, P., 2000. *Einkaufstättenwahl von Konsumenten. Ein präferenztheoretischer Erklärungsansatz*. Wiesbaden: Deutscher Universitätsverlag.
Krentzel, G., 2008. Objectives and trap avoidance for successful global account management. *Velocity*, 10(1), pp. 16–18.
Krentzel, G., 2018a. Connecting the Route to Purchase with the Route to Market. [Online] Available at: www.ama.org/2018/02/14/connecting-the-route-to-purchase-with-the-route-to-market/ [Accessed 13 November 2019].
Krentzel, G., 2018b. Shopper marketing: estrategias de mercado. Madrid: Ra-Ma.
Krentzel, G., 2019a. Getting the Route to Market Right in the New Omni-channel Reality. [Online] Available at: www.ama.org/marketing-news/getting-the-route-to-market-right-in-the-new-omni-channel-reality/ [Accessed 13 November 2019].
Krentzel, G., 2019b. Introducing Strategic Account Management in Organized Retail. *Velocity*, 21(3), pp. 40–6.
Krentzel, G., 2019c. The New Shopping Ecosystem. [Online] Available at: www.ama.org/marketing-news/the-new-shopping-ecosystem/ [Accessed 13 November 2019].
Krueger Jr., N. & Brazael, D., 1994. Entrepreneurial potential and potential entrepreneurs. *Entrepreneurship: Theory & Practice*, 18(3), p. 91.
Krugman, H., 1966. The measurement of advertising involvement. *Public Opinion Quarterly*, 30(4), pp. 583–96.
Krugman, P., 2009. *The return of depression economics and the crisis of 2008*. New York: W.W. Norton.
Kumar, S., 2008. A study of the supermarket industry and its growing logistics capabilities. *International Journal of Retail & Distribution Management*, 36(3), pp. 192–211.
Kumar, V. & Leone, R., 1988. Measuring the effect of retail store promotions on brand and store substitution. *Journal of Marketing Research*, 25(2), pp. 178–85.
Kumar, V., Petersen, J. & Leone, R., 2007. How valuable is word of mouth?. [Online] Available at: https://hbr.org/2007/10/how-valuable-is-word-of-mouth [Accessed 22 October 2016].
Kushwaha, T. & Shankar, V., 2011. Are multichannel customers always the most valuable customers? Working paper, University of North Carolina.
Kushwaha, T. & Venkatesh, S., 2007. Optimal allocation of marketing efforts by customer-channel segment. MSI working paper.
Kuβ, A. & Tomczak, T., 2007. *Käuferverhalten*. 4th ed. Stuttgart: Lucius & Lucius.
Laaksonen, P., 1994. *Consumer involvement: concepts and research*. London: Routledge.
Laczniak, R. & Muehling, D., 1989. Manipulating message involvement in advertising research. *Journal of Advertising*, 19(2), pp. 28–38.

Lang, N., von Szczepanski, K. & Wurzer, C., 2019. *The emerging art of ecosystem management. s.l.*: BCG Henderson Institute.

Lapoule, P. & Colla, E., 2016. The multi-channel impact on the sales forces management. *International Journal of Retail & Distribution Management*, 44(3), pp. 248–65.

Larivière, B., Aksoy, L., Cooil, B. & Keiningham, T., 2011. Does satisfaction matter more if a multichannel customer also is a multicompany customer? *Journal of Service Management*, 22(1), pp. 39–66.

Lastovicka, J. & Gardner, D., 1979. Components of involvement. In: J. Maloney & B. Silverman, eds., *Attitude research plays for high stakes. s.l.*: American Marketing Association Proceedings, pp. 53–73.

Legris, P., Ingham, J. & Collerette, P., 2003. Why do people use information technology? A critical review of the technology acceptance model. *Information & Management*, 40(3), pp. 191–204.

Lenskold Group, 2017. ROI tools. [Online] Available at: www.lenskold.com/tools/LeadGenTool.html [Accessed 1 March 2017].

Lewin, K., 1936. *Principles of topological psychology*. New York and London: McGraw-Hill Company.

Liebmann, H.-P. & Kraigher-Krainer, J., 2003. *Der Zusammenhang zwischen Kognitionen, Emotionen und Stimmungen im Wissensmanagement. Bestandaufnahme und Entwicklung eines theoretischen Bezugsrahmens. s.l.*:Universität Graz, Institut für Handel, Absatz und Marketing.

Lindblad, T., 2019. Snart är de här – butikskamerorna som känner igen kunderna. [Online] Available at: https://sverigesradio.se/sida/artikel.aspx?programid=406&artikel=7230776 [Accessed 22 October 2019].

Liu, Y., 2006. Word-of-mouth for movies: its dynamics and impact on box office revenue. *Journal of Marketing*, 70(3), pp. 74–89.

Locke, E. & Latham, G., 2013. *New developments in goal setting and task performance*. New York: Routledge.

Locker, M., 2019. Hey Google, bring me a chalupa! Hangry people can now order food without a separate app. [Online] Available at: www.fastcompany.com/90355392/how-to-order-food-directly-with-google-ios-or-android [Accessed 22 September 2019].

Lockshin, L., Spawton, A. & Macintosh, G., 1997. Using product, brand and purchasing involvement for retail segmentation. *Journal of Retailing and Consumer Services*, 4(3), pp. 171–83.

Löfgren, M., 2005. Winning at the first and second moments of truth: an exploratory study. *Managing Service Quality*, 15(1), pp. 102–15.

Lord, C., R.M. Paulson, T.L. Sia, J.C. Thomas & M.R. Lepper, 2004. Houses built on sand: effects of exemplar stability on susceptibility to attitude change. *Journal of Personality & Social Psychology*, 87(6), p. 733.

Lucas, R., 2005. *Lecturas sobre crecimiento económico*. Bogotá: Grupo Editorial Norma.

Luna, J., 2018. Why Every Business Will Soon Be a Subscription Business. [Online] Available at: www.gsb.stanford.edu/insights/why-every-business-will-soon-be-subscription-business [Accessed 4 June 2019].

Lutzky, C., 2007. Kaufakzeleration bei konsumentengerichteter Verkaufsförderung (Diss.). Wiesbaden: Deutscher Universitätsverlag.

Madlberger, H., 2011. Vom category management zum shopper management. Vienna: Vortrag beim Praxisdialog an der WU-Wien.

Maechler, N., Neher, K. & Park, R., 2016. From touchpoints to journeys: seeing the world as customers do. [Online] Available at: www.mckinsey.com/businessfunctions/marketing-and-sales/our-insights/from-touchpoints-to-journeys-seeing-the-world-as-customers-do [Accessed 27 March 2020].

Marx, K., Moore, S., Aveling, E. & Engels, F., 1970. *Capital: a critique of political economy. Vol I, capitalist production*. London: Lawrence & Wishart.

Maslow, A. & Ribé, R., 2012. *El hombre autorrealizado hacia una psicología del ser*. Barcelona: Editorial Kairós.

McClelland, D., 2016. *The achieving society*. e-book: Pickle Partners Publishing.

McDonald, M., 11th of June 2005. *Profitable growth and the role of key client management. s.l.*: Cranfield School of Management.
McGregor, D. & Cutcher-Gershenfield, J., 2008. *The human side of enterprise*. New York: McGraw-Hill.
Michaelidou, N. & Dibb, C., 2006. Product involvement: an application in clothing. *Journal of Consumer Behavior*, 5(5), pp. 442–53.
Michaelidou, N. & Dibb, S., 2008. Consumer involvement: a new perspective. *Marketing Review*, 8(1), pp. 83–99.
Millward Brown, 2008. *What are the main influences on purchase decisions? s.l.*: Millward Brown.
Minsait, 2017. Retos estrátegicos del FMCG y del retail. [Online] Available at: https://minsait.com/sites/default/files/newsroom_documents/retosestrategicosfmcgyretail_1.pdf [Accessed 28 February 2017].
Miranda, M. & Jegasothy, K., 2008. Malaysian grocery shoppers' behavioural response to stock-outs. *Asia Pacific Journal of Marketing and Logistics*, 20(4), pp. 396–412.
Mitchell, A., 1979. Involvement: a potentially important mediator of consumer behavior. In: W.L. Wilkie, ed., *Advances in Consumer Research*, vol. VI. Provo, UT: Association for Consumer Research, pp. 191–5.
Mittal, B., 1989. Measuring purchase-decision involvement. *Psychology and Marketing*, 6(2), pp. 147–62.
Mittal, B. & Lee, M., 1987. Separating brand-choice involvement from product involvement via consumer involvement profiles. In: M.J. Houston, ed., *Advances in Consumer Research*, vol. XV. Provo, UT: Association for Consumer Research, pp. 43–9.
Mittal, B. & Lee, M., 1989. A causal model of consumer involvement. *Journal of Economic Psychology*, 10(3), pp. 363–89.
Monbiot, G., 2016. *How did we get into this mess?: politics, equality, nature*. London and Brooklyn, NY: Verso.
Moore, J., 1999. Predators and prey: a new ecology of competition. *Harvard Business Review*, 71(3), pp. 75–86.
Morgan Stanley, 2017. Alexa, what's for dinner tonight? [Online] Available at: www.morganstanley.com/ideas/online-food-delivery-market-expands [Accessed 21 September 2019].
Muncy, J., 1990. Involvement and perceived brand similarities/differences: the need for process oriented models. In: M.E. Goldberg, G. Gorn & R.W. Pollay, eds., *Advances in Consumer Research*, vol. XVII. Provo, UT: Association for Consumer Research, pp. 144–8.
Murray, H., 2008. *Explorations in personality*. Oxford: Oxford University Press.
Murray, K., 1991. A test of services marketing theory: consumer information acquisition activities. *Journal of Marketing*, 55(1), pp. 10–25.
Myerson, P., 2017. E-Commerce Raises Stakes for Supply Chain. [Online] Available at: https://business.lehigh.edu/blog/2017/e-commerce-raises-stakes-supply-chain [Accessed 4 June 2019].
Neelamegham, R. & Jain, D., 1999. Consumer choice process for experience goods. An econometric model and analysis. *Journal of Marketing Research*, 36(3), pp. 373–86.
Neff, J., 2009. Where social media and shopper marketing merge to meet moms. *Advertising Age* (9 July).
Neslin, S., D. Grewal, R. Leghorn & V. Shankar, 2006. Challenges and operations in multichannel management. *Journal of Services Research*, 9(2), pp. 95–113.
Neslin, S. & Shankar, V., 2009. Key issues in multichannel management: current knowledge and future directions. *Journal of Interactive Marketing*, 23(1), pp. 70–81.
Nicholls, J., Roslow, S. & Comer, L., 1994. An Anglo mall and Hispanic patronage. In: A. Vásquez-Párraga, ed., *Bridging the Americas: re-discovery, understanding, partnership. s.l.*: Business Association of Latin American Studies Proceedings, p. 383.
Nicholls, J., Roslow, S. & Dublish, S., 1997. Time and companionship: key factors in Hispanic shopping behavior. *Journal of Consumer Marketing*, 14(3), pp. 194–205.
Nielsen, 2015. *Screen wars: the battle for eye space in a TV-everywhere world. s.l.*: Nielsen.

Nielsen, 2018. The Rise and Rise Again of Private Label. [Online] Available at: www.nielsen.com/eu/en/insights/report/2018/the-rise-and-rise-again-of-private-label/# [Accessed 12 November 2019].
Nielsen, Q1 2011. Nielsen global online survey. [Online] Available at: www.nielsen.com/ca/en/insights/report/2016/global-connected-commerce/ [Accessed 27 March 2020].
Nielsen, Q4 2015. Global connected commercial survey. [Online] Available at: www.nielsen.com/ca/en/insights/report/2011/global-consumer-confidence-survey-q3-2011/ [Accessed 27 March 2020]..
Nielsen, R., 1993. Woolman's "I am We" triple-loop action learning: origin and application in organizational ethics. *Journal of Applied Behavioral Science*, 29(1), pp. 117–38.
Nitzberg, M., 2012. Putting the shopper in your marketing strategy. In: M. Stahlberg & V. Ville Maila, eds., *Shopper marketing: how to increase purchase decisions at the point of sales*. London: Kogan Page, pp. 153–72.
Noor, A. & Ahmmed, K., 2013. Key account management strategy in business-to-business relationship: a proposed research framework. *International Journal of Business, Economics and Law*, 2(1), pp. 70–7.
NPR, 2019. NPR/Marist Poll: Amazon is a colossus in a nation of shoppers. [Online] Available at: www.npr.org/about-npr/617470695/npr-marist-poll-amazon-is-a-colossus-in-a-nation-of-shoppers?t=1573658639167 [Accessed 13 November 2019].
Nsairi, Z., 2012. Managing browsing experience in retail stores through perceived value: implications for retailers. *International Journal of Retail & Distribution Management*, 40(9), pp. 676–98.
Numbeo, 2017. Numbeo.com. [Online] Available at: www.numbeo.com/quality-of-life/rankings_by_country.jsp?title=2017 [Accessed 21 June 2017].
Oakes, S., Patterson, A. & Oakes, H., 2013. Shopping sound tracks: evaluating the musicscape using introspective data. *Arts Marketing: An International Journal*, 3(1), pp. 41–57.
O'Brien, K., 2018. Coca-Cola and UberEats offer free dinner delivery to those who work Christmas Eve. [Online] Available at: www.creativereview.co.uk/coca-cola-uber-eats-ad-homemade-xmas-dinner/ [Accessed 27 March 2020].
Odekerken-Schröder, G., Ouwersloot, H., Lemmink, J. & Semeijn, J., 2003. Consumers' trade-off between relationship, service package and price: an empirical study in the car industry. *European Journal of Marketing*, 37(1/2), pp. 219–42.
O'Keefe, D., 1990. *Persuasion: theory and research*. Newbury Park, CA: Sage.
Olson, J. & Dover, P., 1979. Disconfirmation of consumer expectations through product trial. *Journal of Applied Psychology*, 64(2), pp. 179–89.
Orbell, S., Hodgkins, S. & Sheeran, P., 1997. Implementation intentions and the theory of planned behavior. *Personality and Social Psychology Bulletin*, 23(9), pp. 945–54.
Orth, U., Heinrich, F. & Malkewitz, K., 2012. Servicescape interior design and consumers' personality impressions. *Journal of Services Marketing*, 26(3), pp. 194–203.
Park, C., Iyer, E. & Smith, D., 1989. The effects of situational factors on instore grocery shopping behavior: the role of store environment and time available for shopping. *Journal of Consumer Research*, 15(4), pp. 422–33.
Park, C. & Mittal, B., 1985. A theory of involvement in consumer behavior: problems and issues. In: J. Sheth, ed., *Research in consumer behavior*. Greenwich, CT: JAI Press, pp. 201–31.
Park, M. & Lennon, S., 2009. Brand name and promotion in online shopping contexts. *Journal of Fashion Marketing and Management*, 13(2), pp. 149–60.
Parker, G. & van Alstyne, M., 2018. Innovation, openness, and platform control. *Management Science*, 64(7), pp. 3015–32.
Parsons, A., 2009. Use of scent in a naturally odourless store. *International Journal of Retail & Distribution Management*, 37(5), pp. 440–52.
Parsons, A. & Thompson, A.-M., 2009. Wine recommendations: who do I believe?. *British Food Journal*, 111(9), pp. 1003–15.
Pauwels, K., Hanssens, D. & Siddarth, S., 2002. The long-term effects of price promotions on category incidence, brand choice and purchase quantity. *Journal of Marketing Research*, 39(4), pp. 421–39.

Pavlou, P. & Flygenson, M., 2006. Understanding and predicting electronic commerce adoption: an extension of the theory of planned behavior. *MIS Quarterly*, 30(1), pp. 115–43.

Pettersson, T., 2003. I teknikrevolutionens centrum: företagsledning och utveckling i Facit 1957–1972. Uppsala Papers in Financial and Business History, Report 16.

Petty, R. & Cacioppo, J., 1981. Issue involvement as a moderator of the effects on attitude of advertising content and context. In: K. Monroe, ed., *Advances in Consumer Research*. Provo, UT: Association for Consumer Research, pp. 20–4.

Pew Research Center, 2013. [Online] Available at: www.pewresearch.org/ [Accessed 17 July 2013].

Pew Research Center, 2018. [Online] Available at: www.pewresearch.org/fact-tank/2019/09/11/key-findings-about-the-online-news-landscape-in-america/ [Accessed 28 March 2020].

Peyton, R., Pitts, S. & Kamery, H., 2003. Consumer satisfaction/dissatisfaction (CS/D): a review of the literature prior to the 1990s. *Proceedings of the Academy of Organizational Culture, Communication and Conflict*, 7(2).

Piercy, N., 2012. Positive and negative cross-channel shopping behaviour. *Market Intelligence and Planning*, 30(1), pp. 83–104.

Piketty, T. & Goldhammer, A., 2014. *Capital in the twenty-first century*. Cambridge, MA: The Belknap Press of Harvard University Press.

Pointer Media Network & CMO Council, 2008. Discovering the pivotal point consumer: a milestone study on American shoppers who drive CPG brand volume. *s.l.*: *s.n.*

Porter, M. & Heppelmann, J., 2015. How Smart, Connected Products Are Transforming Companies. *HBR*, 114 (October), pp. 96–112.

Prahalad, C., 2004. *The fortune at the bottom of the pyramid: eradicating poverty through profits*. London: FT Press.

Prahalad, C. & Hart, S., 2002. The fortune at the bottom of the pyramid. *Strategy + Business*, 26 (First Quarter). [Online] Available at: www.strategy-business.com/article/11518?gko=9a4ba [Accessed 27 March 2020].

Pramatari, K. & Miliotis, P., 2008. The impact of collaborative store ordering on shelf availability. *Supply Chain Management: An International Journal*, 13(1), pp. 49–61.

Prasad, C. & Aryasri, A., 2011. Effect of shopper attributes on retail format choice behaviour for food and grocery retailing in India. *International Journal of Retail & Distribution Management*, 39(1), pp. 68–86.

Prud'homme, A., Boyer, K. & Hult, G., 2007. An analysis of operations-oriented drivers of customer loyalty for two service channels. *Direct Marketing: An International Journal*, 1(2), pp. 78–101.

PwC, 2019. Global consumer insights survey 2019. [Online] Available at: www.pwc.com/gx/en/industries/consumer-markets/consumer-insights-survey.html [Accessed 13 November 2019].

Quester, P. & Lim, A., 2003. Product involvement/brand loyalty: is there a link? *Journal of Product and Brand Management*, 12(1), pp. 22–39.

Rahtz, D. & Moore, D., 1989. Product class involvement and purchase intent. *Psychology and Marketing*, 6(2), pp. 13–127.

Rani, L. & Velayudhan, S., 2008. Understanding consumers' attitude towards retail store in stockout situations. *Asia Pacific Journal of Marketing and Logistics*, 20(3), pp. 259–75.

Reagan, C., 2017. Think running retail stores is more expensive than selling online? Think again. [Online] Available at: www.cnbc.com/2017/04/19/think-running-retail-stores-is-more-expensive-than-selling-online-think-again.html [Accessed 14 November 2019].

Reily, J. & White, S., 2018. Alexa: Re-invent my shopping experience. [Online] Available at: www.digitalcommerce360.com/2018/01/02/alexa-re-invent-shopping-experience/ [Accessed 4 November 2019].

Reiss, S. & Bootzin, R., 1985. *Theoretical issues in behavior therapy*. Orlando, FL: Academic Press.

Retail Commission on Shopper Marketing, 2010. *Shopper marketing best practices: a collaborative model for retailers and manufacturers*. *s.l.*: In-Store Marketing Institute.

Skrovan, S., 2017. How shoppers use their smartphones in stores. Retail Dive, 7 June. [Online] Available at: www.retaildive.com/news/how-shoppers-use-their-smartphones-in-stores/444147/ [Accessed 31 March 2020].

Richins, M. & Bloch, P., 1986. After the new wears off: the temporal context of product involvement. *Journal of Consumer Research*, 13(2), pp. 280–5.

Rothschild, M., 1979. Advertising strategies for high and low involvement situations. In: J. Maloney & B. Silverman, eds., *Attitude research plays for high stakes. s.l.*: American Marketing Association Proceedings, pp. 74–93.

Sandell, R., 1968. The effects of attitudinal and situational factors on reported choice behavior. *Journal of Marketing Research*, 5(4), pp. 405–8.

Sansolo, M., 2010. Illogic inside the mind of the shopper. In: M. Stahlberg & V. Maila, eds., *Shopper marketing: how to increase purchase decisions at the point of sales*. London: Kogan Page, pp. 33–7.

Savage, M., F. Devine, N. Cunningham et al., 2013. A new model of social class? Findings from the BBCs Great British class survey experiment. *Sociology*, 47(2), pp. 219–50.

Sayer, R., 2015. *Why we can't afford the rich*. Bristol, UK and Chicago, IL: Policy Press.

Schneider, B. & Rau, G., 2009. *Shopper marketing: 5 strategies for connecting with shoppers at the point of decision. s.l.*: Aisle 7.

Scholz and Friends, 2008. Dramatic shift in marketing reality. [Online] Available at: www.youtube.com/watch?v=ciSrNc1v17M [Accessed 24 March 2020].

Schoolov, K., 2019. Amazon is rapidly expanding its air fleet to handle more of its own shipping. [Online] Available at: www.cnbc.com/2019/02/15/amazon-will-compete-with-fedex-and-ups-to-become-logistics-company.html [Accessed 4 June 2019].

Shafriz, J., Ott, S. & Jang, Y., 2011. *Classics of organizational theory*. 7th ed. Belmont, CA: Wadsworth.

Shankar, V., 2011. *Shopper marketing*. Cambridge, MA: Marketing Science Institute.

Shankar, V. & Balasubramanian, S., 2009. Mobile marketing: a synthesis and prognosis. *Journal of Interactive Marketing*, 23(2), pp. 118–29.

Shankar, V., J. Inman, M. Mantrala, E. Kelley & R. Rizley, 2011. Innovations in shopper marketing: current insights and future research issues. *Journal of Retailing*, 87(Supplement 1), pp. 29–42.

Shankar, V. & Kushwaha, T., 2010. An empirical analysis of cross-channel effects in a multichannel environment. Working Paper, Texas A&M University.

Shankar, V., Venkatesh, A., Hofacker, C. & Naik, P., 2010. Mobile marketing in the retailing environment: current insights and future research avenues. *Journal of Interactive Marketing*, 24(2), pp. 111–20.

Shaw, D. & Shiu, E., 2003. Ethics in consumer choice: a multivariate modelling approach. *European Journal of Marketing*, 37(10), pp. 1485–98.

Shaw, D., Shiu, E. & Clarke, I., 2000. The contribution of ethical obligation and self identity to the theory of planned behavior: an exploration of ethical consumers. *Journal of Marketing Management*, 16(8), pp. 879–94.

Sherif, M. & Sargent, S., 1947. Ego-involvement and the mass media. *Journal of Social Issues*, 3(3), pp. 8–16.

Sherif, C. & Sherif, M., 1967. *Attitude, ego-involvement, and change*. Westport, CT: Greenwood Press.

Sherif, C., Sherif, M. & Nebergall, R., 1965. *Attitude and attitude change: the social judgement involvement approach*. Philadelphia: Saunders.

Shoppermotion, 2019. Why should you analyze your in-store shopping missions? [Online] Available at: https://shoppermotion.com/blog/why-should-you-analyze-your-in-store-shopping-missions/ [Accessed 13 November 2019].

Silveira, P. & Marreiros, C., 2014. Shopper marketing: a literature review. *International Review of Management and Marketing*, 4(1), pp. 90–7.

Simonson, I. & Winer, R., 1992. The influence of purchase quantity and display format on consumer preference for variety. *Journal of Consumer Research*, 19(1), pp. 133–8.

Skinner, B. & Schlinger, H., 2015. *Verbal behavior*. Brattleboro, VT: Echo Point Books & Media.

Slama, M. & Tashchian, A., 1985. Selected socio-economic and demographic characteristics associated with purchasing involvement. *Journal of Marketing*, 49(1), pp. 72–82.

Smith, J. & Bristor, J., 1994. Uncertainty orientation: explaining differences in purchase involvement and external search. *Psychology and Marketing*, 11(6), pp. 587–608.

Smith, J., D.J. Terry, A.S.R. Manstead, W.R. Louis, D. Kotterman & J. Wolfs, 2008. The attitude-behavior relationship in consumer conduct: the role of norms, past behavior and self-identity. *Journal of Social Psychology*, 148(3), pp. 311–34.

Soman, D., 2001. Effects of payment mechanism on spending behavior: the role of rehearsal and immediacy of payments. *Journal of Consumer Research*, 27(4), pp. 460–74.

Sommer, D., 2010. Integrated communications planning for shopper marketing. In: M. Stahlberg & V. Maila, eds., Shopper marketing: how to increase purchase decisions at the point of sales. London: Kogan Page, pp. 68–72.

Speed, R. & Thompson, P., 2000. Determinants of sports sponsorship response. *Journal of the Academy of Marketing Science*, 28(2), pp. 226–38.

Srivastava, R., 1980. Usage-situational influences on the perceptions of product markets response homogeneity and its implications for consumer research. In: J.C. Olson, ed., *Advances in Consumer Research*, vol. VII. Ann Arbor, MI: Association for Consumer Research, pp. 644–9.

Srivastava, R., Shocker, A. & Day, G., 1978. An exploratory study of the influences of usage situations on perceptions of product markets. In: K. Hunt, ed., *Advances in Consumer Research*, vol. V). Ann Arbor, MI: Association for Consumer Research, pp. 32–8.

Stanton, J. & Bonner, P., 1980. An investigation of the differential impact of purchase situation on levels of consumer choice behavior. In: J.C. Olson, ed., *Advances in Consumer Research*, vol. VII. Ann Arbor, MI: Association for Consumer Research, pp. 639–43.

Stassen, R., Mittelstaedt, J. & Mittelstaedt, R., 1999. Assortment overlap: its effect on shopping patterns in a retail market when the distributions of prices and goods are known. *Journal of Retailing*, 75(3), pp. 371–86.

Stengel, J., 2011. *Grow: how ideals power growth and profit at the world's greatest companies*. New York: Crown Business.

Stewart, H., 2010. Consumer spending and the economy. [Online] Available at: fivethirtyeight.blogs.nytimes.com [Accessed 22 October 2017].

Stigler, G., 1975. *The citizen and the states: essays on regulation*. Chicago, IL: University of Chicago Press.

Stilley, K., Inman, J. & Wakefield, K., 2010. Spending on the fly: mental budgets, promotions and spending behavior. *Journal of Marketing*, 70(3), pp. 34–47.

Stockholm International Water Institute, 2008. Saving water: from field to fork curbing losses and wastage in the food chain. *s.l.*: Stockholm International Water Institute.

Stone, R., 1984. The marketing characteristics of involvement. In: T. Kinnear, ed. *Advances in Consumer Research*, vol. XI. Provo, UT: Association for Consumer Research, pp. 210–15.

Stüber, E., 2011. Personalisierung im Internethandel: Die Akzeptanz von Kaufempfehlungen in der Bekleidungsbranche (Diss.). Wiesbaden: Gabler Verlag Research.

Swan, J. & Oliver, R., 1989. Postpurchase communication by consumers. *Journal of Retailing*, 65(4), pp. 516–33.

Swieringa, J. & Wierdsma, A., 1992. *Becoming a learning organization: beyond the learning curve*. Workingham: Addison-Wesley.

Tang, Y.-C., Wang, Y.-M. & Huang, J.-Y., 2014. Optimal promotional strategy for intra-category cross-selling: an application to culinary products in Taiwan. *British Food Journal*, 116(1), pp. 80–90.

Taylor, F., 1947. *The principles of scientific management*. New York: Norton.

Taylor, S. & Todd, P., 1995. Understanding information technology usage: a test of competing models. *Information Systems Research*, 6(2), pp. 144–76.

The Partnering Group, 2018. *E-Commerce category leadership: a new approach to retailer and supplier collaboration for digital and e-Commerce growth*/. *s.l.*: The Partnering Group and sponsored by The Category Management Association.

The World Bank, 2017. World bank world development indicators. [Online] Available at: http://data.worldbank.org/data-catalog/world-development-indicators [Accessed 21 June 2017].

Trading Economics, 2016. [Online] Available at: https://tradingeconomics.com/ [Accessed 2 April 2016].

Turley, L. & Chebat, J., 2002. Linking retail strategy, atmospheric design and shopping behaviour. *Journal of Marketing Management*, 18(1–2), pp. 125–44.

Turley, L. & Milliman, R., 2000. Atmospheric effects on shopping behavior: a review of the experimental evidence. *Journal of Business Research*, 49(2), pp. 193–211.

Tyebjee, T., 1979. Response time, conflict, and involvement in brand choice. *Journal of Consumer Research*, 6(3), pp. 295–304.

Underhill, P., 1999. *Why we buy: the science of shopping*. New York: Simon & Schuster.

van Kenhove, P., de Wule, K. & van Waterschoot, W., 1999. The impact of task definition on store-attribute saliences and store choice. *Journal of Retailing*, 75(1), pp. 125–37.

Vaughn, R., 1980. How advertising works: a planning model. *Journal of Advertising Research*, 20(5), pp. 27–33.

Vaughn, R., 1986. How advertising works: a planning model revised. *Journal of Advertising Research*, 26(1), pp. 57–66.

Venkatesh, V., Morris, M., Davis, G. & Davis, F., 2003. User acceptance of information technology: toward a unified view. *MIS Quarterly*, 27(3), pp. 425–78.

Venkatraman, M., 1988. Investigating differences in the roles of enduring and instrumentally involved consumers in the diffusion process. In: M.J. Houston, ed., *Advances in Consumer Research*, vol. XV. Provo, UT: Association for Consumer Research, pp. 299–303.

Verhoef, P., Kannan, P. & Inman, J.J., 2015. From Multi-Channel Retailing to Omni-Channel Retailing: Introduction to the Special Issue on Multi-Channel Retailing. *Journal of Retailing*, 91(2), pp. 174–81.

Verhoef, P., Neslin, S. & Vroomen, B., 2007. Multichannel customer management: understanding the research shopper phenomenon. *International Journal of Research in Marketing*, 24(2), pp. 129–48.

Vernon, R., 1966. International investment and international trade in the product cycle. *The International Executive*, 8(4), p. 16.

von Hayek, F., 1944. *The road to serfdom*. Chicago, IL: University of Chicago Press.

von Mises, L., 1944. *Bureaucracy*. New Haven, CT: Yale University Press.

Vroom, V. & Jago, A., 1988. *The new leadership: managing participation in organizations*. Englewood Cliffs, NJ: Prentice-Hall.

WAAM, 2019. medium.com. [Online] Available at: https://medium.com/@waamofficial/1-in-3-of-all-products-bought-online-will-be-returned-to-the-retailer-why-and-what-can-be-done-342414e84ccc [Accessed 1 December 2019].

Wade, G., 2013. *Category management mastery: the key to growth! s.l.*: The Category Management Association.

Wakefield, K. & Inman, J., 2003. Situational price sensitivity: the role of consumption occasion, social context and income. *Journal of Retailing*, 79(4), pp. 199–212.

Walter, E. & Reutterer, T., 2009. *How mobile advertising affects consumers: empirical findings from a sms direct marketing campaign*. Nantes: EMAC.

Wang, S., 2014. Category management – common language between retailers and manufacturers. [Online] Available at: www.nielsen.com/tw/en/insights/report/2014/category-management-the-win-win-platform-for-manufacturers-and-retailers/ [Accessed 13 November 2019].

Weber, M., 1980. *Wirtschaft und Gesellschaft*. 5th ed. Tübingen: Mohr.

Weber, W., 2009. Shopper insights and shopper marketing: getting it right. White paper.

Wendt, E., 2010. Sozialer Abstieg und Konsum: Auswirkungen finanzieller Verknappung auf das Konsumverhalten (Diss.). Wiesbaden: Gabler Verlag.

Wid.World, 2017. World Wealth & Income Data Base. [Online] Available at: https://wid.world/ [Accessed 21 June 2017].

Williamson, O., Winter, S. & Coase, R., 1991. *The nature of the firm: origins, evolution, and development*. New York: Oxford University Press.

Wood, S., 2018. Ipsos views: The evolution of shopper behaviour. [Online] Available at: www.ipsos.com/sites/default/files/ct/news/documents/2018-11/ipsos-views-evolution-of-shopper-behaviour-2018.pdf [Accessed 13 November 2019].

Wordpress, 2017. Multichannel vs. omnichannel. [Online] Available at: https://mimeographs.wordpress.com/2013/07/28/multichannel-vs-omnichannel [Accessed 28 February 2017].

World Economic Forum, 2019. Global gender gap report 2020. [Online] Available at: http://reports.weforum.org/global-gender-gap-report-2020/ [Accessed 28 March 2020].

Worrington, P. & Shim, S., 2000. An empirical investigation of the relationship product involvement and brand commitment. *Psychology and Marketing*, 17(9), pp. 761–82.

Wu, W.-Y., Lee, C.-L., Fu, C.-S. & Wang, H.-C., 2014. How can online store layout design and atmospheric influence consumer shopping intention on a website. *International Journal of Retail & Distribution Management*, 42(1), pp. 4–24.

Yavas, U. & Babakus, E., 2009. Retail store loyalty: a comparison of two customer segments. *International Journal of Retail & Distribution*, 37(6), pp. 477–92.

Yoon, S.-J., 2013. Antecedents and consequences of in-store experiences based on experiential typology. *European Journal of Marketing*, 47(5/6), pp. 693–714.

Zaichkowsky, J., 1985. Measuring the involvement construct. *Journal of Consumer Research*, 12(3), pp. 341–52.

Zaichkowsky, J., 1994. The personal involvement inventory: reduction, revision, and application to advertising. *Journal of Advertising*, 23(4), pp. 59–70.

Zhuang, G., A.S.L. Tsang, N. Zhou, F. Li & J.A.F. Nicholls, 2006. Impacts of situational factors on buying decisions in shopping malls: an empirical study with multinational data. *European Journal of Marketing*, 40(1/2), pp. 17–43.

Zidda, P., Lockshin, L. & van der Heart, S., 2008. Channel choice behavior for different usage situations. The case of the wine product category. Working paper.

Index

For Product Safety Concerns and Information please contact our EU
representative GPSR@taylorandfrancis.com
Taylor & Francis Verlag GmbH, Kaufingerstraße 24, 80331 München, Germany

www.ingramcontent.com/pod-product-compliance
Ingram Content Group UK Ltd.
Pitfield, Milton Keynes, MK11 3LW, UK
UKHW051830180425
457613UK00022B/1176

* 9 7 8 0 3 6 7 1 9 2 5 8 7 *